OpenSceneGraph 3.0
Beginner's Guide

Create high-performance virtual reality applications with
OpenSceneGraph, one of the best 3D graphics engines

Rui Wang

Xuelei Qian

open source
community experience distilled

BIRMINGHAM - MUMBAI

OpenSceneGraph 3.0
Beginner's Guide

First published: December 2010

Production Reference: 1081210

Published by Packt Publishing Ltd.
32 Lincoln Road
Olton
Birmingham, B27 6PA, UK.

ISBN 978-1-849512-82-4

www.packtpub.com

Cover Image by Ed Maclean (edmaclean@gmail.com)

Credits

Authors
Rui Wang
Xuelei Qian

Reviewers
Jean-Sébastien Guay
Cedric Pinson

Acquisition Editor
Usha Iyer

Development Editor
Maitreya Bhakal

Technical Editors
Conrad Sardinha
Vanjeet D'souza

Indexers
Tejal Daruwale
Hemangini Bari
Monica Ajmera Mehta

Editorial Team Leader
Akshara Aware

Project Team Leader
Lata Basantani

Project Coordinator
Leena Purkait

Proofreader
Dirk Manuel

Graphics
Nilesh Mohite

Production Coordinator
Adline Swetha Jesuthas

Cover Work
Adline Swetha Jesuthas

Foreword

Scene graphs have been the foundation of real-time graphics applications for the last two decades, whether it is a 3D game on a phone or a professional flight simulator costing millions of pounds, a virtual reality application through to the latest 3D real-time visualization on television, scene graphs are there under the hood, quietly churning out high quality visuals.

However, even powerful tools like scene graphs don't write world leading graphics applications by themselves, they still need developers with the skill and knowledge to make best use of them and the hardware that they run on. This expertise isn't something that you can gain by reading a few pages on the web—graphics hardware and software continues to evolve and you need to keep up with it... It's a journey of learning and exploration undertaken throughout your career.

OpenSceneGraph itself is the world's leading scene graph API, and has been written by, and to fulfil the needs of, professional graphics application developers. It is written to be powerful and productive to use rather than cut down and easy to use. Your first encounter with OpenSceneGraph may well be daunting; it's a professional grade scene graph containing many hundreds of classes and modules. But with this sophistication comes the ability to write very powerful graphics applications quickly so it's well worth the effort in learning how to make best use of it.

The authors of this book are users and contributors to the OpenSceneGraph software and its community. For me it's rewarding to see this open source project reach out across the world and inspire people, such as Rui Wang and Xuelei Qian, not only to use and contribute to the software, but also to write a book about it so that others can start their own journey into real-time graphics.

With this book their aim has been to take you from your first steps through to being able to use advanced features of the OpenSceneGraph and the graphics hardware that it runs on. Learning new concepts and APIs can often be dry and awkward, but once you get your first applications on screen you'll glimpse the potential, and it won't be long before you are seeing complex worlds come life. As a real-time graphics geek myself, I can't think anything more rewarding than immersing yourself in 3D worlds that you help create. Some familiarity with linear algebra, such like 3D vectors, quaternion numbers and matrix transformations, is helpful, too.

Robert Osfield.
OpenSceneGraph Project Lead

About the Authors

Rui Wang is a software engineer at the Chinese Academy of Surveying and Mapping and the manager of osgChina, the largest OSG discussion website in China. He is one of the most active members of the official OSG community, who contributes to the serialization I/O, GPU-based particle functionalities, BVH and animated GIF plugins, and other fixes and improvements to the OSG project. He translated Paul Martz's *OpenSceneGraph Quick Start Guide* into Chinese in 2008, and wrote his own Chinese book *OpenSceneGraph Design and Implementation* in 2009, cooperating with Xuelei Qian. He is also a novel writer and a guitar lover.

Xuelei Qian received his B.Sc. degree in Precision Instrument Engineering from Southeast University, Jiangsu, China, and his Ph.D. degree in applied graphic computing from the University of Derby, Derby, UK in 1998 and 2005, respectively. Upon completion of his Ph.D. degree, he worked as a postdoctoral research fellow in the Dept. of Precision Instrument and Mechanology at Tsinghua University and his current research interests include E-manufacturing, STEP-NC and intelligent CNC, and virtual reality engineering.

Acknowledgement

We'd like to first thank Don Burns and Robert Osfield for their creative efforts in giving birth to OpenSceneGraph, as well as thousands of members in the OSG core community, for their supports and contributions all the time.

Thanks again to Robert Osfield, a pure open source enthusiast and father of a happy family, for his tremendous passion in leading the development the OSG project for so many years (since 1999). He also took time out of his busy schedule to write the foreword for this book.

We must express our deep gratitude to Rakesh Shejwal, Usha Iyer, Leena Purkait, Priya Mukherji, and the entire Packt Publishing team for their talented work in producing yet another product, as well as Jean-Sébastien Guay and Cedric Pinson for reviewing the first drafts of the book and providing insightful feedback.

We would like to acknowledge John F. Richardson and Marek Teichmann, who announced the book at the OpenSceneGraph BOF at SIGGRAPH 2010. We also offer special thanks to Zhanying Wei, Xuexia Chen, Shixing Yang, Peng Xiao, Qingliang Liu, Su Jiang, and a number of other people who contributed to the completion of this book in different ways.

Finally, we owe the most sincere thanks to Paul Martz, who dedicates the first non-commercial book to OSG beginners all over the world and provides great help in supporting the publication of our past and current books.

About the Reviewers

Jean-Sébastien Guay is a software developer from Montréal, Quebec, Canada. After completing a Bachelor's Degree in Software Development and Software Engineering at UQAM, he began a Master's Degree in Computer Graphics at École Polytechnique, where he chose to use OpenSceneGraph for his Master's project. Motivated by the open nature of the project and wanting to contribute, he started learning its inner workings, fixing bugs, improving the Windows build system, and helping others with their problems on the osg-users mailing list. He has been in the top three posters each month ever since. But is that a good thing or just an indication that he talks too much?

Since late 2007, he has worked for CM-Labs Simulations Inc. (http://www.vortexsim.com/), where he develops the Vortex physics toolkit and training simulators for various industries such as construction, subsea, and others. Being the company's dedicated graphics developer allows him to continue using and contributing to OpenSceneGraph. The best part is he gets paid for it, too! Doing so has helped improve his proficiency with C++ as well as allowed him to use other scene graphs such as Vega Prime and OpenSG, which lets him keep an open mind and always see the big picture.

Jean-Sébastien has participated in several OpenSceneGraph user meetings, and he was a presenter at the OpenSceneGraph BOFs at Siggraph in 2008 and 2009. He is also a co-developer of the osgOcean nodekit, an ocean surface rendering add-on library for OpenSceneGraph, which is available at http://osgocean.googlecode.com/. He has also contributed to other open source projects, such as Bugzilla, Yafaray, and others.

Jean-Sébastien currently lives in the suburbs of Montréal, with his lovely wife and their three young boys. His personal website can be found at http://whitestar02.webhop.org/.

Cedric M. Pinson has twelve years of experience in 3D software. He has worked in the video game industry at Nemosoft and Mekensleep, before joining OutFlop, where he has served as the project leader for 3D client technology. He is a contributor to the OpenSceneGraph project and the author and maintainer of osgAnimation. He now does freelance work around OpenGL technologies such as OpenSceneGraph and WebGL.

I would like to thank my friends, Loic Dachary for helping me with his advice, Jeremy Moles for the motivation and comments about OpenSceneGraph, Johan Euphrosine for his support, Olivier Lejade who offered me a place to work, and Amy Jones who helps in many ways.

www.PacktPub.com

Support files, eBooks, discount offers and more

You might want to visit www.PacktPub.com for support files and downloads related to your book.

Did you know that Packt offers eBook versions of every book published, with PDF and ePub files available? You can upgrade to the eBook version at www.PacktPub.com and as a print book customer, you are entitled to a discount on the eBook copy. Get in touch with us at service@packtpub.com for more details.

At www.PacktPub.com, you can also read a collection of free technical articles, sign up for a range of free newsletters and receive exclusive discounts and offers on Packt books and eBooks.

http://PacktLib.PacktPub.com

Do you need instant solutions to your IT questions? PacktLib is Packt's online digital book library. Here, you can access, read and search across Packt's entire library of books.

Why Subscribe?

- ◆ Fully searchable across every book published by Packt
- ◆ Copy and paste, print and bookmark content
- ◆ On demand and accessible via web browser

Free Access for Packt account holders

If you have an account with Packt at www.PacktPub.com, you can use this to access PacktLib today and view nine entirely free books. Simply use your login credentials for immediate access.

Rui Wang dedicates this book to his parents, Lihang Wang and Ximei Bao, and his lovely fiancée Qin Leng, for their patience and moral support during the entire writing.

Xuelei Qian dedicates this book to his wife Yuehui Liu, for her constant love, support, and feels she deserves a major share of this book. He also wants to thank his grandfather Xinmin Zhu, mother Danmu Zhu, and father Gimping Qian, for their hugely spiritual support and encouragement all along.

Table of Contents

Preface

Real-time rendering is in quite demand in computer science today, and OpenSceneGraph, being one of the best 3D graphics toolkits, is being used widely in the fields of virtual reality, scientific visualization, visual simulation, modeling, games, mobile applications, and so on. Although you can use the powerful OpenSceneGraph, which is based on the low-level OpenGL API, to implement applications that simulate different environments in the 3D world, developing picture-perfect applications is easier said than done.

This book has been written with the goal of helping readers become familiar with the structure and main functionalities of OpenSceneGraph, and guiding them to develop virtual-reality applications using this powerful 3D graphics engine. This book covers the essence of OpenSceneGraph, providing programmers with detailed explanations and examples of scene graph APIs.

This book helps you take full advantages of the key features and functionalities of OpenSceneGraph. You will learn almost all of the core elements required in a virtual reality application, including memory management, geometry creation, the structure of the scene graph, realistic rendering effects, scene navigation, animation, interaction with input devices and external user interfaces, file reading and writing, and so on.

With the essential knowledge contained in this book, you will be able to start using OpenSceneGraph in your own projects and research fields, and extend its functionalities by referring to OpenSceneGraph's source code, official examples, and API documentation.

This handy book divides the core functionalities of the proved and comprehensive OpenSceneGraph 3D graphics engine into different aspects, which are introduced in separate chapters. Each chapter can be treated as an individual lesson that covers one important field of OpenSceneGraph programming, along with several examples illustrating concrete usages and solutions. The sequence of the chapters is organized from the easy topics to the more difficult concepts, to help you to gradually build your knowledge and skills in with OpenSceneGraph.

By the end of the whole book, you will have gained a ready-to-use OpenSceneGraph development environment for yourself, and will have the ability to develop OpenSceneGraph -based applications and extend practical functionalities for your own purposes.

With plenty of examples to get you started quickly, you'll master developing with OpenSceneGraph in no time.

What this book covers

Chapter 1, The Journey into OpenSceneGraph introduces the history, structure and features of OpenSceneGraph (OSG), and introduces the general concept of scene graph.

Chapter 2, Compilation and Installation of OpenSceneGraph guides readers through compiling, installing and configuring an OSG development environment, either by using the prebuilt binaries or building an environment wholly from the source code.

Chapter 3, Creating Your First OSG Program shows how to code an OSG-based application, highlighting the utilization of smart pointers, notifying system, object instances and data variances.

Chapter 4, Building Geometry Models explains how to create a geometry entity simply with vertices and the drawing primitives defined within OSG.

Chapter 5, Managing Scene Graph is all about the implementation of a typical scene graph using OSG, and shows the usages of the various types of scene graph nodes with special focus on some commonly-used node types.

Chapter 6, Creating Realistic Rendering Effects introduces some basic knowledge about OSG implementation of rendering states, texture mapping, shaders, and the render-to-texture technique.

Chapter 7, Viewing the World shows the means by which developers can encapsulate the cameras, manipulators, and stereo supports, and have them work together.

Chapter 8, Animating Scene Objects shows OSG's capability of creating animated graphic presentations by using the built-in animation library, and showcases the implementations of path animations, vertex-level animations, state and texture animations, and character animations that a 3D application can use.

Chapter 9, Interacting with Outside Elements focuses on the implementation of human computer interaction using OSG, including input device handling and GUI toolkit integration.

Chapter 10, Saving and Loading Files explains in detail the working mechanism of reading and writing scene data, and gives tips for creating user-customized I/O plugins.

Chapter 11, Developing Visual Components covers a wide range of advanced scene graph components, including billboards, texts, height mapped terrains, shadows, and volume rendering.

Chapter 12, Improving Rendering Efficiency introduces the techniques necessary for building a fast real time rendering system. It helps users to load, organize, and render massive datasets in a very efficient manner.

What you need for this book

To use this book, you will need a graphics card with robust OpenGL support, with the latest OpenGL device driver from your graphics hardware vendor installed.

You will also need a working compiler that can transform C++source code into executable files. Some recommended ones include: `.gcc`, `.mingw32`, and Visual Studio. For Windows users, there is a free Visual Studio Express Edition for use (`http://www.microsoft.com/express/Windows/`). However, you should read the documentation in order to consider its limitations carefully.

Who this book is for

This book is intended for software developers who are new to OpenSceneGraph and are considering using it in their applications. It is assumed that you have basic knowledge of C++ before using this book, especially the standard template library (STL) constructs, of which OSG makes extensive use. Some familiarity with design patterns as implemented in C++ is also useful, but is not required.

You need to be familiar with OpenGL—the standard cross-platform low-level 3D graphics API. We'll meet some math in the book, including geometry and linear algebra. Familiarity with these topics will be great, but you don't need to be a math whiz to use this book.

Conventions

In this book, you will find several headings appearing frequently.

To give clear instructions of how to complete a procedure or task, we use:

Time for action – heading

1. Action 1
2. Action 2
3. Action 3

Instructions often need some extra explanation so that they make sense, so they are followed with:

What just happened?

This heading explains the working of tasks or instructions that you have just completed.

You will also find some other learning aids in the book, including:

Pop quiz – heading

These are questions intended to help you test your own understanding.

Have a go hero – heading

These set practical challenges and give you ideas for experimenting with what you have learned.

You will also find a number of styles of text that distinguish between different kinds of information. Here are some examples of these styles, and an explanation of their meaning.

Code words in text are shown as follows: "CMake will generate an `OpenSceneGraph.sln` file at the root of the build directory".

A block of code is set as follows:

```
#include <osg/PolygonMode>
#include <osg/MatrixTransform>
#include <osgDB/ReadFile>
#include <osgViewer/Viewer>
```

Any command-line input or output is written as follows:

```
# osgviewer --image picture_name.bmp
```

New terms and **important words** are shown in bold. Words that you see on the screen, in menus or dialog boxes for example, appear in the text like this: "Start the installer and you will see the **Choosing Language** dialog, the **Welcome** page, and the **License Agreement** page".

 Warnings or important notes appear in a box like this.

Tips and tricks appear like this.

Reader feedback

Feedback from our readers is always welcome. Let us know what you think about this book—what you liked or may have disliked. Reader feedback is important for us to develop titles that you really get the most out of.

To send us general feedback, simply send an e-mail to feedback@packtpub.com, and mention the book title via the subject of your message.

If there is a book that you need and would like to see us publish, please send us a note in the **SUGGEST A TITLE** form on www.packtpub.com or e-mail suggest@packtpub.com.

If there is a topic that you have expertise in and you are interested in either writing or contributing to a book, see our author guide on www.packtpub.com/authors.

Customer support

Now that you are the proud owner of a Packt book, we have a number of things to help you to get the most from your purchase.

Downloading the example code for this book

You can download the example code files for all Packt books you have purchased from your account at http://www.PacktPub.com. If you purchased this book elsewhere, you can visit http://www.PacktPub.com/support and register to have the files e-mailed directly to you.

Errata

Although we have taken every care to ensure the accuracy of our content, mistakes do happen. If you find a mistake in one of our books—maybe a mistake in the text or the code—we would be grateful if you would report this to us. By doing so, you can save other readers from frustration and help us improve subsequent versions of this book. If you find any errata, please report them by visiting http://www.packtpub.com/support, selecting your book, clicking on the **errata submission form** link, and entering the details of your errata. Once your errata are verified, your submission will be accepted and the errata will be uploaded on our website, or added to any list of existing errata, under the Errata section of that title. Any existing errata can be viewed by selecting your title from http://www.packtpub.com/support.

Piracy

Piracy of copyright material on the Internet is an ongoing problem across all media. At Packt, we take the protection of our copyright and licenses very seriously. If you come across any illegal copies of our works, in any form, on the Internet, please provide us with the location address or website name immediately so that we can pursue a remedy.

Please contact us at `copyright@packtpub.com` with a link to the suspected pirated material.

We appreciate your help in protecting our authors, and our ability to bring you valuable content.

Questions

You can contact us at `questions@packtpub.com` if you are having a problem with any aspect of the book, and we will do our best to address it.

1

The Journey into
OpenSceneGraph

Before looking into various rendering effects and playing with carefully selected code snippets, let us first get a glimpse of the history of OpenSceneGraph, learn about its structures and capabilities, and join a web community to learn and discuss OSG online. You will also have the chance to create a "Hello World" application in OSG style, through which you will gain necessary information about OSG's syntax and structure.

*In this book, **OSG** is short for **OpenSceneGraph**. It will be used from time to time to replace OpenSceneGraph's full name, for convenience.*

In this chapter, we will:

- Have a brief overview of the concept of scene graph and a history of OSG
- Look into the fundamental structure and features of the latest OSG distribution
- Have a first-hand taste of OSG with a very simple example
- Establish a fast connection for interacting with the OSG community

A quick overview of rendering middleware

Before entering the world of OpenSceneGraph, we assume that you are already experienced in OpenGL programming. You work with stacks of matrices, set pipeline states, look for new extensions, call rendering APIs or commands and immediately draw them on a context, no matter if you are enjoying or suffering from the whole process.

A rendering middleware is a solution that raises the level of abstraction and eases the complexity of using a low-level OpenGL API, at the cost of flexibility. The concepts of modularity and object-orientation are often applied to manage graphics primitives, materials, and different visual data sets in user applications, saving much development time and allowing new functionalities to be combined as modules and plugins.

OpenSceneGraph is a well-designed rendering middleware application. It is actually a **retained rendering** (or deferred rendering) system based on the theory of **scene graph**, which records rendering commands and data in a buffer, for executing at some other time. This allows the system to perform various optimizations before rendering, as well as implement a multithreaded strategy for handling complex scenes.

Scene graphs

A **scene graph** is a general data structure that defines the spatial and logical relationship of a graphical scene for efficient management and rendering of graphics data. It is typically represented as **a hierarchical graph**, which contains a collection of graphics nodes including a top-level **root node**, a number of **group nodes** each of which can have any number of **child nodes**, and a set of **leaf nodes** each of which has zero child nodes and that serve together as the bottom layer of the tree. A typical scene graph does not allow a directed cycle (where some nodes are connected in a closed chain) or an isolated element (a node that has no child or parent) inside of itself.

Each **group node** can have any number of children. Grouping these **child nodes** allows them to share the information of the parent and be treated as one unit. By default, an operation performed by a parent propagates its effects to all of its children.

It also happens that certain nodes have more than one **parent node**, in which case the node is considered to be "instanced", and the **scene graph** can be defined as a **directed acyclic graph** (**DAG**). Instancing produces many interesting effects, including data sharing and **multi-pass rendering**.

The concept of scene graph has been widely applied in many modern software and applications, for instance, AutoCAD, Maya, CorelDraw, VRML, Open Inventor, and the one that we are going to investigate—OpenSceneGraph.

The Birth and development of OSG

The OpenSceneGraph project was initiated as an avocation by Don Burns in 1998. He used to work for SGI and is a hang-gliding enthusiast. He wrote a simplified SGI Performer-like **scene graph** API on a humble Linux PC, named SG, which was the prototype of OSG.

In 1999, Robert Osfield, a design consultant for a hang-glider manufacturer, started to take part in this young project. He suggested continuity to develop SG as a standalone, **open source** project and soon ported its elements to Windows. At the end of the year, Robert took over the project and changed its name to OpenSceneGraph. The project was then fully rewritten to take advantage of C++ standards and design patterns.

In 2001, in response to the growing interest in the project, Robert set up *OpenSceneGraph Professional Services*. He gave up the opportunity to work for other companies, and went full-time providing both commercial and free OSG services. Don also formed his own company, *Andes Computer Engineering,* and continues to support the development of OSG.

The first OpenSceneGraph birds-of-a-feather (BOF) meeting occurred the same year, at SIGGRAPH 2001, with only 12 people attending. After that, attendance at the OSG BOF continues to grow every year, with more and more people getting to know this great OpenGL-based API.

The **Producer** library, which was initially created to provide windowing and multi-pipe graphic system integrations for customer's needs, was added, along with other two important libraries, **osgText** and **osgFX**, in 2003. Then, in 2005, OSG 1.0 was announced, to the delight of over 1,100 members in the mailing list.

In 2007, a totally new OSG 2.0 was released, with improved multi-core, multi-GPU support, and three important new libraries: **osgViewer**, **osgManipulator**, and **osgShadow**. From then on, the unified build system CMake was used to simplify the build process. Then the old **Producer** was deprecated and maintained by *Andes Computer Engineering* as an independent project. The first two OSG books, *OpenSceneGraph Quick Start Guide* and *OpenSceneGraph Reference Manuals*, were available, too. Paul Martz dedicated them to all developers who were new to scene graph technology.

How time flies! Years have slipped away and OSG is developing at an incredible speed all the time: **osgWidget** was first introduced in 2008; **osgVolume** and **osgAnimation** came out in 2009; and **osgQt** was born in 2010, with the coming 3.0 release and the amazing OpenGL ES and OpenGL 3.0 support.

Today, several hundred high-performance applications are using OSG to render complex scenes and manage massive datasets. With the great efforts made by 432 core contributors and the continuous support of software developers around the world, it can be anticipated that OSG has a very bright future ahead of it.

Components

The computing infrastructure of OSG is designed to be highly scalable in order to enable runtime access to extended functionalities. In addition to the standard **core libraries**, a set of additional modular libraries known as **NodeKits** have been delivered to meet specific development requirements.

The core OSG functionality consists of four libraries:

1. **The OpenThreads library**: This library is intended to provide a minimal and complete Object-Oriented (OO) thread interface for C++ programmers. It is used by OSG as the main threading model implementation.

2. **The osg library**: This library provides basic elements used to build scene graphs, such as nodes, geometries, rendering states and textures, as well as related management tools and methods. It also contains a few necessary math classes, which are used to implement vector and matrix operations that are commonly used in two-dimensional and three-dimensional spaces.

3. **The osgDB library**: This library provides a plugin mechanism for reading and writing 2D and 3D files, with a derivable class containing access to data files and stream I/O operations. Its built-in database pager also supports dynamic loading and unloading of scene graph segments, in order to achieve the scheduling of huge collections of user data.

4. **The osgUtil library**: This library is designed for building the OSG rendering backend, which traverses the scene tree, performs culling in each frame, and finally converts the OSG scene into a series of OpenGL calls. There are also functionalities for user intersections, and polygon modification algorithms.

The extra **NodeKits** and utilities available with current OSG distributions are:

- **The osgAnimation library**: This library provides a range of general purpose utilities for various animations, including skeleton and morphing. It uses generic templates to construct multiple kinds of key frames and animation channels.

- **The osgFX library**: This library has a framework for implementing special effects in the 3D space, and contains several useful effect classes.

- **The osgGA library**, which stands for **OSG GUI abstraction**: This library is an abstract user interface on top of various windowing systems. It helps to handle interactive events from peripheral devices, for example, a keyboard or mouse.

- **The osgManipulator library**: This library extends the scene graph to support 3D interactive manipulation, such as moving, rotating, and scaling of transformable nodes.

- **The osgParticle library**: This library makes it possible to render explosions, fire, smoke, and other particle-based effects.

- **The osgShadow library**: This library provides a framework for various shadow rendering techniques.

- **The osgSim library**: This library meets some special requirements from simulation systems, especially from the OpenFlight databases.

- **The osgTerrain library**: This library provides geographic terrain rendering support using height field and imagery data.

- **The osgText library**: This library fully supports the rendering of TypeType and a series of other font formats, based on the FreeType project. It can draw 2D and 3D texts in 3D space or on the screen.

- **The osgViewer library**: This library defines a set of viewer-related classes, and therefore integrates OSG scene graphs and renders the backend with a wide variety of windowing systems, including Win32, X11, Carbon, and Cocoa, as well as providing indirect support for many other famous GUI toolkits.

- **The osgVolume library**: This library includes an initial support for volume rendering techniques.

- **The osgWidget library**: This library extends the core OSG elements and provides a 2D GUI widget set for 3D applications.

- **The osgQt library**: This library embeds the Qt GUI into scene graphs and thus has the ability to display web pages and common Qt widgets in space.

All OSG **core libraries** and **NodeKits**, no matter what kind of features they implement or who contributed them, have the same prefix "osg", and a short word or abbreviation followed as the keyword.

The whole OSG architecture can be illustrated as follows:

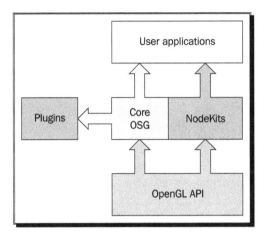

In most cases, the **osg**, **osgDB**, **osgUtil**, and **osgViewer** libraries are the major components of an OSG-based application, and will be discussed in more detail in the following chapters of this book, while other less frequently used **NodeKits** may also be mentioned in specific chapters.

Why OSG?

The OSG project is open sourced and released under a modified GNU Lesser General Public License (LGPL), named OSGPL. It brings about significant benefits to its users:

- **Rigorous structure**: OSG makes full use of the Standard Template Library (STL) and multiple design patterns. It also takes advantage of the open source development model in order to provide a legacy-free and user-centric application programming interface.

- **Superior performance**: A series of scene graph techniques are already well-implemented in OSG, including view-frustum and occlusion culling, level of detail (LOD) configuration, rendering state sorting, particle and shadow supports, and complete encapsulation of OpenGL extensions and the shader language.

- **High scalability**: The core OSG functionalities are clean and highly extensible. This makes it easy for users to write their own NodeKits and file I/O plugins, and integrate them into scene graphs and applications.

- **Software and hardware portability**: The core OSG is already designed to have minimal dependency on any specific platform or windowing system, requiring only Standard C++ and OpenGL. This provides great convenience in being able to rapidly port OSG-based applications to Windows, Linux, Mac OSX, FreeBSD, Solaris, and even embedded platforms.

- **Latest activity**: With an active developer community, OSG is growing at an incredible speed. It supports the latest OpenGL and OpenGL ES extensions and various graphics concepts and techniques, along with a great deal of feedback in the development cycle.

- **Open source**: In modern industry, open source means co-intelligence, quality and flexibility, rather than merely inexpensive. Users and companies also don't have to worry about software patent violations when using OSG in their own applications.

Who uses OSG?

The following is a rough list of some of the organizations that are using or have used OSG as a development tool for their applications and products:

Organization name	Download link (if downloadable)	Purpose using OSG
Boeing	-	Flight simulation
Delta 3D	www.delta3d.org	Game engine
Flight Gear	www.flightgear.org	Flight simulation
Intra	-	Train simulation
Magic Earth	-	Oil and gas probing
NASA	-	Earth simulation
Norcontrol	-	Maritime simulation
ossimPlanet	www.ossim.org/OSSIM/ossimPlanet.html	Geo-spatial visualization
Virtual Terrain Project	www.vterrain.org	CAD and GIS related fields
VR Juggler	www.vrjuggler.org	Virtual reality system

Other customers include ESA, Landmark Graphics, Sony, STN Atlas, Northrop Grumman, and even the military sectors. To learn more about the large number of OSG-based projects and outcome, just search the whole web, and always keep in contact with developers all over the world through the web community.

Have a quick taste

Before sitting down and coding, you should have already set up an OSG development environment consisting of **header files** and **libraries**, either by obtaining a prebuilt package compliant to your compiler version, or building everything with the source code. Please refer to *Chapter 2, Compilation & Installation of OpenSceneGraph* for details.

Time for action – say "Hello World" OSG style

Can't wait to have a taste of OSG programming? Here is the simplest example, which shows how to load an existing model file and render it on the screen. It is much more interesting than just printing a "Hello World" text on the console:

1. Create a new project with any source code editor:

```
#include <osgDB/ReadFile>
#include <osgViewer/Viewer>
int main( int argc, char** argv )
{
    osgViewer::Viewer viewer;
    viewer.setSceneData( osgDB::readNodeFile("cessna.osg") );
    return viewer.run();
}
```

2. Specify the OSG **header** location and **dependent libraries**. You need to tell the linker to link your project with five libraries: **OpenThreads**, **osg**, **osgDB**, **osgUtil**, and **osgViewer**. You will learn more about configuring an OSG application in the next chapter.

3. Build your project. Make sure the file `cessna.osg` already exists in the same directory as the executable file, or in the path specified with the **OSG_FILE_PATH** environment variable.

4. Check it out! You get a full-screen display with a flight model shown in the middle:

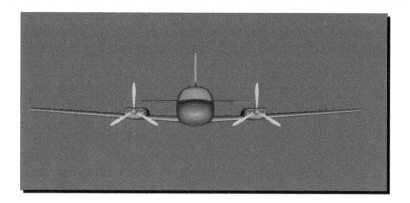

5. Try to make some changes to what you are observing simply with your mouse. Press and hold the left, middle, and right mouse buttons when you are moving the mouse, to rotate, move, and scale the Cessna. Note that you are not actually modifying the model but changing the virtual view point instead.

What just happened?

An easy-to-read example was just created to show how powerful and clear OSG is. The `osgDB::readNodeFile()` function is used to read an existing **node file**, that is, a **scene graph** that represents the Cessna model. The `osgViewer::Viewer` instance is then created to set the scene data and provide a simulation loop for the application.

Here, *osgDB* and *osgViewer* are namespaces, and *Viewer* is a class name. The naming style of a function or class member uses the same convention as the famous "camel-case", that is, the first word of the function name starts with a lowercase letter, and additional ones start with upper-case letters.

Live in community

Everyone interested in learning and making use of OSG is welcome to join the community at any time. There are several ways to get in touch with the core developing team and thousands of OSG programmers.

The preferred way is to use one of the two major **public mailing lists**. A mailing list here is a list of subscribers who have discussions on the same particular topic, via e-mail. To subscribe to an OSG mailing list, follow the appropriate links mentioned:

Mailing list	Subscription link	Description
osg-users	`http://lists.openscenegraph.org/listinfo.cgi/osg-users-openscenegraph.org`	General technique support and discussions
osg-submissions	`http://lists.openscenegraph.org/listinfo.cgi/osg-submissions-openscenegraph.org`	Submission of code changes and bug fixes only

The forum, which is already linked to the mailing lists, is also provided for people who like this form: `http://forum.openscenegraph.org/`.

You will find a greater variety of OSG discussion groups on the internet, such as IRC channel, Google group, LinkedIn, and even a Chinese mirror:

◆ `irc.freenode.net #openscenegraph`

◆ `http://groups.google.com/group/osg-users/topics`

◆ `http://www.linkedin.com/e/gis/61724/6F710C14EBAF`

◆ `http://bbs.osgchina.org/`

Companies and individuals may ask for professional services, too, by making the appropriate payments. A number of professional OSG contractors are listed here as a reference: `http://www.openscenegraph.org/projects/osg/wiki/Community/Contractors`.

Finally, remember to visit the wiki website and developer blog at any time. This contains an enormous wealth of information, including the latest news and download links for OSG distributions:

◆ `http://www.openscenegraph.org/`

◆ `http://blog.openscenegraph.org/`

Summary

This chapter gave a bird's eye view of OSG, in which we have drawn in mind a rough image about what we are going to learn about this widely used 3D graphics API. We sincerely hope the following chapters of this small book will serve as a ladder to help the readers, rung by rung, to get into the world of OSG-based programming.

In this chapter, we specially covered:

◆ The cornerstone and funder of OSG

◆ The basic structure of OSG including various functional modular libraries

◆ A quick view of how to write OSG-style applications

◆ The way to join the OSG community and obtain the latest news

2
Compilation and Installation of OpenSceneGraph

It is usually a painstaking process to create binary files completely from the source code in order to construct an efficient development environment. There are two different ways to set up the OSG working environment: for beginners, an easy-to-use prebuilt package installer can be obtained from the official OSG website, which may help with installing particular versions of OSG (not all versions have a corresponding installer); and for developers with more experience, there is a more flexible way to work with the OSG source code— using the CMake build system, which is also presented in detail.

In this chapter, we will tell you:

- How to obtain OSG prebuilt packages with the quick installer
- How to make use of application utilities provided by the installed OSG distribution
- How to get familiar with the CMake build system and how to set compilation options properly
- How to build OSG and set up a working environment from the source code on Windows and UNIX platforms
- How to configure development environment variables

System requirements

OSG can run on most computers, as well as mobile devices with OpenGL ES installed which is a subset of OpenGL 3D Graphical API that was specially designed for embedded devices. OSG has been designed to take advantage of multi-processor and multi-core architectures, and works fine on both 32 and 64 bit processors.

Since OSG is an OpenGL-based scene graph API, it is recommended that you have **an AGP or PCI-Express graphics card** which guarantees satisfying OpenGL performance. In fact, most professional and consumer grade graphics hardware on the market nowadays should suffice for development needs. OSG is capable of working with a very low version OpenGL and limited graphics RAM, at the price of losing particular rendering features and functional extensions. Therefore, it is suggested that you have **the latest version of the device driver** installed on your machine before programming with OSG. A graphics card with 256 MB or 512 MB of memory will be a good start, too.

The needs for disk space and system memory depend on specific application requirements and the scale of the datasets to be rendered. Basically, the core OSG binary and library file size is up to **30 MB**, without any debug information. The size of the executable file will be even smaller and only those shared library files are necessary at runtime.

Note that developers who decide to build OSG completely from the source code have to make sure there is **at least 3GB of free disk space** available for storage of intermediate files generated during the compilation process.

Using the installer

It is easy and fast to use a prebuilt OSG package to deploy the binaries and libraries necessary for creating your own programs. A typical prebuilt binary package is designed, compiled, and tested by a third party, and often includes run-time executables, shared libraries, static-link libraries, headers, third-party dependencies, documentation, and other useful resources, and is available to developers in the form of a freeware or a commercial product.

To quickly set up your OSG development environment, you may get an OSG installer with the following URL: `http://www.openscenegraph.org/files/dev/OpenSceneGraph-Installer.exe`

This tiny and simple installer will check your computer's configuration and automatically download the previously mentioned prebuilt binary packages from the official OSG website. The installer will read from a `.ini` configuration file first, which will be updated as soon as new prebuilt packages are released. In this way, users can keep their OSG version up-to-date simply by re-executing the installer.

Time for action – installing OSG

The installer is designed to make the installation process flow more efficiently. If you are not familiar with the process of compiling a project from source code, or just want to have an initial impression of the OSG utilities, the following instructions may help you to install an OSG development environment step by step by using the installer.

Note that **only Microsoft Windows developers** can benefit from the installer at present. Users of Linux, Mac OS X, and other systems should refer to the *Cross-platform building* section.

1. Start the installer and you will see the **Choosing Language** dialog, the **Welcome** page, and the **License Agreement** page. Read the OpenSceneGraph license carefully, select **I accept the terms of the License Agreement**, then click on **Next** to continue:

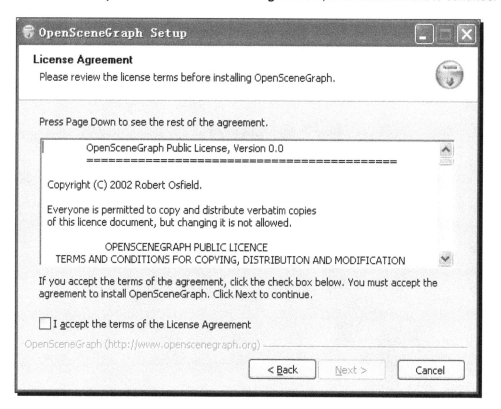

2. If you have already installed a previous OSG version, the installer will pop up a warning dialog box and ask if you want to continue with the installation, or quit and uninstall the old version first. Please note that it may cause unexpected trouble if you have different versions of OSG installed on the same machine, because an application developed with one specific OSG version may incorrectly link to shared libraries created by another during the linking process. To avoid link errors or runtime exceptions, each time before you install a new version of OSG, it is suggested that you remove the old version, because OSG is backwards compatible. Here we assume it is the first time that you installed OSG; please select **Yes** to ignore and continue:

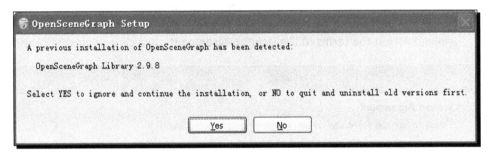

3. There will be one or more distributions listed on this page, in addition to an entry panel for selection of the Visual C++ product directory. Select a distribution and specify the C++ working directory and click on **Next**.

Make sure that the displayed building environment of the item goes with your system and development settings. For example, you should have installed Visual Studio 2008 Service Pack 1 on a 32-bit Windows XP system, in order to make use of the OSG 3.0 prebuilt packages shown in the following image, either with dynamic debug or release configuration.

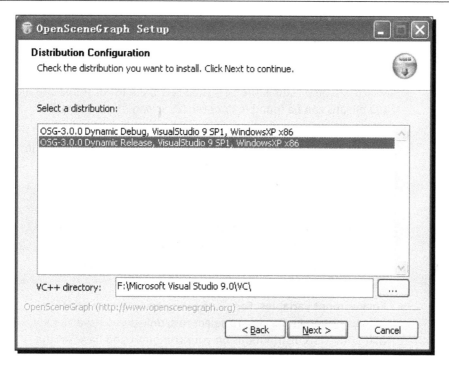

4. The massage box below will show up if the processor architecture, operating system, or the IDE is mismatched with the distribution's requirements. Don't ignore it unless you have specific requirements and know what will happen.

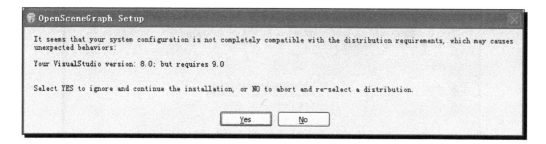

5. Now it is time to decide the components to be installed, which have been classified into eight categories by the installer. Users are allowed to select one or more of them according to their individual requirements. A grayed out (disabled) section means that that part is not included in the current distribution:

    □   **Binaries**: Core runtime libraries (DLL), key plugins and utilities, which will be placed in the `bin` subdirectory of the installation directory.

- **Developer files**: Headers and static-link libraries for developing OSG-based applications, placed in the `include` and `lib` subdirectories.

- **Extra plugins**: Extra plugins and related runtime dependencies, which will be placed in the `bin` subdirectory. A list of supported file I/O plugins can be found in *Chapter 10, Saving and Loading Files*.

- **Sample data**: Sample datasets for demonstrations and experiments. Some of the sample data will be used many times in this book. It will be installed in the `data` subdirectory.

- **Documentation**: The API documentation in HTML help file format (`.chm`), which will be easy to read on Windows platforms.

- **Examples**: A great deal of useful examples and tests, installed in the `examples` subdirectory of the installation directory.

- **Visual Studio project wizard**: See *Using the project wizard* for details. Be sure to select this.

- **Environment variables**: See *Configuring environment variables* below, for details. Be sure to select this, unless you have already had other OSG distributions on your computer and have set the environment variables yourself.

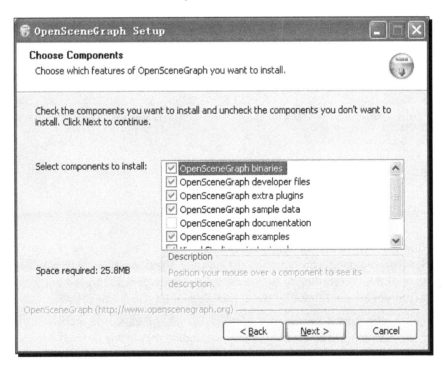

6. What we need to do in the next few steps is quite simple: decide upon the installation directory, specify the start menu folder, and launch the installation! Make sure the Internet connection remains alive during the entire installation process.

7. Click on **Finish** and if everything progresses well, you will see a Cessna model in the middle of a deep blue background. This installer's demo is actually what *Chapter 1, The Journey into OpenSceneGraph* is going to demonstrate in the "Hello World" example!

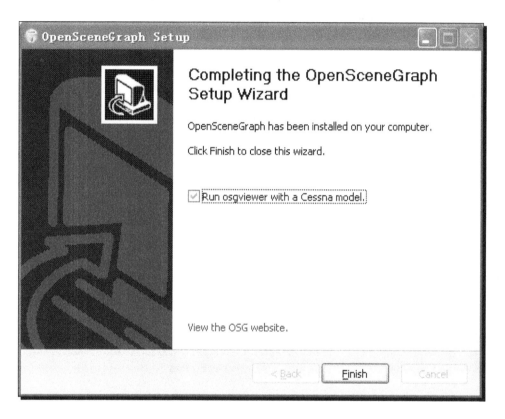

What just happened?

The installer will generate a few subdirectories under the installation directory (hereafter INSTDIR) and copy files into those subdirectories. Binaries and plugins will be copied to INSTDIR/bin, header files to INSTDIR/include, static-link libraries to INSTDIR/lib, sample data to INSTDIR/data, documentation to INSTDIR/doc, and examples to INSTDIR/share.

Running utilities

OSG comes with a few command-line tools that can be used to quickly view models and images, and convert them into other file formats. Run the command prompt first:

- On Windows platforms, you can access the command prompt simply by going to the **Start Menu** and typing in the command cmd in the **Run command box**.

- For a Mac OS X system, open the **Terminal** application, which is located by default inside the **Applications | Utilities** folder

- On a Linux console, type the commands directly and see the output results

Now enter the following command at the prompt:

```
# osgversion
```

Here, the pound sign (#) is used to indicate the prompt itself. Other kinds of user prompts may include the current directory, the username, and the printing time. You shall also explicitly provide a path in the command line for your executables on a UNIX shell.

The osgversion application will output the working OSG version, for example:

```
OpenSceneGraph Library 3.0.0
```

Moreover, OSG provides a flexible and powerful model and image viewing tool—osgviewer, as well as a model format converter—osgconv.

Time for action – playing with osgviewer

If you have chosen to download the sample data and configured environment variables by using the installer, it is time to load and display a sample model. Here we will reproduce the "Hello World" example of the first chapter. Developers who have trouble compiling the example code are suggested to look into the osgviewer first.

1. Start the osgviewer utility by issuing the following command:

```
# osgviewer cessna.osg
```

2. The displayed result will be nearly the same as our "Hello World" example and the installer's demo. Don't forget to change the view point with your mouse. Pressing the space bar at any time will return you to the initial view.

3. Besides that, osgviewer provides lots of shortcuts to switch between different display modes and gather rendering performance information as well. To have a first-hand experience of them, press the *Esc* key to quit the currently running osgviewer, and type in:

```
# osgviewer cow.osg
```

4. Now you will see a cow with a beautiful reflection map:

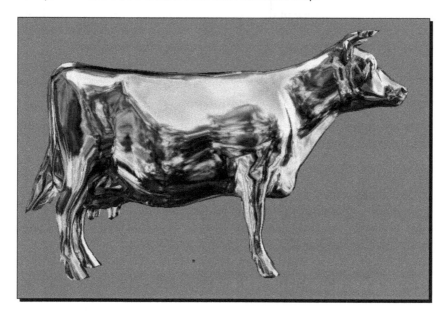

5. **Press the W key** to switch polygon modes, which include filled (by default), wireframe, and points.

6. **Press the T key** to toggle textures on or off to activate or deactivate the reflection map.

7. **Press the I key** to enable or disable lighting. Scenery loaded in `osgviewer` are lighted by default.

8. **Press the F key** to change between full-screen and windowed display.

9. **Press the S key** repeatedly to display real-time rendering statistics, which are very useful for optimizing graphics. The following image illustrates the current frame rate and traversal time, which was displayed by pressing the *S* key twice:

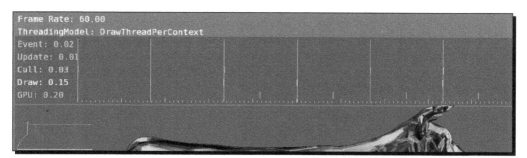

What just happened?

We have already had an overview of the osgviewer. The osgviewer is a fundamental but feature-rich scene graph viewing tool, which is used for loading models and images, and fully observing them by taking advantage of a series of auxiliary functionalities.

To load a picture with osgviewer, issue the following command:

```
# osgviewer --image picture_name.bmp
```

To learn more about the osgviewer command-line arguments, start the shell prompt again without any arguments, and read the output text carefully:

```
# osgviewer
```

Please try more models and image files in different formats, and you will find that osgviewer supports a great number of data formats, including but not limited to .3ds, .obj, .stl, .bmp and .dds. For the external data formats that OSG supports, you can find out more details in *Chapter 10, Saving and Loading Files*.

Pop quiz – dependencies of osgviewer

Copy the osgviewer utility and the data file cessna.osg (which is in the data subfolder of the installation directory) to another computer on which OSG has never been installed. Do you think it can work properly this time? OSG-based applications depend heavily on related dynamic libraries. Could you find out which libraries are required by osgviewer while reading cessna.osg?

Some dependent modules locator software may help a lot in finishing such work. For example, you may download the free *Dependency Walker* utility from http://www.dependencywalker.com/.

Have a go hero – playing with osgconv

Another tool named osgconv is mainly used for converting between formats. To summarize the usage, osgconv can import graphical contents in order to export to different file formats. It supports as many input formats as osgviewer. Please note that whether a given format can be written depends on the plugin, which means that some formats can only be read while others can be read and written. We will discuss this later in *Chapter 10, Saving and Loading Files*. Now, you can try to convert a .osg file to a .3ds file by using the following command, and then open the new file with any 3D modeling software such as 3dsmax, on your own, if you like:

```
# osgconv cessna.osg cessna.3ds
```

Using the project wizard

If you are a Windows user, and have experience in developing with the Visual Studio IDE, you may obtain the OSG prebuilt packages installer and select the item *Visual Studio project wizard* when selecting components to install. Wait until the package installation is successfully done, and then a new Visual Studio project wizard will appear. This can help beginners to configure their OSG-based applications and start tasting OSG programming quickly.

Time for action – creating your solution with one click

At present, the project wizard can only work with Visual Studio 7 (2003), 8 (2005), 9 (2008), and 10 (2010) under Windows. If you have any problems using it, contact the author directly.

1. Open your Visual Studio IDE and start a new project. You will find a new project template named **OSG Wizard** in the Visual C++ project types, which is illustrated as follows:

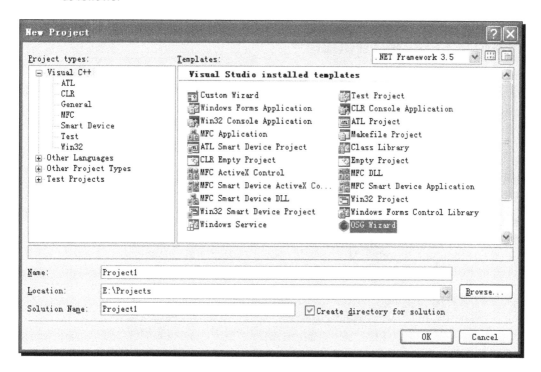

2. Enter the project name, click on **OK**, and create your solution with the OSG wizard in one step! After that, you will have a ready-to-use working environment.

What just happened?

So far you have created your solution with the OSG wizard and also established a ready-to-use working environment. Try programming and debugging the example code, then open the project property page, and have a look at the pre-configured items in **C/C++ | General | Additional Include Directories**, **Linker | General | Additional Library Directories**, and **Linker | Input | Additional Dependencies**, which will be useful for constructing your own project in the next chapter.

A non-Windows or non-Visual Studio developer will never see the wizard interface and thus is not necessary to have the related installer option selected.

Have a go hero – constructing "Hello World" with the wizard

Do you still have problems compiling the "Hello World" example in *Chapter 1, The Journey into OpenSceneGraph*? Now it is time to finish this work with the help of the Visual Studio wizard. You may also compare your own project's properties with the ones in the generated project, and try to point out problems, if any.

Prebuilts making trouble?

There are several inconveniences when using prebuilt packages and installers. First, these prebuilts are often compiler-dependent, platform-dependent, and even architecture-dependent. For example, you can never run `osgviewer.exe` on a UNIX system if the executable was built under Windows XP and Visual Studio 2008. One more example: although a 32-bit OSG application is capable of running on 64-bit Windows servers, a 64-bit OSG application compiled specifically for 64-bit Windows will only run on 64-bit Windows. In these cases, you will have to wait until others who are using the same computing environment with you have their OSG package built and published.

Secondly, the prebuilts are seldom made from the latest version. Their creators may think of using a more stable distribution, or some specified ones instead, intending to meet their own development requirements. This is of course a pain for developers to be stalled from adopting new releases, especially those including exciting features and important bug fixes.

Last but not least, it is more customizable, flexible, and sometimes interesting to compile binaries and developer files from the source code, under different platforms and configurations. OSG is open sourced, so why not to think and act from open source perspective?

Cross-platform building

From the 2.0 version, OSG starts to make use of a powerful build system—**CMake**. This can be used to configure software compilation processes with a compiler-independent scripting language. With simple configuration files, CMake can generate native makefiles and workspaces that can be applied to various compilation environments and platforms. That is why an increasing number of projects, such as KDE, VTK, Boost, MySql, and OpenSceneGraph, choose CMake for cross-platform building.

You may download the CMake binaries or source code at:
`http://www.cmake.org/cmake/resources/software.html`.

After that, you may start to download the latest OSG source package or any previous version you are interested in. Be aware that there are usually two different kinds of OSG versions: **stable releases** and **developer releases**. For end-users, the former is preferred because of their stability. And for software developers and community contributors, the latter will be at the cutting edge and will always contain exciting new features, although you may occasionally see build and runtime errors on particular platforms.

OSG uses **odd minor version numbers** to denote developer releases and **even minor version numbers** for stable ones. For example, OpenSceneGraph 2.8 was the previous stable release branch, based on the work that was done in the 2.7.x versions. Then the 2.9.x versions were intermediate versions leading to the latest stable release family, named OpenSceneGraph 3.0. The patch version after the minor version number is used to denote very minor changes and bug fixes.

Stable source code can be downloaded from:
`http://www.openscenegraph.org/projects/osg/wiki/Downloads`.

And for early adopters, remember to keep track of the latest developments at: `http://www.openscenegraph.org/projects/osg/wiki/Downloads/DeveloperReleases`.

The link to the SVN repository, which is even more bleeding-edge but requires a subversion client (for example, TortoiseSVN) to check out the source code:
`http://www.openscenegraph.org/projects/osg/wiki/Downloads/SVN`.

Starting CMake

The steps for using CMake for cross-platform compiling are nearly the same in different system environments. In following sections, we will take Windows and Visual Studio 2010 Express as an example. The steps can be easily transposed to UNIX and Mac OS X, too.

Time for action – running CMake in GUI mode

After Cmake has been installed on your system, you can run it from the command line, or choose to run in GUI mode, which allows you to edit the options in a much easier way.

1. Find the executalbe `cmake-gui.exe` from the start menu folder and run it. A GUI will show up with two entry panels for specifying the source and binary directories, as well as a couple of text boxes.

2. To make it work with the OpenSceneGraph source code, you should first identify the place where the source code is: drag the file `CMakeLists.txt` from the **OSG root directory**, and drop it onto the CMake window. The contents of two entry panels will change at the same time, and, to the same absolute path value, which indicates that the platform-dependent workspaces or makefiles will be generated directly in the source code directory, and the compilation process will start at the same place, too. In short, this is an **in-source** build.

3. Conversely, an **out-of-source** build will export the generated files into a completely separate directory, with the source code unchanged. For that purpose, you should modify the path value of **Where to build the binaries**, and designate the expected path. Out-of-source is always recommended because it will keep the source code clear, and make it possible to generate multiple variants of project configurations.

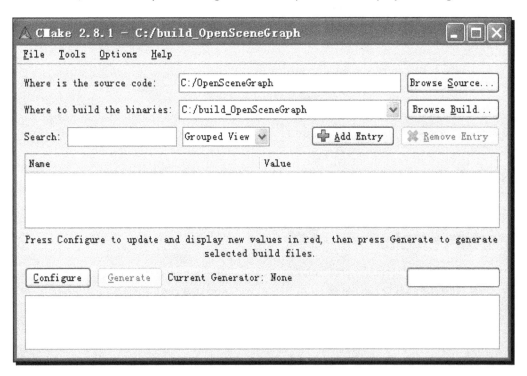

4. Assuming that you have already downloaded the OSG source code to
C:\OpenSceneGraph, and set the binary directory to C:\build_
OpenSceneGraph, as shown in the previous image, the next step is to
click on **Configure**, and select a suitable generator for your system in following
pop-up dialog:

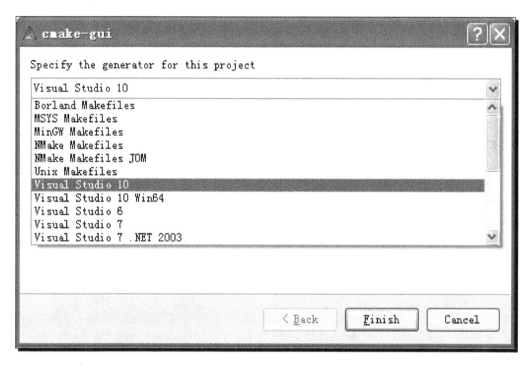

5. Please do not specify a generator that does not exist on your system. CMake
will automatically search for an available compiler and a linker according to
your selection, and report any errors if this fails. Select **Visual Studio 10**, or any
other generator in the list. Beginners can download the free **Visual Studio 10
(2010) Express** from http://www.microsoft.com/express/Windows/.

6. Press the **Finish** button to continue. After that you will see the blank text box filling with red-highlighted building options. Choose **Grouped View** in the central combo box and rearrange the options in tree structures, as shown:

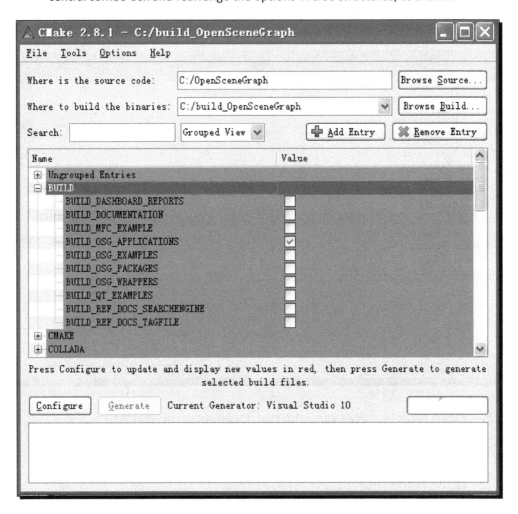

7. Try opening a top-level tree item, for instance, the **BUILD** group. Now it is time to set up building options and get ready to create your **Visual Studio 10** solutions. See the section *Setting up options* below, for more details.

8. After all of the options are selected and accepted, click on **Generate** in order to generate the Visual Studio solutions or UNIX makefiles,\ according to your previous selection:

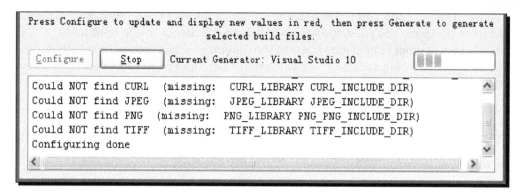

9. Close the CMake GUI, and navigate to `C:\build_OpenSceneGraph`—the predetermined place to build the binaries. If everything progressed properly, you will find that the solution file has already been created. Open the freshly-baked `OpenSceneGraph.sln` file, and start to compile OSG binaries and libraries at once!

What just happened?

CMake will generate makefiles and cache files in the `Where to build the binaries` directory. The cache files are used to keep the build settings, and will remember the user's choices for future rebuilding, which means that options don't have to be repeated if CMake is running on the same build directory the next time.

Setting up options

There exist three kinds of options:

♦ **Check box**: Provide an option list for the user to select. The state can be defined as ON or OFF, each of which may lead to different additional options and building behaviors.

♦ **Search box**: Provide an entry panel and a file browser for the user to specify a directory or file. It may also search the path automatically in applicable cases. The result will be used as an include path or dependency of a project.

♦ **Text box**: Provide an entry panel, the text value of which may work as a macro definition or compiling flag .

As an OSG beginner, you don't have to learn and configure all of the options immediately. In *Chapter 10*, *Saving and Loading Files*, you will have the chance to add third-party dependencies in order to configure some of the OSG plugins, and recompile the whole solution again. However, at present, we will simply have a look at several important options in the following table, and then build your first package from the source code:

Group	CMake options	Values	Description
BUILD	BUILD_OSG_APPLICATIONS	ON/OFF	Set to ON to build OSG utilities (osgviewer, osgconv, etc.).
	BUILD_OSG_EXAMPLES	ON/OFF	Set to ON to build OSG native examples, which are great for learning advanced topics in OSG.
CMake	CMAKE_BUILD_TYPE	String	For UNIX, the type will be Debug or Release. For Windows, this field contains all possible configurations, and developers can select which one to build in Visual Studio after opening the solution file.
	CMAKE_DEBUG_POSTFIX	String	Sometimes it's annoying to have the same library name for Debug and Release configurations, because people can hardly differentiate them at first sight. This option can set a postfix (default is 'd') for Debug building outputs.
	CMAKE_INSTALL_PREFIX	String	This specifies the installation prefix, which determines the base installation path of the created runtime files and development files.
OSG	OSG_MSVC_VERSIONED_DLL	ON/OFF	Use versioned names for shared libraries. In some cases, this may not be convenient. Set to OFF to avoid this behavior.
WIN32	WIN32_USE_DYNAMICBASE	ON/OFF	If you are still working with Windows 7 Beta Version, then you users may meet a linker error while building. This option may help to solve it.
	WIN32_USE_MP	ON/OFF	Build with multiple processes, which can reduce the total time to compile the source files.

Not all options are shown at the beginning. Each time you change the values and click on **Configure** to update, you may see some more new options being displayed in red. Decide whether you want to modify them or not, and press **Configure** again, until all of the options turn gray.

The generating process will apply all user options when creating the build files, based on the CMake script files, that is the `CMakeLists.txt` file, in each subdirectory.

Generating packages using Visual Studio

The Microsoft Visual Studio IDE provides a truly high-end compiler that is used for building binaries from source code under Windows. It uses a solution file (.sln) to organize a set of projects. CMake will generate an OpenSceneGraph.sln file at the root of the build directory. Open the solution file and start building OSG with the Visual Studio compiler.

Time for action – building with a Visual Studio solution

There are only two steps left in order to build the Visual Studio solution and create your own OSG packages, which will include runtime binaries, headers, static-link libraries, utilities, and examples.

1. First, select a build type (Debug, Release, RelWithDebInfo, or MinSizeRel), and build the **ALL_BUILD** project. This may take an extremely long time during first-time building, but will save a lot of time in subsequent compilations, unless you have cleared all intermediate files and decided to rebuild the solution completely from scratch.

2. When the building process has finished, switch to the **INSTALL** project and "build" it. The compiler will traverse a series of post-build events that install all of the built files into the directory defined by the **CMAKE_INSTALL_PREFIX** option.

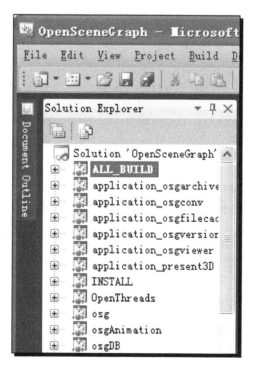

What just happened?

Everything is done as if you are working on your own Visual Studio solutions! The only difference is that every subproject will include an extra `CMakeLists.txt` file, which will check if the source files or settings were modified in the pre-build step, and automatically regenerate the project if necessary.

Go to your installation directory to see if all of the necessary files are already there. Then run the `osgversion` and `osgviewer` commands in the binary directory to see if the new package performs correctly. Do not forget to hide or uninstall the prebuilt packages generated by the quick installer in order to avoid any confusion caused by the coexistence of more than one binary package.

Please note that, when using `Debug` build type, the installed filename will have a postfix, of d. For example, `osgviewer.exe` will be renamed to `osgviewerd.exe`, to be distinct from the `Release` distribution. This behavior can be changed by setting the **CMAKE_DEBUG_POSTFIX** option and re-configuring the solution.

Pop quiz – the difference between ALL_BUILD and 'build all'

Some developers may love the following steps for building their Visual Studio solutions: open the **Batch Build** dialog box, select all projects in the current solution for inclusion in the batch build, start the build process, and go and have a cup of coffee (maybe more). Do you think this will produce the same result as using **ALL_BUILD** and then the **INSTALL** project? Will they take the same time?

Generating packages using gcc

Most UNIX systems adopt the **GNU compiler collection (gcc)** as the major compiler system. The gcc uses makefiles to build and manage projects, which is a little more complex than Visual Studio solutions, but is extremely powerful.

Time for action – building with a UNIX makefile

With a desktop system like KDE and Gnome, a UNIX developer may execute the **cmake-gui** application and work the way described above. The only difference is that the generator should be set to *Unix Makefiles,* and a makefile hierarchy will be generated instead of Visual Studio solutions.

1. After closing the CMake GUI, start a terminal (make sure you are logged in as root unless **CMAKE_INSTALL_PREFIX** has been set to a path in the user's home directory), and then type:

   ```
   # make
   # make install
   ```

2. Built files will be exported to the specified place, usually /usr/local or the path defined by **CMAKE_INSTALL_PREFIX**.

What just happened?

You will find that **cmake-gui** is able to work on most windowing systems, if you have downloaded a ready-made binary package for your platform. Or you can use the curses-based **ccmake**. This is a text-mode GUI with the same interface as **cmake-gui**. You can set options with it visually, switch binary choices from TRUE to FALSE via the *Enter* key, and then when you are done, press *c* for configure and *g* for generate. However, on a console, the whole process should start from the **cmake** command-line. Take a Linux console—for example, assuming source in /home/OpenSceneGraph and the binary directory in /home/build_OpenSceneGraph, **you may have to build OSG source code in the following way:**

```
# cd /home/build_OpenSceneGraph
# cmake -DCMAKE_BUILD_TYPE=Release ,,/OpenSceneGraph
# make
# make install
```

More options could be added as command-line arguments here.

Have a go hero – checking mis-compiled parts

So far you have finished the compilation of OSG from the source code. Before starting to use this for future development, spend a little more time to compare the outcomes of using a quick installer and compiling from the source code. Look into the two installation directories and try to find if there is any difference among files and subfolders.

- **The bin subfolder** contains all of the utilities and shared libraries of the core OSG, as well as an osgPlugins-x.x.x subdirectory made up of dozens of file I/O plugins. Here, x.x.x refers to the OSG distribution version. Note that, shared libraries and plugins will go into the lib subfolder on UNIX.

- **The include subfolder** contains the C++ headers that declare the exported OSG classes, functions, and identifiers that are usable in user applications.

- **The lib subfolder** contains all of the static-link libraries that will be used as dependencies in user applications, and import libraries when using DLLs on Windows.

- **The share subfolder** contains an `OpenSceneGraph/bin` subdirectory full of example executables, all of which could be run to test various features.

Note that the `osgPlugins-x.x.x` subdirectory may be placed in the `lib` folder in UNIX systems.

Configuring environment variables

The last but not least thing to do before programming with the installed OSG is to configure some important environment variables. It is OK if you ignore this section and continue to the next chapter, but understanding what environment variables do and how to make use of them will bring about significant benefits.

Environment variables are a set of global values that may affect a program's starting behaviors. OSG has defined a number of environment variables that can be used to change its internal running states and display settings. Due to limited textual length, only the most commonly-used variables are introduced here. These are automatically set for the **Current User** if you are using the installer on Windows:

- **OSG_FILE_PATH** identifies the location of the sample data. According to the path value kept by it, OSG could directly find and read any file archived in the specified path, otherwise you may have to enter an absolute path like `C:/Programs Files/OpenSceneGraph/data/cessna.osg`.

- **OSG_NOTIFY_LEVEL** sets a value that controls the verbosity level of debugging messages displayed by OSG. The default value is **NOTICE**. We will discuss this variable, and the notification mechanism, in more detail in *Chapter 3, Creating Your First OSG Program*.

- **OSG_ROOT** is not used by OSG itself. It defines the OSG installation path, which is quite useful for other independent projects that use OSG and the CMake build system.

To set environment variables manually, you can either change the profiles for permanent modification, or start the command-line shell for temporary changes during set-up. On Windows, an environment variable dialog can be found by right-clicking the **My Computer** icon and selecting **Properties | Advanced**, but to set a temporary one you can type `set VARIABLE=value` in the shell before running the application. On UNIX, use start-up profiles and the `export/setenv` commands instead.

Summary

This chapter taught us how to compile, install, and configure an OSG development environment, either by using the prebuilt binaries or completely from the source code. It also illustrated how to make use of the application utilities provided by the OSG distribution.

More specifically, in this chapter we covered:

- ◆ The minimum system requirements for building up an OSG development environment
- ◆ How to utilize the quick installer in order to set up an OSG development environment in a very efficient manner
- ◆ How to set up an OSG development environment from the source code and the CMake tools on different operating systems
- ◆ How to use the scene graph viewer and converter that are distributed with OSG

We have also discussed how to configure environment variables in order to facilitate future programming. Now you are ready to create your first OSG program.

3
Creating Your First OSG Program

This chapter demonstrates a common method to create your own OSG applications. The CMake build system, which has already been discussed in the last chapter, will be used for quickly generating solutions and makefiles on different platforms. The native memory management mechanism of OSG is also explained in detail, which is designed to avoid memory leaks at run-time, OSG also supports a refined argument parser and a debugging message notifier, both of which will be introduced.

In this chapter, we will:

- Show how to build and run your first OSG program with the CMake tool
- Discuss the utilization of OSG native smart pointers for automatic garbage collection and memory deallocation
- Introduce the argument parser that will read arguments from the command line
- Work with the message notifier tool to trace and debug OSG programs

Constructing your own projects

To build an executable program from your own source code, a platform-dependent solution or makefile is always required. For Windows developers, we have already introduced a project wizard tool in the last chapter. But this doesn't work for UNIX and Mac OS X developers, or even those who are using MinGW and Cygwin under Windows.

At the beginning of this chapter, we are going to introduce another way to construct platform-independent projects with the CMake system, by which means, we are able to focus on interacting with the code and ignore the painstaking compiling and building process.

Time for action – building applications with CMake

Before constructing your own project with CMake scripts, it could be helpful to keep the headers and source files together in an empty directory first. The second step is to create a CMakeLists.txt file using any text editor, then and start writing some simple CMake build rules.

1. The following code will implement a project with additional OSG headers and dependency libraries. Please enter them into the newly-created CMakeLists.txt file:

```
cmake_minimum_required( VERSION 2.6 )
project( MyProject )

find_package( OpenThreads )
find_package( osg )
find_package( osgDB )
find_package( osgUtil )
find_package( osgViewer )

macro( config_project PROJNAME LIBNAME )
    include_directories( ${${LIBNAME}_INCLUDE_DIR} )
    target_link_libraries( ${PROJNAME} ${${LIBNAME}_LIBRARY} )
endmacro()

add_executable( MyProject main.cpp )
config_project( MyProject OPENTHREADS )
config_project( MyProject OSG )
config_project( MyProject OSGDB )
config_project( MyProject OSGUTIL )
config_project( MyProject OSGVIEWER )
```

2. We have only added a `main.cpp` source file here, which is made up of the "Hello World" example and will be compiled to generate an executable file named `MyProject`. This small project depends on five major OSG components. All of these configurations can be modified to meet certain requirements and different user applications, as explained in the following chapters.

3. Next, start `cmake-gui` and drag your `CMakeLists.txt` into the GUI. You may not be familiar with the CMake scripts to be executed, at present. However, the CMake wiki will be helpful for further understanding: `http://www.cmake.org/Wiki/CMake`.

4. Follow the step-by-step instructions provided in the last chapter to create and build a Visual Studio solution or a makefile.

5. The only point is that you have to ensure that your CMake software version is equal to or greater than 2.6, and make sure you have the `OSG_ROOT` environment variable set. Otherwise, the `find_package()` macro may not be able to find OSG installations correctly. The following image shows the unexpected errors encountered because OSG headers and libraries were not found in the path indicated by `OSG_ROOT` (or the variable was just missed):

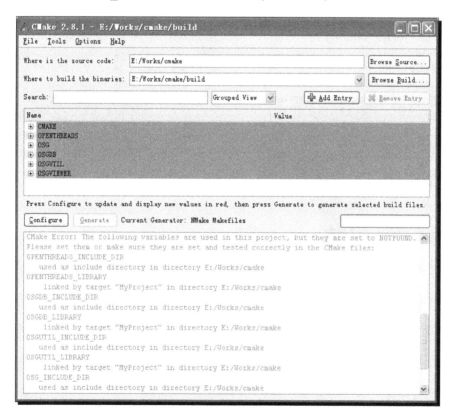

6. Note that, there is no INSTALL project in the Visual Studio solution, or any make install command to run at this time, because we don't write such CMake scripts for post-build installations. You could just run the executable file in the build directory directly.

What just happened?

CMake provides easy-to-read commands to automatically find dependencies for user projects. It will check preset directories and environment variables to see if there are any headers and libraries for the required package.

The environment variable OSG_ROOT (OSG_DIR is OK, too) will facilitate in looking for OSG under Windows and UNIX, as CMake will first search for valid paths defined in it, and check if there are OSG prebuilt headers and libraries existing in these paths.

Pop quiz – configuring OSG path options yourselves

Your CMake may not be able to find the OSG headers and development files for special reasons, for instance, the headers and libraries may be placed in different places, or you just intend to use a distribution different from the one set by OSG_ROOT or OSG_DIR.

Can you set CMake options yourselves at this time? There are often three options in each OSG-related group (OPENTHREADS, OSG, OSGDB, and so on), such as OSG_INCLUDE_DIR, OSG_LIBRARY, and OSG_LIBRARY_DEBUG. What do they mean, in your opinion?

Have a go hero – testing with different generators

Just try a series of tests to generate your project, using Visual Studio, MinGW, and the UNIX gcc compiler. You will find that CMake is a convenient tool for building binary files from source code on different platforms. Maybe this is also a good start to learning programming in a multi-platform style.

Using a root node

Now we are going to write some code and build it with a self-created CMake script. We will again make a slight change to the frequently-used "Hello World" example.

Time for action – improving the "Hello World" example

The included headers, `<osgDB/ReadFile>` and `<osgViewer/Viewer>`, do not need to be modified. We only add a root variable that provides the runtime access to the Cessna model and assigns it to the `setSceneData()` method.

1. In the main entry, record the Cessna model with a variable named `root`:

```
osg::ref_ptr<osg::Node> root = osgDB::readNodeFile("cessna.osg");
osgViewer::Viewer viewer;
viewer.setSceneData( root.get() );
return viewer.run();
```

2. Build and run it at once:

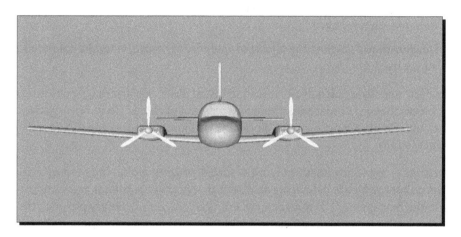

3. You will see no difference between this example and the previous "Hello World". So what actually happened?

What just happened?

In this example, we introduced two new OSG classes: `osg::ref_ptr<>` and `osg::Node`. The `osg::Node` class represents the basic element of a **scene graph**. The variable `root` stands for the **root node** of a Cessna model, which is used as the scene data to be visualized.

Meanwhile, an instance of the `osg::ref_ptr<>` class template is created to manage the node object. It is a **smart pointer**, which provides additional features for the purpose of efficient **memory management**.

Understanding memory management

In a typical programming scenario, the developer should create a pointer to the **root node**, which directly or indirectly manages all other **child nodes** of the scene graph. In that case, the application will traverse the **scene graph** and delete each node and its internal data carefully when they no longer need to be rendered. This process is tiresome and error-prone, debugging dozens of bad trees and wild pointers, because developers can never know how many other objects still keep a pointer to the one being deleted. However without writing the management code, data segments occupied by all scene nodes will never be deleted, which will lead to unexpected memory leaks.

This is why **memory management** is important in OSG programming. A basic concept of **memory management** always involves two topics:

1. **Allocation**: Providing the memory needed by an object, by allocating the required memory block.

2. **Deallocation**: Recycling the allocated memory for reuse, when its data is no longer used.

Some modern languages, such as C#, Java, and Visual Basic, use a garbage collector to free memory blocks that are unreachable from any program variables. That means to store the number of objects reaching a memory block, and deallocate the memory when the number decrements to zero.

The standard C++ approach does not work in such a way, but we can mimic it by means of a **smart pointer**, which is defined as an object that acts like a pointer, but is much smarter in the management of memory. For example, the `boost` library provides the `boost::shared_ptr<>` class template to store pointers in order to dynamically allocated related objects.

ref_ptr<> and Referenced classes

Fortunately, OSG also provides a native **smart pointer**, `osg::ref_ptr<>`, for the purpose of automatic garbage collection and deallocation. To make it work properly, OSG also provides the `osg::Referenced` class to manage reference-counted memory blocks, which is used as the base class of any classes that may serve as the template argument.

The `osg::ref_ptr<>` class template re-implements a number of C++ operators as well as member functions, and thus provides convenient methods to developers. Its main components are as follows:

♦ `get()`: This public method returns the managed pointer, for instance, the `osg::Node*` pointer if you are using `osg::Node` as the template argument.

- `operator*()`: This is actually a dereference operator, which returns **l-value** at the pointer address, for instance, the `osg::Node&` reference variable.

- `operator->()` and `operator=()`: These operators allow a user application to use `osg::ref_ptr<>` as a normal pointer. The former calls member functions of the managed object, and the latter replaces the current managed pointer with a new one.

- `operator==()`, `operator!=()`, and `operator!()`: These operators help to compare smart pointers, or check if a certain pointer is invalid. An `osg::ref_ptr<>` object with NULL value assigned or without any assignment is considered invalid.

- `valid()`: This public method returns true if the **managed pointer** is not NULL. The expression `some_ptr.valid()` equals to `some_ptr!=NULL` if `some_ptr` is defined as a **smart pointer**.

- `release()`: This public method is useful when returning the managed address from a function. It will be discussed later.

The `osg::Referenced` class is the pure base class of all elements in a scene graph, such as nodes, geometries, rendering states, and any other allocatable scene objects. The `osg::Node` class actually inherits from `osg::Referenced` indirectly. This is the reason why we program as follows:

```
osg::ref_ptr<osg::Node> root;
```

The `osg::Referenced` class contains an integer number to handle the memory block allocated. The **reference count** is initialized to 0 in the class constructor, and will be increased by 1 if the `osg::Referenced` object is referred to by an `osg::ref_ptr<>` **smart pointer**. On the contrary, the number will be decreased by 1 if the object is removed from a certain **smart pointer**. The object itself will be automatically destroyed when no longer referenced by any smart pointers.

The `osg::Referenced` class provides three main member methods:

- The public method `ref()` increases the **referenced counting number** by 1

- The public method `unref()` decreases the **referenced counting number** by 1

- The public method `referenceCount()` returns the value of the current **referenced counting number**, which is useful for code debugging

These methods could also work for classes that are derived from `osg::Referenced`. Note that it is very rarely necessary to call `ref()` or `unref()` directly in user programs, which means that the reference count is managed manually and may conflict with what the `osg::ref_ptr<>` is going to do. Otherwise, OSG's internal garbage collecting system will get the wrong number of smart pointers in use and even crash when managing memory blocks in an improper way.

Collecting garbage: why and how

Here are some reasons for using smart pointers and the garbage collection system in programming:

- **Fewer bugs**: Using smart pointers means the automatic initialization and cleanup of pointers. No dangling pointers will be created because they are always reference-counted.

- **Efficient management**: Objects will be reclaimed as soon as they are no longer referenced, which gives more available memory to applications with limited resources.

- **Easy to debug**: We can easily obtain the **referenced counting number** and other information on objects, and then apply other optimizations and experiments.

For instance, a scene graph tree is composed by a **root node** and multiple levels of child nodes. Assuming that all children are managed with `osg::ref_ptr<>`, user applications may only keep the pointer to the **root node**. As is illustrated by the following image, the operation of deleting the **root node** pointer will cause a *cascading effect* that will destroy the whole node hierarchy:

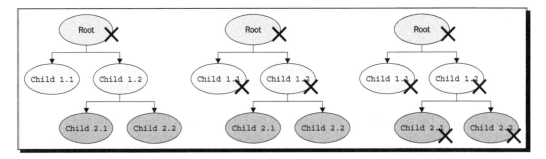

Each node in the example scene graph is managed by its parent, and will automatically be unreferenced during the deletion of the **parent node**. This node, if no longer referenced by any other nodes, will be destroyed immediately, and all of its children will be freed up. The entire scene graph will finally be cleaned without worries after the last **group node** or **leaf node** is deleted.

The process is really convenient and efficient, isn't it? Please make sure the OSG **smart pointer** can work for you, and use a class derived from `osg::Referenced` as the `osg::ref_ptr<>` template argument, and correctly assign newly-allocated objects to smart pointers.

A **smart pointer** can be used either as a local variable, a global variable, or a class member variable, and will automatically decrease the **referenced counting number** when reassigned to another object or moved out of the smart pointer's declaration scope.

It is strongly recommended that user applications always use smart pointers to manage their scenes, but there are still some issues that need special attention:

- `osg::Referenced` and its derivatives should be created from the heap only. They cannot be used as local variables because class destructors are declared **protected** internally for safety. For example:

  ```
  osg::ref_ptr<osg::Node> node = new osg::Node; // this is legal
  osg::Node node; // this is illegal!
  ```

- A regular C++ pointer is still workable temporarily. But user applications should remember to assign it to `osg::ref_ptr<>` or add it to a **scene graph** element (almost all OSG scene classes use smart pointers to manage child objects) in the end, as it is always the safest approach.

  ```
  osg::Node* tmpNode = new osg::Node; // this is OK
  ...
  osg::ref_ptr<osg::Node> node = tmpNode; // Good finish!
  ```

- Don't play with reference cycles, as the garbage collecting mechanism cannot handle it. A **reference cycle** means that an object refers to itself directly or indirectly, which leads to an incorrect calculation of the **referenced counting number**.

The scene graph shown in the following image contains two kinds of reference cycles, which are both invalid. The node **Child 1.1** directly adds itself as the **child node** and will form a dead cycle while traversing to its children, because it is the child of itself, too! The node **Child 2.2**, which also makes a **reference cycle** indirectly, will cause the same problem while running:

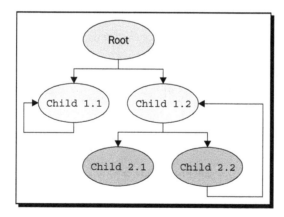

Now let's have a better grasp of the basic concepts of memory management, through a very simple example.

Tracing the managed entities

The main point that we are interested in is how `osg::ref_ptr<>` binds and handles an `osg::Referenced` object, and when the managed object will be destroyed. What we have already learnt is: the managed object will be automatically destroyed when it is no longer referenced by any smart pointers, or when its referrer is out of the declaration scope. Now let's see how this is performed in practice.

Time for action – monitoring counted objects

We will first declare a customized class that is derived from `osg::Referenced`. This can benefit from the garbage collecting system by using the **smart pointer**. After that, let's take a look at the initialization and cleanup procedures of our referenced objects.

1. Include the necessary headers:

```
#include <osg/ref_ptr>
#include <osg/Referenced>
#include <iostream>
```

2. Define the customized `MonitoringTarget` class with a unique name, `_id`. We will simply use the standard output to print out verbose information when constructing and destructing:

```
class MonitoringTarget : public osg::Referenced
{
public:
    MonitoringTarget( int id ) : _id(id)
    { std::cout << "Constructing target " << _id << std::endl; }

protected:
    virtual ~MonitoringTarget()
    { std::cout << "Destroying target " << _id << std::endl; }

    int _id;
};
```

3. In the main function, we will first create a new `MonitoringTarget` object, and assign it to two different smart pointers, `target` and `anotherTarget`, and see if the referenced count changed:

```
osg::ref_ptr<MonitoringTarget> target = new MonitoringTarget(0);
std::cout << "Referenced count before referring: "
        << target->referenceCount() << std::endl;
osg::ref_ptr<MonitoringTarget> anotherTarget = target;
std::cout << "Referenced count after referring: "
        << target->referenceCount() << std::endl;
```

4. A second experiment is to create new objects in a cycle, but never delete them. Do you think this will cause memory leaks or not?

```
for ( unsigned int i=1; i<5; ++i )
{
    osg::ref_ptr<MonitoringTarget> subTarget =
        new MonitoringTarget(i);
}
```

5. The result is printed as shown in the following screenshot. As the construction and destruction processes both write to the standard output, a list of texts will be produced in the console.

```
Constructing target 0
Referenced count before referring: 1
Referenced count after referring: 2
Constructing target 1
Destroying target 1
Constructing target 2
Destroying target 2
Constructing target 3
Destroying target 3
Constructing target 4
Destroying target 4
Destroying target 0
```

What just happened?

A new `MonitoringTarget` object was created with the ID 0 and assigned to the **smart pointer** `target`. Another **smart pointer**, `anotherTarget`, immediately refers to the target and thus increases the referenced count of the `MonitoringTarget` object to 2, which means that the object is referenced by two smart pointers at the same time. It won't be deleted until all referrers are redirected or destroyed, as illustrated:

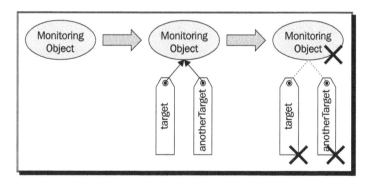

After that, we were going to try constructing MonitoringTarget objects with the ID 1 to 4 in a cycle. Every time, the allocated object was set to an osg::ref_ptr<> pointer, but without any explicit deletion. You will notice that the MonitoringTarget object was automatically deleted at the end of each loop, and would never cause memory leaks.

Another interesting issue is to decide the best time to actually delete an unreferenced object. Most osg::Referenced-based classes define their destructors as protected members, so the C++ delete operator can't be used directly in user programs. The deletion process will be performed internally when the **reference count** decreases to 0. But this may still cause serious problems if some other threads are working on the object at the same time when it is being deleted. That is to say, the garbage collecting system may not be thread-safe for massive use!

Fortunately, OSG has already provided an object deletion scheduler in response to the problem. This deletion scheduler, named osg::DeleteHandler, will not perform the deleting operation at once, but defer it for a while. All objects to be deleted will be stored temporarily, until it is a safe time to release them. The osg::DeleteHandler class is managed by the OSG rendering backend. User applications should always pay little attention to this class, unless you have to implement another deletion handler yourselves, some day.

Have a go hero – returning from a function

We have already mentioned that there is a release() method that can be used when returning from a function. The following code will tell more about its usage:

```
MonitoringTarget* createMonitoringTarget( unsigned int id )
{
osg::ref_ptr<MonitoringTarget> target = new
    MonitoringTarget(i);
return target.release();
}
```

Try replacing the new MonitoringTarget(i) statements in the last example with this function. It is for the purpose of returning from a function and has no side effects.

Pop quiz – release a smart pointer

The release() method of osg::ref_ptr<> will prevent the **smart pointer** from managing the memory that it points to. In the function mentioned in the *Have a go hero* section, release() will first decrease the **reference count** to 0. After that, instead of deleting the memory, it directly returns the actual pointer. As long as the calling code stores the returned pointer in another osg::ref_ptr<>, there will be no memory leaks.

So, what will happen if the function returns `target.get()` instead of `target.release()`? Can you figure out why `release()` is always preferred for returning the allocated address in a function?

Parsing command-line arguments

Command-line arguments to the main function define different parameters for user applications. The main function declaration always looks like this:

```
int main( int argc, char** argv );
```

The `argc` and `argv` arguments form a string array containing the application name and other necessary arguments. OSG provides a fast and safe `osg::ArgumentParser` to read and make use of them.

Time for action – reading the model filename from the command line

The most common public method of `osg::ArgumentParser` is the overloaded `read()` function. In this example, we are going to read command-line arguments with a special format and apply the parsing result to the `osgDB::readNodeFile()` function.

1. Include the necessary headers:

    ```
    #include <osgDB/ReadFile>
    #include <osgViewer/Viewer>
    ```

2. In the main function, try reading `--model` and the `filename` from the input arguments:

    ```
    osg::ArgumentParser arguments( &argc, argv );
    std::string filename;
    arguments.read( "--model", filename );
    ```

3. Read `Node` from the specified file and initialize the viewer. This is very similar to some previous examples except that it replaces the `const` string `"Cessna.osg"` with a `std::string` variable:

    ```
    osg::ref_ptr<osg::Node> root = osgDB::readNodeFile( filename );
    osgViewer::Viewer viewer;
    viewer.setSceneData( root.get() );
    return viewer.run();
    ```

4. Build and start this example! Assuming that your executable file is `MyProject.exe`, type the following command in the prompt:

```
# MyProject.exe --model dumptruck.osg
```

5. We will see more than a Cessna model now. It is a dump truck loaded from the disk! Please be aware that you should have the OSG sample data installed, and the environment variable `OSG_FILE_PATH` set.

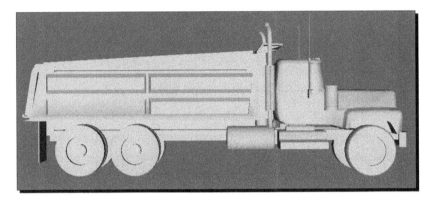

What just happened?

The dump truck model is loaded and rendered on the screen. Here, the most important point is that the filename `dumptruck.osg` is obtained from the command-line argument. The `read()` function, which consists of a format string parameter and a result parameter, helps to successfully find the first occurrence of the user-defined option `--model` and the filename argument that follows.

The `read()` function of the `osg::ArgumentParser` class is overloaded. You may obtain integers, float and double values, and even mathematical vectors, in addition to strings, from its parameters. For instance, to read a customized option `--size` with a single precision value from the command line, just use the following code:

```
float size = 0.0f;
arguments.read( "--size", size );
```

The initial value of `size` will not be changed if there is no such argument, `--size`.

Tracing with the notifier

The OSG notifier mechanism provides a novel method of outputting verbose debugging messages, either from the OSG rendering backend or from the user level. It is really an important and time-honored method for tracing and debugging programs. In addition, the notifier is also used throughout the OSG core functionalities and plugins to show errors, warning messages, or information about the work in progress. Developers may simply insert debugging print functions liberally in the source code files. The print function, `osg::notify()`, is designed to accept different levels of messages and send them to the console or user-defined controllers.

The `osg::notify()` function can be used as the standard output stream `std::cout`. It requires a `NotifySeverity` argument to indicate the message level, which can be `ALWAYS`, `FATAL`, `WARN`, `NOTICE`, `INFO`, `DEBUG_INFO`, and `DEBUG_FP`, sorted from the most severity to the least. For instance:

```
osg::notify(osg::WARN) << "Some warn message." << std::endl;
```

This will print out a line of the warning message by default. Here `osg::WARN` is used to indicate the notify level to the OSG notifier system.

A series of macro definitions, such as `OSG_FATAL`, `OSG_WARN`, and `OSG_NOTICE`, will do the same work as the `osg::notify()` function, with different severity levels.

Redirecting the notifier

The OSG output message always includes important information about the running state, graphics system extensions, and possible problems in the OSG backend and user applications. This is also important as a reference source for debugging OSG-based programs.

In some cases, there is no console output in an application, which prevents us from reading notifier messages and finding possible bugs. However, the `osg::NotifyHandler` derived class can be used to redirect the notifier to another output stream, such as files or GUI widgets.

Time for action – saving the log file

We will make use of the `std::ofstream` class to redirect the OSG internal notify messages to an external log file. The virtual function `notify()` of the `osg::NotifyHandler` derived class should be overridden to apply standard file stream operations, and a global function `osg::setNotifyHandler()` is called before everything starts as well.

1. Include the necessary headers:

```
#include <osgDB/ReadFile>
#include <osgViewer/Viewer>
#include <fstream>
```

2. Implement the derived class `LogFileHandler`, which will redirect notify messages to the file stream:

```
class LogFileHandler : public osg::NotifyHandler
{
public:
    LogFileHandler( const std::string& file )
    { _log.open( file.c_str() ); }
    virtual ~LogFileHandler() { _log.close(); }

    virtual void notify(osg::NotifySeverity severity,
                        const char* msg)
    { _log << msg; }

protected:
    std::ofstream _log;
};
```

3. Now set a new notify handler to the entire OSG system, and work under the **INFO** level to see more verbose messages. The function `osgDB::readNodeFiles` here directly reads all usable filenames from the command line and merges them into the root node. We also add an `OSG_FATAL` macro to check if there is no scene graph data loaded:

```
int main( int argc, char** argv )
{
    osg::setNotifyLevel( osg::INFO );
    osg::setNotifyHandler( new LogFileHandler("output.txt") );

    osg::ArgumentParser arguments( &argc, argv );
    osg::ref_ptr<osg::Node> root = osgDB::readNodeFiles(
        arguments );
    if ( !root )
```

```
    {
        OSG_FATAL << arguments.getApplicationName()
                    <<": No data loaded." << std::endl;
        return -1;
    }

    osgViewer::Viewer viewer;
    viewer.setSceneData( root.get() );
    return viewer.run();
}
```

4. Build and start the example. All information will be saved in the log file output.txt, which is also indicated in the example. Try the command line with the newly-generated executable MyProject.exe this time:

```
# MyProject.exe dumptruck.osg
```

5. Press the *Esc* key to quit, and then open the resulting log file in the working directory with notepad (on Windows) or any text editor:

```
[INFO]: Opened DynamicLibrary osgPlugins-2.9.8/osgdb_osg.dll
[INFO]: CullSettings::readEnvironmentalVariables()
[INFO]: CullSettings::readEnvironmentalVariables()
[INFO]: Constructing PixelBufferObject for image=025AA488
[INFO]: Opened DynamicLibrary osgPlugins-2.9.8/osgdb_deprecated_osg.dll
[INFO]: OSGReaderWriter wrappers loaded OK
[INFO]: CullSettings::readEnvironmentalVariables()
[INFO]: DatabasePager::addDatabaseThread() HANDLE_NON_HTTP
[INFO]: DatabasePager::addDatabaseThread() HANDLE_ONLY_HTTP
[INFO]: CullSettings::readEnvironmentalVariables()
[INFO]: CullSettings::readEnvironmentalVariables()
[INFO]: CullSettings::readEnvironmentalVariables()
[INFO]: CullSettings::readEnvironmentalVariables()
[INFO]: View::setSceneData() Reusing exisitng scene025B8DB0
[INFO]: Viewer::realize() - No valid contexts found, setting up view across all screens.
[INFO]: GraphicsContext::getWindowingSystemInterface() 0259BC90 00F48A20
[INFO]: GraphicsContext::registerGraphicsContext 026623E0
[INFO]: GraphicsContext::createNewContextID() creating contextID=0
[INFO]: Updating the MaxNumberOfGraphicsContexts to 1
[INFO]:    GraphicsWindow has been created successfully.
[INFO]: osg::State::_maxTexturePoolSize=0
[INFO]: osg::State::_maxBufferObjectPoolSize=0
[INFO]: Viewer::startThreading() - starting threading
[INFO]: Viewer::startThreading() - contexts.size()=1
[INFO]: Making scene thread safe
```

6. Don't be discouraged if you can't read and understand all of the information listed here. It only shows how OSG is starting and getting every part to work properly. It will be of great help in future development.

What just happened?

By default, OSG will send messages to the standard output stream `std::cout` and error stream `std::cerr`. However, these messages can be easily redirected to other streams and even the GUI text windows. A log file here is friendly to end users and helps them a lot, while sending feedbacks.

Besides, setting the `osg::setNotifyLevel()` function will make the notify level reset to the specified level or a higher level. The notifier system then ignores statements from lower levels and prints nothing to the output stream. For instance, assuming that you have the following lines in your application:

```
osg::setNotifyLevel( osg::FATAL );
…
osg::notify(osg::WARN) << "Some warn message." << std::endl;
```

The message with the notifier level lower than `FATAL` will not be printed any more.

The environment variable `OSG_NOTIFY_LEVEL`, which was mentioned in the previous chapter, can be used to control the displayed message level, too, for any OSG-based applications.

Summary

This chapter provided a simple guide to creating your own simple OSG program with the CMake tool, and introduced some practical utilities. OSG **uses** smart pointers **heavily** for efficient manipulation of operating system resources allocated for each **scene graph** node at run time, which is crucial to the performance of these safety-critical programs. To help understand the working principle of smart pointers, we spent much of the chapter explaining the use of `osg::ref_ptr<>` and how to calculate the referenced count, and discussing various situations that may occur when managing OSG scene elements.

In this chapter, we specifically covered:

- How to write a simple CMake script file and make it work with your own source code and OSG dependencies
- The principle of smart pointers and the garbage collection mechanism of OSG
- Advantages and notes on using the native smart pointers with scene graph objects
- Some other useful classes and functions for parsing command-line arguments, and tracing and debugging your source code

4

Building Geometry Models

The basic operation of OpenGL's graphical pipeline is to accept vertex data (points, lines, triangles, and polygons) and pixel data (graphical image data), convert them into fragments and store them in the frame buffer. The frame buffer serves as a major interface between developers and the computer display, which maps each frame of graphic contents into memory space for read-write operation. OSG encapsulates the whole OpenGL vertex transformation and primitive assembly operations in order to manage and send vertex data to the OpenGL pipeline, as well as some data transmission optimizations and additional polygonal techniques for improving rendering performance.

In this chapter, we just focus on how to draw and render geometry models through a fast path, and will cover the following topics:

- How to quickly draw basic objects with a few necessary parameters
- How to set vertices and vertex attribute arrays to construct a geometry object
- The reason and methods of indexing vertex data with primitives
- How to make use of different polygon techniques to optimize rendering
- How to get access to geometry attributes and primitives
- Integrate OpenGL drawing calls into your OSG-based applications

How OpenGL draws objects

OpenGL uses **geometry primitives** to draw different objects in the 3D world. A geometry primitive, which may be a set of points, lines, triangles, or polygonal faces, determines how OpenGL sorts and renders its associated vertex data. The easiest way to render a primitive is to specify a list of vertices between the `glBegin()` and `glEnd()` pair, which is called **immediate mode**, but it is inefficient in most cases.

The vertex data, including vertex coordinates, normals, colors, and texture coordinates, can also be stored in various arrays. Primitives will be formed by dereferencing and indexing the array elements. This method, named **vertex array**, reduces redundant shared vertices and thus performs better than **immediate mode**.

Display lists also significantly improve application performance, because all vertex and pixel data are compiled and copied into the graphics memory. The prepared primitives can be reused repeatedly, without transmitting data over and over again. It helps a lot in drawing static geometries.

The **vertex buffer object** (**VBO**) mechanism allows **vertex array** data to be stored in high-performance memory. This provides a more efficient solution for transferring dynamic data.

By default, OSG uses **vertex arrays** and **display lists** to manage and render geometries. However, this may change depending on different data types and rendering strategies.

We would like to also call attention to the removal of **immediate mode** and **display lists** in OpenGL ES and OpenGL 3.x, for the purpose of producing a more lightweight interface. Of course OpenGL 3.x and further versions will keep these deprecated APIs for backward compatibility. However, they are not recommended to be used in new code.

Geode and Drawable classes

The `osg::Geode` class corresponds to the **leaf node** of a scene graph. It has no child nodes, but always contains geometry information for rendering. Its name `Geode` is short for *geometry node*.

The geometry data to be drawn are stored in a set of `osg::Drawable` objects managed by `osg::Geode`. The non-instantiable `osg::Drawable` class is defined as a pure virtual class. It has several subclasses for rendering models, images, and texts to the OpenGL pipeline. These renderable elements are collectively called **drawables**.

The `osg::Geode` class provides a few methods to attach and detach **drawables**, as well as collect information about them:

1. The public method `addDrawable()` takes an `osg::Drawable` pointer as its parameter and attaches a **drawable** to the `osg::Geode` instance. All **drawables** added are internally managed by the `osg::ref_ptr<>` smart pointer.

2. The public methods `removeDrawable()` and `removeDrawables()` will detach one or more **drawables** from the current `osg::Geode` object, and decrease their **referenced counting number** as well. The `removeDrawable()` method uses an `osg::Drawable` pointer as the only parameter, and `removeDrawables()` accepts two parameters: the zero-based index of the start element, and number of elements to be removed.

3. The `getDrawable()` method returns the `osg::Drawable` object stored at the specified zero-based index.

4. The `getNumDrawables()` method returns the total number of attached **drawables**. Developers are then able to traverse each **drawable** in a cycle with the `getDrawable()` method, or remove all **drawables** at once by using the following code:

    ```
    geode->removeDrawables( 0, geode->getNumDrawables() );
    ```

Rendering basic shapes

OSG provides an `osg::ShapeDrawable` class, which inherits from the `osg::Drawable` base class, to render basic geometry shapes quickly with plain parameters. An `osg::ShapeDrawable` instance always includes an `osg::Shape` object to indicate the specified geometry's type and properties.

The `setShape()` method is usually used to allocate and set a shape. For example:

```
shapeDrawable->setShape( new osg::Box(osg::Vec3(1.0f, 0.0f, 0.0f),
                         10.0f, 10.0f, 5.0f) );
```

It will assign a box with a center point at (1.0, 0.0, 0.0) in its local coordinate space, width and height of `10`, and depth of `5`. Here, the class `osg::Vec3` represents a three-element vector in OSG. Other predefined classes such as `osg::Vec2` and `osg::Vec4` will also help when defining vertices, colors, normals, and texture coordinates.

Note that `osg::Vec3` means a float type vector, and `osg::Vec3d` means a double type one, as do `osg::Vec2` and `osg::Vec2d`, `osg::Vec4` and `osg::Vec4d`, and so on.

The most frequently used basic shapes defined in OSG are: `osg::Box`, `osg::Capsule`, `osg::Cone`, `osg::Cylinder`, and `osg::Sphere`. Their appearances can be well defined by passing parameters directly to constructors.

Time for action – quickly creating simple objects

It is easy to create simple objects by using an osg::Shape subclass. We will take three typical shapes as examples: a box with different width, height, and depth values, a sphere with a radius value, and a cone with a radius and a height.

1. Include necessary headers:

```
#include <osg/ShapeDrawable>
#include <osg/Geode>
#include <osgViewer/Viewer>
```

2. Add three osg::ShapeDrawable objects successively, each with a type of basic shape. We set these shapes to different positions to make them visible to viewers at the same time, and for the reason of distinguishing them from each other, we color the latter two shapes green and respectively, blue by using the setColor() method of osg::ShapeDrawable:

```
osg::ref_ptr<osg::ShapeDrawable> shape1 = new osg::ShapeDrawable;
shape1->setShape( new osg::Box(osg::Vec3(-3.0f, 0.0f, 0.0f),
                               2.0f, 2.0f, 1.0f) );

osg::ref_ptr<osg::ShapeDrawable> shape2 = new osg::ShapeDrawable;
shape2->setShape( new osg::Sphere(osg::Vec3(3.0f, 0.0f, 0.0f),
                                  1.0f) );
shape2->setColor( osg::Vec4(0.0f, 0.0f, 1.0f, 1.0f) );

osg::ref_ptr<osg::ShapeDrawable> shape3 = new osg::ShapeDrawable;
shape3->setShape( new osg::Cone(osg::Vec3(0.0f, 0.0f, 0.0f),
                                1.0f, 1.0f) );
shape3->setColor( osg::Vec4(0.0f, 1.0f, 0.0f, 1.0f) );
```

3. An osg::Geode object is created, and all the **drawables** are added to it. Note that the **drawables** and the geometry node are all managed by the osg::ref_ptr<> smart pointer here. The osg::Geode object is finally used as the scene root of the viewer:

```
osg::ref_ptr<osg::Geode> root = new osg::Geode;
root->addDrawable( shape1.get() );
root->addDrawable( shape2.get() );
root->addDrawable( shape3.get() );

osgViewer::Viewer viewer;
viewer.setSceneData( root.get() );
return viewer.run();
```

4. Now it's time to see if these shapes are rendered properly. We don't have to care about the actual drawing work of vertex positions, normals, and colors here, which brings convenience for debugging and quick shape viewing:

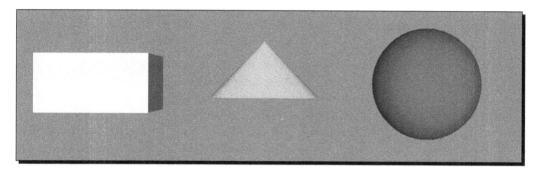

What just happened?

The `osg::ShapeDrawable` class is useful for quick display, but it is not an efficient way of drawing **geometry primitives**. It should only be used for quick prototyping and debugging when you develop 3D applications. To create geometries with high performance computation and visualization requirements, the `osg::Geometry` class, which is going to be introduced, is always a better choice.

OSG has an internal `osg::GLBeginEndAdapter` class that is used to perform basic shape drawing operations. This class enables the use of **vertex arrays** in the style of a `glBegin()` and `glEnd()` pair, which makes the implementation of basic shapes easy to understand and extend.

To get and use an initialized `osg::GLBeginEndAdapter` object, you should define a class derived from the `osg::Drawable` base class and re-implement its `drawImplementation()` method, and start programming as if you are writing the classic OpenGL 1.0 drawing calls:

```
void drawImplementation( osg::RenderInfo& renderInfo ) const
{
    osg::GLBeginEndAdapter& gl =
        renderInfo.getState()->getGLBeginEndAdapter();
    gl.Begin( … );
    gl.Vertex3fv( … );
    gl.End();
}
```

More information about re-implementing the `osg::Drawable` class can be found in the *Implementing your own drawables* section of this chapter.

Storing array data

As already mentioned in earlier chapters, OSG supports **vertex arrays** and **VBO** to speed up the rendering process. To manage the vertex data used in these two mechanisms, OSG defines a basic `osg::Array` class and a few derived classes for commonly used array and index array types.

The `osg::Array` class can't be instantiated, but it declares interfaces to exchange with OpenGL calls and buffer data modifiers. Its subclasses (`osg::Vec2Array`, `osg::Vec3Array`, `osg::UIntArray`, etc.) inherit the characteristics of the *Standard Template Library* vector class, and can thus make use of all of the `std::vector` members, including `push_back()`, `pop_back()`, `size()`, and STL algorithms and iterators.

The following code will add a three-element vector to an existing `osg::Vec3Array` object named *vertices*:

```
vertices->push_back( osg::Vec3(1.0f, 0.0f, 0.0f) );
```

The OSG built-in array classes should be allocated from heap and managed by **smart pointers**. However, it is not necessary for the array elements such as `osg::Vec2` and `osg::Vec3` to follow this rule, as they are very basic data types.

The `osg::Geometry` class acts as the high-level wrapper of the OpenGL vertex array functionality. It records different types of arrays and manages a geometry primitive set to render these vertex data in an orderly manner. It is derived from `osg::Drawable` class and can be added to an `osg::Geode` object at any time. This class accepts arrays as basic data carriers and uses them to produce simple or complex geometry models.

Vertices and vertex attributes

The Vertex is the atomic element of geometry primitives. It uses several numeric attributes to describe a point in 2D or 3D spaces, including vertex position, color, normal and texture coordinates, fog coordinate, and so on. The position value is always required, and other attributes will help to define the nature of the point. OpenGL accepts up to 16 generic attributes to be specified per vertex, and can create different arrays in which to store each of them. All attribute arrays are supported by the `osg::Geometry` class with the corresponding `set*Array()` methods.

A table of built-in vertex attributes in OpenGL is listed below:

Attribute	Suggested data type	osg::Geometry method	Equivalent OpenGL call
Position	3D vectors	`setVertexArray()`	`glVertexPointer()`
Normal	3D vectors normalized to the range [0, 1]	`setNormalArray()`	`glNormalPointer()`
Color	4D vectors normalized to the range [0, 1]	`setColorArray()`	`glColorPointer()`
Secondary color	4D vectors normalized to the range [0, 1]	`setSecondaryColorArray()`	`glSecondaryColor PointerEXT()`
Fog coordinate	Float values	`setFogCoordArray()`	`glFogCoordPointerEXT()`
Texture coordinates	2D or 3D vectors	`setTexCoordArray()`	`glTexCoordPointer()`
Other general attributes	User-defined values	`setVertexAttribArray()`	`glVertexAttrib PointerARB()`

A vertex usually contains eight texture coordinates and three general attributes in current OpenGL graphics systems. In principle, each vertex should set all of its attributes to certain values, and form a set of arrays with exactly the same size; otherwise the undefined ones may cause unexpected problems. OSG provides binding methods to make the work more convenient. For instance, developers may call the public method `setColorBinding()` of an `osg::Geometry` object geom, and take an enumerate as the parameter:

```
geom->setColorBinding( osg::Geometry::BIND_PER_VERTEX );
```

This indicates that the color and the vertex are put into a one-to-one relationship. However, see the following code:

```
geom->setColorBinding( osg::Geometry::BIND_OVERALL );
```

It will apply a single color value to the entire geometry. There are `setNormalBinding()`, `setSecondaryColorBinding()`, `setFogCoordBinding()`, and `setVertexAttribBinding()`, which do the similar work for other attribute types.

Specifying drawing types

The next step after setting vertex attribute arrays is to tell the `osg::Geometry` object how to render them. The virtual base class `osg::PrimitiveSet` is used to manage a **geometry primitive** set which records the rendering order information of vertices. The `osg::Geometry` provides a few public methods to operate on one or more primitive sets:

1. The `addPrimitiveSet()` method takes an `osg::PrimitiveSet` pointer as the parameter and attaches a primitive set to the `osg::Geometry` object.

2. The `removePrimitiveSet()` requires a zero-based index parameter and the number of primitive sets to remove. It will remove one or more attached primitive sets.

3. The `getPrimitiveSet()` returns the `osg::PrimitiveSet` pointer at the specified index.

4. The `getNumPrimitiveSets()` returns the total number of primitive sets.

The `osg::PrimitiveSet` class is unable to be instantiated directly, but it brings out a few subclasses that are used to encapsulate OpenGL's `glDrawArrays()` and `glDrawElements()` entries, for example `osg::DrawArrays` and `osg::DrawElementsUInt`.

The `osg::DrawArrays` class uses a number of sequential elements from **vertex arrays** to construct a sequence of **geometry primitives**. It can be created and attached to an `osg::Geometry` object geom via the following declaration:

```
geom->addPrimitiveSet( new osg::DrawArrays(mode, first, count) );
```

The first parameter mode specifies what kind of primitives to render. Like the OpenGL `glDrawArrays()` entry, `osg::DrawArrays` usually accepts ten kinds of primitives: GL_POINTS, GL_LINE_STRIP, GL_LINE_LOOP, GL_LINES, GL_TRIANGLE_STRIP, GL_TRIANGLE_FAN, GL_TRIANGLES, GL_QUAD_STRIP, GL_QUADS, and GL_POLYGON.

The second and third parameters indicate that the primitive set begins at index *first* and has *count* elements altogether. Developers should make sure that there are at least *first + count* elements in the vertex array. OSG won't audit if the total number of vertices meets the requirement of the primitive set, which could cause crashes.

Time for action – drawing a colored quad

Let's work on a common shape in order to see the steps to complete a renderable geometry model. We will create a quadrangle with only four vertices as the four corners, and use GL_QUADS mode to draw these vertices. The GL_QUADS mode tells OpenGL to combine the first four coordinates in the vertex array as one quad, the second four as the second quad, and so on.

1. Include the necessary headers:

```
#include <osg/Geometry>
#include <osg/Geode>
#include <osgViewer/Viewer>
```

2. Create the vertex array and push the four corner points to the back of the array by using `std::vector` like operations:

```
osg::ref_ptr<osg::Vec3Array> vertices = new osg::Vec3Array;
vertices->push_back( osg::Vec3(0.0f, 0.0f, 0.0f) );
vertices->push_back( osg::Vec3(1.0f, 0.0f, 0.0f) );
vertices->push_back( osg::Vec3(1.0f, 0.0f, 1.0f) );
vertices->push_back( osg::Vec3(0.0f, 0.0f, 1.0f) );
```

3. We have to indicate the normal of each vertex; otherwise OpenGL will use a default (0, 0, 1) normal vector and the lighting equation calculation may be incorrect. The four vertices actually face the same direction, so a single normal vector is enough. We will also set the `setNormalBinding()` method to `BIND_OVERALL` later.

```
osg::ref_ptr<osg::Vec3Array> normals = new osg::Vec3Array;
normals->push_back( osg::Vec3(0.0f,-1.0f, 0.0f) );
```

4. We will indicate a unique color value to each vertex and make them colored. By default, OpenGL will use smooth coloring and blend colors at each vertex together:

```
osg::ref_ptr<osg::Vec4Array> colors = new osg::Vec4Array;
colors->push_back( osg::Vec4(1.0f, 0.0f, 0.0f, 1.0f) );
colors->push_back( osg::Vec4(0.0f, 1.0f, 0.0f, 1.0f) );
colors->push_back( osg::Vec4(0.0f, 0.0f, 1.0f, 1.0f) );
colors->push_back( osg::Vec4(1.0f, 1.0f, 1.0f, 1.0f) );
```

5. Next, we create the `osg::Geometry` object and set the prepared vertex, normal, and color arrays to it. We also indicate that the single normal should be bound to the entire geometry and that the colors should be bound per vertex:

```
osg::ref_ptr<osg::Geometry> quad = new osg::Geometry;
quad->setVertexArray( vertices.get() );
quad->setNormalArray( normals.get() );
quad->setNormalBinding( osg::Geometry::BIND_OVERALL );
quad->setColorArray( colors.get() );
quad->setColorBinding( osg::Geometry::BIND_PER_VERTEX );
```

6. The last step required to finish a geometry and add it to the scene graph is to specify the primitive set. A newly allocated `osg::DrawArrays` instance with the drawing mode set to `GL_QUADS` is used here, in order to render the four vertices as quad corners in a counter-clockwise order:

```
quad->addPrimitiveSet( new osg::DrawArrays(GL_QUADS, 0, 4) );
```

7. Add the geometry to an `osg::Geode` object and render it in the scene viewer:

```
osg::ref_ptr<osg::Geode> root = new osg::Geode;
root->addDrawable( quad.get() );

osgViewer::Viewer viewer;
viewer.setSceneData( root.get() );
return viewer.run();
```

8. Our program finally results in a nice colored quad, as shown in the following screenshot:

What just happened?

We assume that you are familiar with the following OpenGL code snippets:

```
static const GLfloat vertices[][3] = { … };
glEnableClientState( GL_VERTEX_ARRAY );
glVertexPointer( 4, GL_FLOAT, 0, vertices );
glDrawArrays( GL_QUADS, 0, 4 );
```

The array variable `vertices` is used to define the coordinates to be rendered. The OpenGL function `glDrawArrays()` will draw the **geometry primitive** of the mode `GL_QUADS` with four sequential elements in the array, that is, a quadrangle in the 3D space.

The `osg::Geometry` class encapsulates the entire process mentioned above, mainly by using the `setVertexArray()` and `addPrimitiveSet()` methods. Actually, these vertex data and primitive sets settings are not performed as soon as a user application calls these methods, but will be applied when the geometry is reached during the next drawing traversal of the scene graph. This makes it possible to use most `osg::Geometry` methods like properties, which can be read and modified without forcing the scene to render back and forth.

Pop quiz – results of different primitive types

In the previous example, we defined the *mode*, *start*, and *count* parameters of the primitive and generated a quad as the result. It is important for you to understand how geometry vertices are interpreted by one or more primitive sets. Can you list the ten mode symbols (`GL_TRIANGLES`, `GL_QUADS`, and so on) and their major behaviors in a table? For example, do you know how each mode treats vertices and indices, and what shape is going to be drawn in the final stage?

Indexing primitives

The `osg::DrawArrays` works fine when reading vertex data straight through the arrays, without any skipping and hopping. However, it tends to be a little inefficient if there are lots of shared vertices. For example, in order to make `osg::DrawArrays` draw a cube with eight vertices in the `GL_TRIANGLES` mode, the vertex array should repeat each vertex a couple of times and should increase the array size to 36 (12 triangle faces) at last:

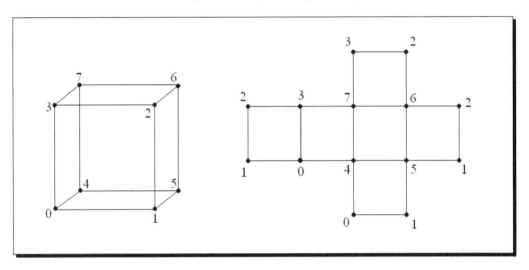

The `osg::DrawElementsUInt` class, as well as `osg::DrawElementsUByte` and `osg::DrawElementsUShort` classes, are used as index arrays in order to solve the above problem. They all derive from `osg::PrimitiveSet` and encapsulate OpenGL's `glDrawElements()` function, with different data types. The index array saves indices of vertex array elements. In this case, the cube's vertex array is able to be resized to eight, with an associated indexing primitive set.

The `osg::DrawElements*` classes are designed to work just like `std::vector`, so any vector-related methods are compatible for use. For instance, to add indices to a newly allocated `osg::DrawElementsUInt` object, we could code like following:

```
osg::ref_ptr<osg::DrawElementsUInt> de =
    new osg::DrawElementsUInt( GL_TRIANGLES );
de->push_back( 0 ); de->push_back( 1 ); de->push_back( 2 );
de->push_back( 3 ); de->push_back( 0 ); de->push_back( 2 );
```

This will specify the front face of our cube shown in the last image.

Time for action – drawing an octahedron

An octahedron is a polyhedron having eight triangle faces. It is really a nice example to show why primitive indexing is important. We will first sketch the octahedron structure, as shown in the following image:

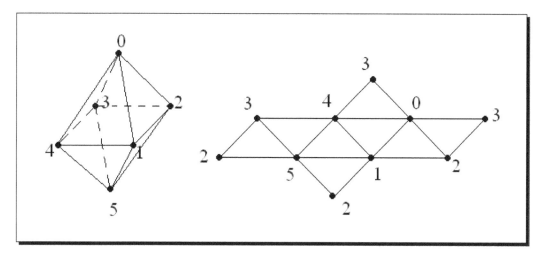

The octahedron has six vertices, each shared by four triangles. We would have to create a vertex array with 24 elements to render all eight faces when using `osg::DrawArrays`. However, with the help of an index array and the `osg::DrawElementsUInt` class, we can allocate a vertex array with only six elements and thus improve the efficiency of drawing the geometry.

1. Include the necessary headers:

   ```
   #include <osg/Geometry>
   #include <osg/Geode>
   #include <osgUtil/SmoothingVisitor>
   #include <osgViewer/Viewer>
   ```

2. As we have discussed before, the `osg::Vec3Array` class inherits the characteristics of `std::vector` and can construct using a predetermined size parameter and work with `operator[]` directly.

   ```
   osg::ref_ptr<osg::Vec3Array> vertices = new osg::Vec3Array(6);
   (*vertices)[0].set( 0.0f, 0.0f, 1.0f);
   (*vertices)[1].set(-0.5f,-0.5f, 0.0f);
   (*vertices)[2].set( 0.5f,-0.5f, 0.0f);
   (*vertices)[3].set( 0.5f, 0.5f, 0.0f);
   (*vertices)[4].set(-0.5f, 0.5f, 0.0f);
   (*vertices)[5].set( 0.0f, 0.0f,-1.0f);
   ```

3. The `osg::DrawElementsUInt` accepts a size parameter besides the drawing mode parameter, too. After that, we will specify the indices of vertices to describe all eight triangle faces.

```
osg::ref_ptr<osg::DrawElementsUInt> indices =
    new osg::DrawElementsUInt(GL_TRIANGLES, 24);
(*indices)[0]  = 0;  (*indices)[1]  = 1;  (*indices)[2]  = 2;
(*indices)[3]  = 0;  (*indices)[4]  = 2;  (*indices)[5]  = 3;
(*indices)[6]  = 0;  (*indices)[7]  = 3;  (*indices)[8]  = 4;
(*indices)[9]  = 0;  (*indices)[10] = 4;  (*indices)[11] = 1;
(*indices)[12] = 5;  (*indices)[13] = 2;  (*indices)[14] = 1;
(*indices)[15] = 5;  (*indices)[16] = 3;  (*indices)[17] = 2;
(*indices)[18] = 5;  (*indices)[19] = 4;  (*indices)[20] = 3;
(*indices)[21] = 5;  (*indices)[22] = 1;  (*indices)[23] = 4;
```

4. In order to create a geometry with a default white color, we will only set the vertex array and the `osg::DrawElementsUInt` primitive set. The normal array is also required but is not easy to compute manually. We will use a smoothed normal calculator to automatically obtain it. This calculator will be described in the next section, *Using polygonal techniques*.

```
osg::ref_ptr<osg::Geometry> geom = new osg::Geometry;
geom->setVertexArray( vertices.get() );
geom->addPrimitiveSet( indices.get() );
osgUtil::SmoothingVisitor::smooth( *geom );
```

5. Add the geometry to an `osg::Geode` object and make it the scene root:

```
osg::ref_ptr<osg::Geode> root = new osg::Geode;
root->addDrawable( geom.get() );

osgViewer::Viewer viewer;
viewer.setSceneData( root.get() );
return viewer.run();
```

6. The generated octahedron is illustrated as shown in the following screenshot:

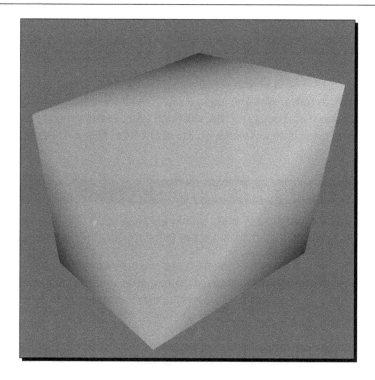

What just happened?

The **vertex array** mechanism reduces the number of OpenGL function calls. It stores vertex data in the application memory, which is called the **client side**. The OpenGL pipeline on the **server side** gets access to different **vertex arrays**.

As can be seen from the following image, OpenGL obtains data from the vertex buffer on the client side and assembles primitive data in an orderly manner.

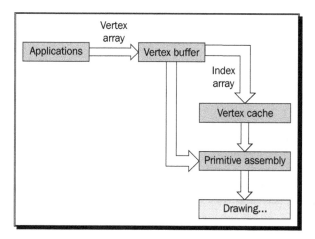

The vertex buffer here is used to manage data specified by `set*Array()` methods of the `osg::Geometry` class. `osg::DrawArrays` marches straight through these arrays and draw them.

However, `osg::DrawElements*` classes also provide an index array in order to reduce the number of vertices to transfer. The index array then allows a new vertex cache on the **server side** for temporary storage. OpenGL will fetch vertices from the cache directly, rather than read from the vertex buffer, which is on the **client side**. This will largely increase the performance.

Pop quiz – optimizing indexed geometries

The octahedron that we just drew is made up of only six vertices. Can you figure out how many vertices will be actually used if we are not going to index the geometry any more?

In many situations, you will find that triangle strips can provide better performance in rendering continuous pieces of mesh faces. Assuming that we choose `GL_TRIANGLE_STRIPS` instead of `GL_TRIANGLES` in the previous example, how could we construct the index array this time?

Have a go hero – challenges with cubes and pyramids

Now it is your turn to draw some other polyhedrons, for example, a cube or a pyramid. The structure of a cube is discussed at the beginning of the section *Indexing primitives*. It contains six vertices and 12 triangle faces, which is a good demonstration of indexing vertices.

A pyramid usually has one polygon base and several triangle faces meeting at an "*apex*". Take the square pyramid as an example: it contains five vertices and six triangle faces (the square base consists of two triangles). Each vertex is shared by three or four triangles:

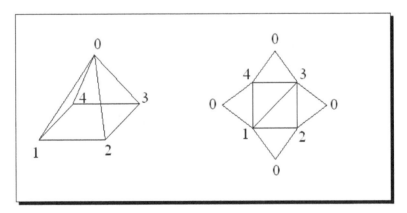

Create a new `osg::Geometry` object and add vertices and normals as arrays. The `osgUtil::SmoothingVisitor` will also calculate smoothed normals. Specify an `osg::DrawElementsUInt` primitive set with the `GL_TRIANGLES` drawing mode. For advanced study, you may even add multiple primitive sets with different drawing modes, for instance, rendering the pyramid base with `GL_QUADS`, and triangle faces with `GL_TRIANGLE_FAN`.

Using polygonal techniques

OSG supports various polygonal techniques for manipulating the geometry objects. These pre-processing methods, such as polygon reduction and tessellation, are often used to create and improve polygonal models for rendering at a later time. They are designed to have a simple interface and be easy to use, but may perform complex calculations backstage. They are not suggested to be used on-the-fly because of possibly massive computations.

A few polygonal technique implementations in OSG are listed as follows:

1. `osgUtil::Simplifier`: This reduces the number of triangles in geometries. The public method `simplify()` can be used to simply enter a geometry object.

2. `osgUtil::SmoothingVisitor`: This calculates normals for any geometries containing primitives, for instance, the octahedron that we have just seen. The public static method `smooth()` can be used to generate smoothed normals of a geometry, instead of reallocating and setting the normal array yourselves.

3. `osgUtil::TangentSpaceGenerator`: This generates arrays containing the tangent-space basis vectors for geometry vertices. It passes the geometry object as a parameter to the `generate()` method and saves the results in `getTangentArray()`, `getNormalArray()`, and `getBinormalArray()`. The results can be used as varying vertex attributes in GLSL.

4. `osgUtil::Tessellator`: This uses the OpenGL Utility (glu) tessellation routines to break complex primitives into simple ones. It provides a `retessellatePolygons()` method to change the primitive sets of the input geometry to tessellated ones.

5. `osgUtil::TriStripVisitor`: This converts geometry surface primitives into triangle strips, which allows faster rendering and more efficient memory usage. The public method `stripify()` is used to convert primitives in the input geometry into `GL_TRIANGLE_STRIP` types.

All of the methods introduced can be used with an `osg::Geometry&` reference parameter, such as:

```
osgUtil::TriStripVisitor tsv;
tsv. stripify( *geom );
```

Here `geom` means an `osg::Geometry` object managed by the **smart pointer**.

The `osgUtil::Simplifier, osgUtil::SmoothingVisitor,` and `osgUtil::TriStripVisitor` classes are also accepted by scene graph nodes. For example:

```
osgUtil::TriStripVisitor tsv;
node->accept( tsv );
```

The variable `node` represents an `osg::Node` object. The `accept()` operation will traverse the node's children until all **leaf nodes** are reached, and find out and process all of the geometries stored in these `osg::Geode` nodes.

Time for action – tessellating a polygon

Complex primitives will not be rendered correctly by the OpenGL API directly. This includes concave polygons, self-intersecting polygons, and polygons with holes. Only after being subdivided into convex polygons, these non-convex polygons can be accepted by the OpenGL rendering pipeline. The `osgUtil::Tessellator` class can be used for the tessellation work in this case.

1. Include necessary headers:

```
#include <osg/Geometry>
#include <osg/Geode>
#include <osgUtil/Tessellator>
#include <osgViewer/Viewer>
```

2. We will create a concave polygon by using the `osg::Geometry` class. A simple polygon is concave if any of its internal edge angles is greater than 180 degrees. Here, the example geometry represents a quad with a cave on the right-hand side. It is drawn as a `GL_POLYGON` primitive.

```
osg::ref_ptr<osg::Vec3Array> vertices = new osg::Vec3Array;
vertices->push_back( osg::Vec3(0.0f, 0.0f, 0.0f) );
vertices->push_back( osg::Vec3(2.0f, 0.0f, 0.0f) );
vertices->push_back( osg::Vec3(2.0f, 0.0f, 1.0f) );
vertices->push_back( osg::Vec3(1.0f, 0.0f, 1.0f) );
vertices->push_back( osg::Vec3(1.0f, 0.0f, 2.0f) );
vertices->push_back( osg::Vec3(2.0f, 0.0f, 2.0f) );
```

```
vertices->push_back( osg::Vec3(2.0f, 0.0f, 3.0f) );
vertices->push_back( osg::Vec3(0.0f, 0.0f, 3.0f) );

osg::ref_ptr<osg::Vec3Array> normals = new osg::Vec3Array;
normals->push_back( osg::Vec3(0.0f,-1.0f, 0.0f) );

osg::ref_ptr<osg::Geometry> geom = new osg::Geometry;
geom->setVertexArray( vertices.get() );
geom->setNormalArray( normals.get() );
geom->setNormalBinding( osg::Geometry::BIND_OVERALL );
geom->addPrimitiveSet( new osg::DrawArrays(GL_POLYGON, 0, 8) );
```

3. If we immediately add the `geom` variable to an `osg::Geode` object and view it with `osgViewer::Viewer`, we will get an incorrect result, as shown in the following screenshot:

4. To render the concave polygon correctly, we should use an `osgUtil::Tessellator` to re-tessellate it:

```
osgUtil::Tessellator tessellator;
tessellator.retessellatePolygons( *geom );
```

5. Now the `geom` variable is already modified. Add it to a geometry node again and start the scene viewer:

```
osg::ref_ptr<osg::Geode> root = new osg::Geode;
root->addDrawable( geom.get() );

osgViewer::Viewer viewer;
viewer.setSceneData( root.get() );
return viewer.run();
```

6. This time we have got a nice result:

What just happened?

A concave polygon without any tessellations will not be rendered as we expect in most cases. In order to optimize performance, OpenGL will treat them as simple polygons or just ignore them, and this always generates unexpected results.

The `osgUtil::Tessellator` uses OpenGL tessellation routines to process concave polygons saved in `osg::Geoemtry` objects. It decides on the most efficient primitive type while performing tessellation. For the previous case, it will use `GL_TRIANGLE_STRIP` to triangulate the original polygon, that is, to separate it into a few triangles.

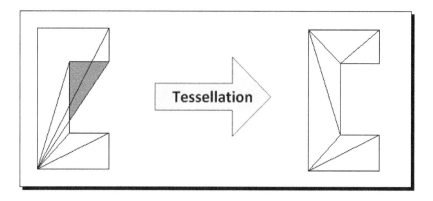

Like the OpenGL tessellation routines, the `osgUtil::Tessellator` class also handles polygons with holes and self-intersecting polygons. Its public method `setWindingType()` accepts different winding rules , such as `GLU_TESS_WINDING_ODD` and `GLU_TESS_WINDING_NONZERO`, which determine the inside and outside regions of a complex polygon.

Rereading geometry attributes

The `osg::Geometry` manages lots of vertex data by using **vertex arrays**, and renders these vertices and vertex attributes with ordered primitive sets. However, an `osg::Geometry` object doesn't have any topological elements, such as faces, edges, and their relationships. This sometimes prevents it from implementing complex polygonal techniques and being edited freely (dragging a certain face or edge to manipulate the model, and so on).

OSG doesn't support algorithmic topology functionalities at present, probably because it seems a little weird for a rendering API to implement this. But OSG has already implemented a series of functors to reread geometry attributes and primitives from any existing **drawables**, and make use of them for the purpose of topological mesh modeling and so on.

A **functor** is always realized as a class but executed like a function. The **functor** can mimic some known interface with the same return-type and calling parameters, but all attributes passed to the **functor** will be captured and handled in a customized way.

The `osg::Drawable` class accepts four kinds of functors:

1. `osg::Drawable::AttributeFunctor` reads vertex attributes as array pointers. It has a number of virtual methods to apply to vertex attributes of different data types. To make use of this functor, you should inherit the class and re-implement one or more of the virtual methods, and do something that you want inside:

   ```
   virtual void apply( osg::Drawable::AttributeType type,
                       unsigned int size, osg::Vec3* ptr )
   {
   ```

```
            // Read 3-elements vectors with the ptr and size parameters.
            // The first parameter determines the attribute type,
            // for example, osg::Drawable::VERTICES.
            ...
        }
```

2. `osg::Drawable::ConstAttributeFunctor` is a read-only version of `osg::Drawable::AttributeFunctor`. The only difference is that it uses constant array pointers as parameters of virtual `apply()` methods.

3. `osg::PrimitiveFunctor` mimics the OpenGL drawing routines, such as `glDrawArrays()`, `glDrawElements()`, and the immediate mode. It will pretend that the drawable is rendered, but call the functor methods instead. `osg::PrimitiveFunctor` has two important template subclasses: `osg::TemplatePrimitiveFunctor<>` and `osg::TriangleFunctor<>`, which can be put into actual usage. These two classes receive result *drawn* vertices per primitive and send them to user-defined `operator()` methods.

4. `osg::PrimitiveIndexFunctor` mimics the OpenGL drawing routines, too. Its subclass, `osg::TriangleIndexFunctor<>`, will receive vertex indices per primitive and make use of them.

The `osg::Drawable` derived classes, such as `osg::ShapeDrawable` and `osg::Geometry`, have the `accept()` method to accept different functors.

Customizing a primitive functor

It is abstract to conceive a scenario using a **functor** with the previous information. We will take the collection of triangle faces as an example. Although we use **vertex arrays** and primitive sets to manage rendering data of `osg::Geometry`, we still would like to collect all of its triangle faces and face points. We can thus maintain incidence information of the geometry vertices, edges, and faces and build the geometry data structure by using the collector.

Time for action – collecting triangle faces

The `osg::TriangleFunctor<>` **functor** class is ideal for collecting information on triangle faces. It will convert primitive sets of an `osg::Drawable` object to triangles whenever possible. The template argument must implement an `operator()` with three `const` `osg::Vec3&` parameters and a `bool` parameter, which will be called for every triangle when the **functor** is applied.

1. We will implement the template argument as a structure including an `operator()`. The first three 3D vector parameters represent the triangle vertices, and the last one indicates whether these vertices come from a temporary vertex array or not:

```
struct FaceCollector
{
    void operator()( const osg::Vec3& v1, const osg::Vec3& v2,
                     const osg::Vec3& v3, bool )
    {
        std::cout << "Face vertices: " << v1 << "; " << v2 << "; "
                  << v3 << std::endl;
    }
};
```

2. We will create a wall-like object by using `GL_QUAD_STRIP`, which means that the geometry was not originally formed by triangles. This object includes eight vertices and four quad faces:

```
osg::ref_ptr<osg::Vec3Array> vertices = new osg::Vec3Array;
vertices->push_back( osg::Vec3(0.0f, 0.0f, 0.0f) );
vertices->push_back( osg::Vec3(0.0f, 0.0f, 1.0f) );
vertices->push_back( osg::Vec3(1.0f, 0.0f, 0.0f) );
vertices->push_back( osg::Vec3(1.0f, 0.0f, 1.5f) );
vertices->push_back( osg::Vec3(2.0f, 0.0f, 0.0f) );
vertices->push_back( osg::Vec3(2.0f, 0.0f, 1.0f) );
vertices->push_back( osg::Vec3(3.0f, 0.0f, 0.0f) );
vertices->push_back( osg::Vec3(3.0f, 0.0f, 1.5f) );
vertices->push_back( osg::Vec3(4.0f, 0.0f, 0.0f) );
vertices->push_back( osg::Vec3(4.0f, 0.0f, 1.0f) );

osg::ref_ptr<osg::Vec3Array> normals = new osg::Vec3Array;
normals->push_back( osg::Vec3(0.0f,-1.0f, 0.0f) );

osg::ref_ptr<osg::Geometry> geom = new osg::Geometry;
geom->setVertexArray( vertices.get() );
geom->setNormalArray( normals.get() );
geom->setNormalBinding( osg::Geometry::BIND_OVERALL );
geom->addPrimitiveSet( new osg::DrawArrays(GL_QUAD_STRIP, 0, 10)
);
```

3. You may first view the object by using an `osg::Geode` scene root and the `osgViewer::Viewer`. It is nothing special when compared to previous geometries:

```
osg::ref_ptr<osg::Geode> root = new osg::Geode;
root->addDrawable( geom.get() );

osgViewer::Viewer viewer;
viewer.setSceneData( root.get() );
viewer.run();
```

The screenshot is as follows:

4. Now, add the user-defined `FaceCollector` structure as the template argument of `osg::TriangleFunctor<>`, and apply it to the `osg::Geometry` object:

```
osg::TriangleFunctor<FaceCollector> functor;
geom->accept( functor );
```

5. Start the program in the console, and you will see a list of face vertices printed at the command-line prompt:

```
Face vertices: 0 0 0; 0 0 1; 1 0 0
Face vertices: 0 0 1; 1 0 1.5; 1 0 0
Face vertices: 1 0 0; 1 0 1.5; 2 0 0
Face vertices: 1 0 1.5; 2 0 1; 2 0 0
Face vertices: 2 0 0; 2 0 1; 3 0 0
Face vertices: 2 0 1; 3 0 1.5; 3 0 0
Face vertices: 3 0 0; 3 0 1.5; 4 0 0
Face vertices: 3 0 1.5; 4 0 1; 4 0 0
```

What just happened?

The **functor** simply mimics the OpenGL calls in the `accept()` implementation of `osg::Geometry`. It reads vertex data and primitive sets by using `setVertexArray()` and `drawArrays()` methods, which have the same input parameters as OpenGL's `glVertexPointer()` and `glDrawArrays()` functions. However, the `drawArrays()` method doesn't actually draw objects in the 3D world. It will call a member method of the template class or structure in which we can perform different kinds of customized operations, such as collecting vertex data.

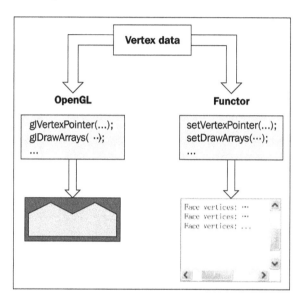

The `osg::TemplatePrimitiveFunctor<T>` not only collects triangle faces of a certain **drawable**; it also has interfaces for obtaining a point, a line, and a quadrangle. It requires implementations of these operators in the template argument:

```
void operator()( const osg::Vec3&, bool );
void operator()( const osg::Vec3&, const osg::Vec3&, bool );
void operator()( const osg::Vec3&, const osg::Vec3&,
                 const osg::Vec3&, bool );
void operator()( const osg::Vec3&, const osg::Vec3&,
                 const osg::Vec3&, const osg::Vec3&, bool );
```

Have a go hero – analyzing topology of a geometry

Have you figured out how to analyze the topology of a geometry? You may need a shared list of vertices and a list of faces storing these vertices, or a list of edges, each with information of the two vertices touched and the two faces bordered.

The **functor** will help you to get all of this information while collecting the triangle faces of any **drawables**. The only question is what data structure you will prefer to use in order to construct a topological polygon mesh; and it is your decision now.

Implementing your own drawables

There are two very important virtual methods in the osg::Drawable pure class:

◆ The computeBound() constant method computes the bounding box around the geometry, which will be used in the view frustum culling process to decide whether to cull the geometry or not

◆ The drawImplementation() constant method actually draws the geometry with OSG and OpenGL calls

To customize a user-defined **drawable** class, you have to re-implement these two methods and add your own drawing code at the appropriate place.

The computeBound() constant method returns an osg::BoundingBox value as the geometry's bounding box. The simplest way to create a bounding box is to set its minimum and maximum extents, both of which are three-element vectors. A bounding box from (0, 0, 0) to (1, 1, 1) can be defined like this:

```
osg::BoundingBox bb( osg::Vec3(0, 0, 0), osg::Vec3(1, 1, 1) );
```

Note that osg::BoundingBox is not managed by the **smart pointer**, and neither is the bounding sphere class osg::BoundingSphere which will be introduced in the next chapter.

The drawImplementation() constant method is the actual implementation of different drawing calls. It has an input osg::RenderInfo& parameter, which stores the current rendering information for the OSG rendering backend. This method is called internally by the draw() method of osg::Drawable. The latter will automatically save OpenGL calls in drawImplementation() in order to a display list, and reuse it repeatedly in the following frames. This means that the drawImplementation() method of an osg::Drawable instance will be invoked only once!

To avoid using display lists, you can turn off related options while allocating a new **drawable**:

```
drawable->setUseDisplayList( false );
```

The customized OpenGL calls will be executed every time after that. This is useful if there are geometry morphing actions or animations in the `drawImplementation()` method.

Using OpenGL drawing calls

You can add any OpenGL functions in the implementation of `drawImplementation()`. The rendering context is created and the OpenGL **make current** operation is already complete before entering this method. Don't release the OpenGL rendering context, because it may be used by other **drawables** soon.

Time for action – creating the famous OpenGL teapot

The GLUT library has the ability to render a solid teapot model directly. Both the teapot surface normals and texture coordinates are automatically generated. And the teapot is generated by using OpenGL evaluators as well.

You may want to download the GLUT library first, which is designed as a third-party project of OpenGL. The source code can be found at either of the following websites:

◆   http://www.opengl.org/resources/libraries/glut/

◆   http://www.xmission.com/~nate/glut.html

The prebuilt binaries, header files, and libraries can also be downloaded, which include everything you need to get started with GLUT.

1.   We have to modify the CMake script file to find GLUT and add it as a dependency of our OSG-based project:

```
find_package( glut )
add_executable( MyProject teapot.cpp )
config_project( MyProject OPENTHREADS )
config_project( MyProject OSG )
config_project( MyProject OSGDB )
config_project( MyProject OSGUTIL )
config_project( MyProject GLUT )
```

2. The CMake system is able to search for the GLUT library directly by using a `find_package()` macro, but sometimes it may come away empty-handed. You should set the `GLUT_INCLUDE_DIR` to the parent directory of `gl/glut.h` and `GLUT_glut_LIBRARY` to the GLUT static-link library, for example, `glut32.lib` on Windows. Click on *Configure* and *Generate* in order to generate your solution or makefile after that.

Name	Value
⊞ CMAKE	
⊟ GLUT	
GLUT_INCLUDE_DIR	E:/3rdParty/include
GLUT_glut_LIBRARY	E:/3rdParty/include/glut32.lib
⊞ OPENTHREADS	
⊞ OSG	
⊞ OSGDB	
⊞ OSGUTIL	
⊞ OSGVIEWER	

3. Include the necessary headers. At this time, remember to add the GLUT header as well:

```
#include <gl/glut.h>
#include <osg/Drawable>
#include <osg/Geode>
#include <osgViewer/Viewer>
```

4. We declare a complete new class named `TeapotDrawable`, which is derived from the `osg::Drawable` class. To make sure that it compiles, we have to use an OSG macro definition `META_Object` to implement some basic properties of the class. A copy constructor is also created to help instantiate our `TeapotDrawable` class.

```
class TeapotDrawable : public osg::Drawable
{
public:
    TeapotDrawable( float size=1.0f ) : _size(size) {}
    TeapotDrawable( const TeapotDrawable& copy,
                const osg::CopyOp&
                copyop=osg::CopyOp::SHALLOW_COPY )
    : osg::Drawable(copy, copyop), _size(copy._size) {}
    META_Object( osg, TeapotDrawable );

    virtual osg::BoundingBox computeBound() const;
    virtual void drawImplementation( osg::RenderInfo& ) const;
protected:
    float _size;
};
```

5. To implement the `computeBound()` method in a simple way, we can use the member variable `_size`, which represents the relative size of teapot, in order to construct a large enough bounding box. A box from the minimum point (`-_size, -_size, -_size`) to the maximum point (`_size, _size, _size`) should always contain the teapot surface:

```
osg::BoundingBox TeapotDrawable::computeBound() const
{
    osg::Vec3 min(-_size,-_size,-_size), max(_size, _size, _size);
    return osg::BoundingBox(min, max);
}
```

6. The implementation of `drawImplementation()` is uncomplicated, too. For the purpose of face culling, we render the GLUT teapot with its front-facing polygon vertices winding clockwise, which will benefit from OpenGL's default back face culling mechanism:

```
void TeapotDrawable::drawImplementation( osg::RenderInfo&
renderInfo ) const
{
    glFrontFace( GL_CW );
    glutSolidTeapot( _size );
    glFrontFace( GL_CCW );
}
```

7. The `TeapotDrawable` object can be added to an `osg::Geode` node and then viewed by the viewer, which has already been done many times:

```
osg::ref_ptr<osg::Geode> root = new osg::Geode;
root->addDrawable( new TeapotDrawable(1.0f) );

osgViewer::Viewer viewer;
viewer.setSceneData( root.get() );
return viewer.run();
```

8. Now build and start the application. Press and hold the left mouse button to rotate your scene to a suitable position, and have a look at the fine teapot model:

What just happened?

Here, the copy constructor is used to create a new TeapotDrawable as a copy of an existing one. It is not needed in the previous example, but is required by any osg::Drawable derived classes.

Another macro definition META_Object is also necessary for implementing a customized **drawable**. It has two parameters which indicate the library name is osg, and the class type and name is TeapotDrawable. You can always fetch the two string values by using the following methods:

```
const char* lib = obj->libraryName();
const char* name = obj->className();
```

OSG classes with the META_Object macro will re-implement these two methods, including almost all scene-related classes.

User-defined drawables should always have a copy constructor and the META_Object macro, and should also override the computeBound() and drawImplementation() methods, otherwise it may cause compiling errors instead.

Summary

This chapter explained how to create geometry entities simply with vertices and the drawing primitives defined with OSG. These geometries are stored in `osg::Geode` objects, which are recognized as the **leaf nodes** of a scene graph. All scene managements and updates in the 3D world serve the purpose of modifying geometry behaviors and transmitting vertex data and geometry primitives, in order to gain different rendering results.

In this chapter, we specially covered:

- The basic concepts of OpenGL **immediate mode**, **display lists**, and **vertex arrays**, and their implementations in OSG.

- How to render simple shapes for quick tests by using the `osg::ShapeDrawable` class.

- How to create and render various shapes in a more efficient way by using the `osg::Geometry` class.

- How to operate on vertex attribute's arrays, index arrays, and geometry primitive sets.

- How to use **functors** to retrieve vertex properties, primitives, and index data, and, through inheritance and rewriting of the member function, realize the customization of vertex data.

- A feasible way to integrate OpenGL calls into customized `osg::Drawable` derived classes, which will help OSG and other OpenGL-based libraries work together.

5
Managing Scene Graph

Scene graph *is a hierarchy graph of nodes representing the spatial layout of graphic and state objects. It encapsulates the lowest-level graphics primitives and state combined to visualize anything that can be created through a low-level graphical API. OpenSceneGraph has leveraged the strength of* **scene graph** *and developed optimized mechanisms to manage and render 3D scenes, thus allowing the developers to use simple but powerful code in a standard way, in order to realize things such as object assembling, traversal, transform stack, culling of the scene, level-of-detail management, and other basic or advanced graphics characteristics.*

In this chapter, we will cover the following topics:

◆ Understanding the concept of group nodes and leaf nodes

◆ How to handle parent and child node interfaces

◆ Making use of various nodes, including the transformation node, switch node, level-of-detail node, and proxy node

◆ How to derive your own nodes from the basic node class

◆ How to traverse the scene graph structure of a loaded model

The Group interface

The osg::Group type represents the **group nodes** of an OSG **scene graph**. It can have any number of **child nodes**, including the osg::Geode **leaf nodes** and other osg::Group nodes. It is the most commonly-used base class of the various **NodeKits**—that is, nodes with various functionalities.

The osg::Group class derives from osg::Node, and thus indirectly derives from osg::Referenced. The osg::Group class contains a children list with each child node managed by the **smart pointer** osg::ref_ptr<>. This ensures that there will be no memory leaks whenever deleting a set of cascading nodes in the **scene graph**.

The osg::Group class provides a set of public methods for defining interfaces for handling children. These are very similar to the **drawable** managing methods of osg::Geode, but most of the input parameters are osg::Node pointers.

1. The public method addChild() attaches a node to the end of the children list. Meanwhile, there is an insertChild() method for inserting nodes to osg::Group at a specific location, which accepts an integer index and a node pointer as parameters.

2. The public methods removeChild() and removeChildren() will remove one or more child nodes from the current osg::Group object. The latter uses two parameters: the zero-based index of the start element, and the number of elements to be removed.

3. The getChild() returns the osg::Node pointer stored at a specified zero-based index.

4. The getNumChildren() returns the total number of children.

You will be able to handle the child interface of osg::Group with ease because of your previous experience of handling osg::Geode and **drawables**.

Managing parent nodes

We have already learnt that osg::Group is used as the **group node**, and osg::Geode as the **leaf node** of a **scene graph**. Their methods were introduced in the last chapter, and are also used in this chapter. Additionally, both classes should have an interface for managing **parent nodes**.

OSG allows a node to have multiple parents, as will be explained later. In this section, we will first have a glimpse of parent management methods, which are declared in the osg::Node class directly:

1. The method getParent() returns an osg::Group pointer as the parent node. It requires an integer parameter that indicates the index in the parent's list.

2. The method `getNumParents()` returns the total number of parents. If the node has a single parent, this method will return 1, and only `getParent(0)` is available at this time.

3. The method `getParentalNodePaths()` returns all possible paths from the root node of the scene to the current node (but excluding the current node). It returns a list of `osg::NodePath` variables.

The `osg::NodePath` is actually a `std::vector` object of node pointers, for example, assuming we have a graphical scene:

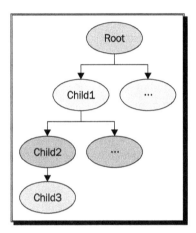

The following code snippet will find the only path from the scene root to the node **child3**:

```
osg::NodePath& nodePath = child3->getParentalNodePaths()[0];
for ( unsigned int i=0; i<nodePath.size(); ++i )
{
    osg::Node* node = nodePath[i];
    // Do something...
}
```

You will successively receive the nodes **Root**, **Child1**, and **Child2** in the loop.

We don't need to use the memory management system to reference a node's parents. When a **parent node** is deleted, it will be automatically removed from its **child nodes'** records as well.

A node without any parents can only be considered as the **root node** of the scene graph. In that case, the `getNumParents()` method will return 0 and no parent node can be retrieved.

Time for action – adding models to the scene graph

In the past examples, we always loaded a single model, like the Cessna, by using the
`osgDB::readNodeFile()` function. This time we will try to import and manage multiple
models. Each model will be assigned to a node pointer and then added to a **group node**. The
group node, which is defined as the scene root, is going to be used by the program to render
the whole scene graph at last:

1. Include the necessary headers:

    ```
    #include <osg/Group>
    #include <osgDB/ReadFile>
    #include <osgViewer/Viewer>
    ```

2. In the main function, we will first load two different models and assign them to
    `osg::Node` pointers. A loaded model is also a sub-scene graph constructed with
    group and leaf nodes. The `osg::Node` class is able to represent any kind of sub
    graphs, and if necessary, it can be converted to `osg::Group` or `osg::Geode` with
    either the C++ `dynamic_cast<>` operator, or convenient conversion methods like
    `asGroup()` and `asGeode()`, which are less time-costly than `dynamic_cast<>`.

    ```
    osg::ref_ptr<osg::Node> model1 = osgDB::readNodeFile(
        "cessna.osg" );
    osg::ref_ptr<osg::Node> model2 = osgDB::readNodeFile( "cow.osg" );
    ```

3. Add the two models to an `osg::Group` node by using the `addChild()` method:

    ```
    osg::ref_ptr<osg::Group> root = new osg::Group;
    root->addChild( model1.get() );
    root->addChild( model2.get() );
    ```

4. Initialize and start the viewer:

    ```
    osgViewer::Viewer viewer;
    viewer.setSceneData( root.get() );
    return viewer.run();
    ```

5. Now you will see a cow getting stuck in the Cessna model! It is a little incredible
    to see that in reality, but in a virtual world, these two models just belong to
    uncorrelated child nodes managed by a **group node**, and then rendered separately
    by the scene viewer.

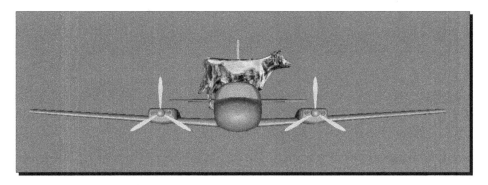

What just happened?

Both osg::Group and osg::Geode are derived from the osg::Node base class.
The osg::Group class allows the addition of any types of child nodes, including the
osg::Group itself. However, the osg::Geode class contains no group or leaf nodes.
It only accepts **drawables** for rendering purposes.

It is convenient if we can find out whether the type of a certain node is osg::Group,
osg::Geode, or other derived type especially those read from files and managed by
ambiguous osg::Node classes, such as:

```
osg::ref_ptr<osg::Node> model = osgDB::readNodeFile( "cessna.osg" );
```

Both the dynamic_cast<> operator and the conversion methods like asGroup(),
asGeode(), among others, will help to convert from one pointer or reference type
to another. Firstly, we take the dynamic_cast<> operator as an example. This can
be used to perform **downcast** conversions of the class inheritance hierarchy, such as:

```
osg::ref_ptr<osg::Group> model =
    dynamic_cast<osg::Group*>( osgDB::readNodeFile("cessna.osg") );
```

The return value of the osgDB::readNodeFile() function is always osg::Node*, but
we can also try to manage it with an osg::Group pointer. If, the root node of the Cessna
sub graph is a **group node**, then the conversion will succeed, otherwise it will fail and the
variable model will be NULL.

You may also perform an **upcast** conversion, which is actually an implicit conversion:

```
osg::ref_ptr<osg::Group> group = ...;
osg::Node* node1 = dynamic_cast<osg::Node*>( group.get() );
osg::Node* node2 = group.get();
```

On most compilers, both node1 and node2 will compile and work fine.

The conversion methods will do a similar job. Actually, it is preferable to use those methods instead of `dynamic_cast<>` if one exists for the type you need, especially in a performance-critical section of code:

```
// Assumes the Cessna's root node is a group node.
osg::ref_ptr<osg::Node> model = osgDB::readNodeFile("cessna.osg");
osg::Group* convModel1 = model->asGroup();  // OK!
osg::Geode* convModel2 = model->asGeode();  // Returns NULL.
```

Pop quiz – fast dynamic casting

In C++ programs, the `dynamic_cast<>` can perform typecasts with a safety at runtime check, which requires the **run-time type information (RTTI)** to be enabled. It is sometimes not recommended to compare with the `osg::Node` class's converting methods, which have been overridden by subclasses like `osg::Group` and `osg::Geode`. Can you tell the reason? When would you prefer to use `asGroup()` and `asGeode()`, and when would you use the `dynamic_cast<>`?

Traversing the scene graph

A typical traversal consists of the following steps:

1. First, start at an arbitrary node (for example, the **root node**).

2. Move down (or sometimes up) the **scene graph** recursively to the **child nodes**, until a **leaf node** is reached, or a node with no children is reached.

3. Backtrack to the most recent node that doesn't finish exploring, and repeat the above steps. This can be called a **depth-first search** of a scene graph.

Different updating and rendering operations will be applied to all scene nodes during traversals, which makes traversing a key feature of scene graphs. There are several types of traversals, with different purposes:

1. An **event traversal** firstly processes mouse and keyboard inputs, and other user events, while traversing the nodes.

2. An **update traversal** (or application traversal) allows the user application to modify the **scene graph**, such as setting node and geometry properties, applying node functionalities, executing **callbacks**, and so on.

3. A **cull traversal** tests whether a node is within the viewport and worthy of being rendered. It culls invisible and unavailable nodes, and outputs the optimized **scene graph** to an internal rendering list.

4. A **draw traversal** (or rendering traversal) issues low-level OpenGL API calls to actually render the scene. Note that it has no correlation with the **scene graph**, but only works on the rendering list generated by the **cull traversal**.

In the common sense, these traversals should be executed per frame, one after another. But for systems with multiple processors and graphics cards, OSG can process them in parallel and therefore improve the rendering efficiency.

The **visitor pattern** can be used to implement traversals. It will be discussed later in this chapter.

Transformation nodes

The `osg::Group` nodes do nothing except for traversing down to their children. However, OSG also supports the `osg::Transform` family of classes, which is created during the traversal-concatenated transformations to be applied to geometry. The `osg::Transform` class is derived from `osg::Group`. It can't be instantiated directly. Instead, it provides a set of subclasses for implementing different transformation interfaces.

When traversing down the scene graph hierarchy, the `osg::Transform` node always adds its own transformation to the current transformation matrix, that is, the OpenGL **model-view matrix**. It is equivalent to concatenating OpenGL matrix commands such as `glMultMatrix()`, for instance:

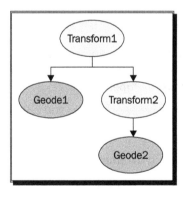

This example **scene graph** can be translated into following OpenGL code:

```
glPushMatrix();
    glMultMatrix( matrixOfTransform1 );
    renderGeode1();  // Assume this will render Geode1
    glPushMatrix();
        glMultMatrix( matrixOfTransform2 );
        renderGeode2();    // Assume this will render Geode2
```

```
    glPopMatrix();
glPopMatrix();
```

To describe the procedure using the concept of **coordinate frame**, we could say that Geode1 and Transform2 are under the **relative reference frame** of Transform1, and Geode2 is under the relative frame of Transform2. However, OSG also allows the setting of an **absolute reference frame** instead, which will result in the behavior equivalent to the OpenGL command glLoadMatrix():

```
transformNode->setReferenceFrame( osg::Transform::ABSOLUTE_RF );
```

And to switch back to the default coordinate frame:

```
transformNode->setReferenceFrame( osg::Transform::RELATIVE_RF );
```

Understanding the matrix

The osg::Matrix is a basic OSG data type which needs not be managed by smart pointers. It supports an interface for 4x4 matrix transformations, such as translate, rotate, scale, and projection operations. It can be set explicitly:

```
osg::Matrix mat( 1.0f, 0.0f, 0.0f, 0.0f,
                 0.0f, 1.0f, 0.0f, 0.0f,
                 0.0f, 0.0f, 1.0f, 0.0f,
                 0.0f, 0.0f, 0.0f, 1.0f ); // Just an identity matrix
```

Other methods and operators include:

1. The public methods postMult() and operator*() post multiply the current matrix object with an input matrix or vector parameter. And the method preMult() performs pre-multiplications.

2. The makeTranslate(), makeRotate(), and makeScale() methods reset the current matrix and create a 4x4 translation, rotation, or scale matrix. Their static versions, translate(), rotate(), and scale(), can be used to allocate a new matrix object with specified parameters.

3. The public method invert() inverts the matrix. Its static version inverse() requires a matrix parameter and returns a new inversed osg::Matrix object.

You will notice that OSG uses **row-major** matrix to indicate transformations. It means that OSG will treat vectors as rows and pre-multiply matrices with row vectors. Thus, the way to apply a transformation matrix mat to a coordinate vec is:

```
osg::Matrix mat = ...;
osg::Vec3 vec = ...;
osg::Vec3 resultVec = vec * mat;
```

The order of OSG row-major matrix operations is also easy to understand when concatenating matrices, for example:

```
osg::Matrix mat1 = osg::Matrix::scale(sx, sy, sz);
osg::Matrix mat2 = osg::Matrix::translate(x, y, z);
osg::Matrix resultMat = mat1 * mat2;
```

Developers can always read the transformation process from left to right, that is, the resultMat means to first scale a vector with mat1, and then translate it with mat2. This explanation always sounds clear and comfortable.

The osg::Matrixf class represents a 4x4 float type matrix. It can be converted by using osg::Matrix using overloaded set() methods directly.

The MatrixTransform class

The osg::MatrixTransform class is derived from osg::Transform. It uses an osg::Matrix variable internally to apply 4x4 double type matrix transformations. The public methods setMatrix() and getMatrix() will assign an osg::Matrix parameter onto the member variable of osg::MatrixTransform.

Time for action – performing translations of child nodes

Now we are going to make use of the transformation node. The osg::MatrixTransform node, which multiplies the current **model-view matrix** with a specified one directly, will help to transfer our model to different places in the viewing space.

1. Include the necessary headers:
    ```
    #include <osg/MatrixTransform>
    #include <osgDB/ReadFile>
    #include <osgViewer/Viewer>
    ```

2. Load the Cessna model first:
    ```
    osg::ref_ptr<osg::Node> model = osgDB::readNodeFile(
      "cessna.osg" );
    ```

3. The osg::MatrixTransform class is derived from osg::Group, so it can use the addChild() method to add more children. All child nodes will be affected by the osg::MatrixTransform node and be transformed according to the presetting matrix. Here, we will transform the loaded model twice, in order to obtain two instances displayed separately at the same time:
    ```
    osg::ref_ptr<osg::MatrixTransform> transformation1 = new
    osg::MatrixTransform;
    ```

```
transform1->setMatrix( osg::Matrix::translate(
  -25.0f, 0.0f, 0.0f) );
transform1->addChild( model.get() );

osg::ref_ptr<osg::MatrixTransform> transform2 = new
osg::MatrixTransform;
transform2->setMatrix( osg::Matrix::translate(
  25.0f, 0.0f, 0.0f) );
transform2->addChild( model.get() );
```

4. Add the two transformation nodes to the root node and start the viewer:

```
osg::ref_ptr<osg::Group> root = new osg::Group;
root->addChild( transformation1.get() );
root->addChild( transformation2.get() );

osgViewer::Viewer viewer;
viewer.setSceneData( root.get() );
return viewer.run();
```

5. The Cessna model, which is initially placed at the axis origin, is duplicated and shown at different positions. One is transformed to the coordinate (-25.0, 0.0, 0.0), and the other to (25.0, 0.0, 0.0):

What just happened?

You may be puzzled by the **scene graph** structure because the model pointer is attached to two parent nodes. In a typical tree structure, a node should have at most one parent, so sharing child nodes is impossible. However, OSG supports the object sharing mechanism, that is, a child node (the model pointer), can be instantiated by different ancestors (transform1 and transform2). Then there will be multiple paths leading from the root node to the instantiated node while traversing and rendering **scene graph**, which causes the instanced node to be displayed more than one time.

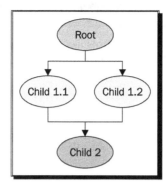

This is extremely useful for reducing the scene memory, because the application will keep only one copy of the shared data and simply call the implementation method (for instance, `drawImplementation()` of `osg::Drawable` derived classes) many times in different contexts managed by its multiple parents.

Each parent of a shared child node keeps its own `osg::ref_ptr<>` pointer to the child. In that case, the **referenced counting number** will not decrease to 0 and the child will not be released until all of its parents unreference it. You will find that the `getParent()` and `getNumParents()` methods are helpful in managing multiple parents of a node.

It is suggested that we share leaf nodes, geometries, textures, and OpenGL rendering states in one application as much as possible.

Pop quiz – matrix multiplications

As we have discussed, OSG uses row vectors and **row-major** matrices to perform pre-multiplications (vector * matrix) under the right-hand rule. However, OpenGL is said to use **column-major** matrices and column vectors to perform post-multiplications (matrix * vector). So, what do you think is important when converting OpenGL transformations to OSG ones?

Have a go hero – making use of the PositionAttitudeTransform class

The `osg::MatrixTransform` class performs like the OpenGL `glMultMatrix()` or `glLoadMatrix()` functions, which can realize almost all kinds of space transformations, but is not easy to use. The `osg::PositionAttitudeTransform` class, however, works like an integration of the OpenGL `glTranslate()`, `glScale()`, and `glRotate()` functions. It provides public methods to transform child nodes in the 3D world, including `setPosition()`, `setScale()`, and `setAttitude()`. The first two both require the `osg::Vec3` input value, and `setAttitude()` uses an `osg::Quat` variable as the parameter. The `osg::Quat` is a quaternion class, which is used to represent an orientation. Its constructor can apply a float angle and an `osg::Vec3` vector as the parameters. Euler rotations (rotating about three fixed axes) is also acceptable, using the `osg::Quat` overloaded constructor:

```
osg::Quat quat(xAngle, osg::X_AXIS,
               yAngle, osg::Y_AXIS,
               zangle, osg::Z_AXIS); // Angles should be radians!
```

Now, let's rewrite the last example to replace the `osg::MatrixTransform` nodes with `osg::PositionAttitudeTransform` ones. Use `setPosition()` to specify the translation, and `setRotate()` to specify the rotation of child models, and see if it is more convenient to you in some cases.

Switch nodes

The `osg::Switch` node is able to render or skip specific children conditionally. It inherits the methods of `osg::Group` super class and attaches a Boolean value to each child node. It has a few useful public methods:

1. The overloaded `addChild()` method is able to have a Boolean parameter in addition to the `osg::Node` pointer. When the Boolean parameter is set to false, the added node will be invisible to the viewer.

2. The `setValue()` method will set the visibility value of the child node at the specified index. It has two parameters: the zero-based index and the Boolean value. And `getValue()` can get the value of child node at the input index.

3. The `setNewChildDefaultValue()` method sets the default visibility for new children. If a child is simply added without specifying a value, its value will be decided by `setNewChildDefaultValue()`, for instance:

```
switchNode->setNewChildDefaultValue( false );
switchNode->addChild( childNode ); // Turned off by default now!
```

Time for action – switching between the normal and damaged Cessna

We are going to construct a scene with the `osg::Switch` node. It can even be used to implement state-switching animations and more complicated work, but at present we will only demonstrate how to predefine the visibilities of child nodes before the scene viewer starts.

1. Include the necessary headers:

```
#include <osg/Switch>
#include <osgDB/ReadFile>
#include <osgViewer/Viewer>
```

2. We will read two models from files and use a switch to control them. We can find a normal Cessna and a damaged one in the OSG sample data directory. They are good for simulating different states (normal/damaged) of an aircraft:

```
osg::ref_ptr<osg::Node> model1= osgDB::readNodeFile("cessna.osg");
osg::ref_ptr<osg::Node> model2= osgDB::readNodeFile("cessnafire.
osg");
```

3. The `osg::Switch` node is able to display one or more children and hide others. It does not work like the `osg::Group` parent class, which always displays all of its children while rendering the scene. This functionality will be quite useful if we are going to develop a flight game, and would like to manage some aircraft objects which may be destroyed at any time. The following code will set `model2` (the damaged Cessna) to visible when adding it to root, and hide `model1` (the normal one) at the same time:

```
osg::ref_ptr<osg::Switch> root = new osg::Switch;
root->addChild( model1.get(), false );
root->addChild( model2.get(), true );
```

4. Start the viewer:

```
osgViewer::Viewer viewer;
viewer.setSceneData( root.get() );
return viewer.run();
```

5. Now you will see an afire Cessna instead of the normal one:

What just happened?

The `osg::Switch` class adds a switch value list, in addition to the children list managed by its super class `osg::Group`. The two lists have the same size, and each element of one list is put into a one-to-one relationship with the element of another list. Thus, any changes in the switch value list will take effects on the related children nodes, turning their visibilities on or off.

The switch value changes that are triggered by `addChild()` or `setValue()` will be saved as properties and performed in the next rendering frame, while the OSG backend traverses the scene graph and applies different **NodeKit**'s functionalities. In the following code fragment, only the last switch values of child nodes at index 0 and 1 will be put into actual operation:

```
switchNode->setValue( 0, false );
switchNode->setValue( 0, true );
switchNode->setValue( 1, true );
switchNode->setValue( 1, false );
```

Redundant calls of setValue() methods will simply be overwritten and will not affect the scene graph.

Level-of-detail nodes

The **level-of-detail** technique creates levels of detail or complexity for a given object, and provides certain hints to automatically choose the appropriate level of the object, for instance, according to the distance from the viewer. It decreases the complexity of the object's representation in the 3D world, and often has an unnoticeable quality loss on a distant object's appearance.

The osg::LOD node is derived from osg::Group and will use child nodes to represent the same object at varying levels of detail, ordered from the highest level to the lowest. Each level requires the minimum and maximum visible ranges to specify the ideal opportunity to switch with adjacent levels. The result of an osg::LOD node is a discrete amount of children as levels, which can also be named **discrete LOD**.

The osg::LOD class can either specify ranges along with the addition of children, or make use of the setRange() method on existing child nodes:

```
osg::ref_ptr<osg::LOD> lodNode = new osg::LOD;
lodNode->addChild( node2, 500.0f, FLT_MAX );
lodNode->addChild( node1 );
...
lodNode->setRange( 1, 0.0f, 500.0f );
```

In the previous code snippet, we first add a node, node2, which will be displayed when the distance to the eye is greater than 500 units. After that, we add a high-resolution model, node1, and reset its visible range for close observation by using setRange().

Time for action – constructing a LOD Cessna

We will create a **discrete LOD** node with a set of predefined objects to represent the same model. These objects are used as child nodes of the osg::LOD node and displayed at different distances. We will use the internal polygon reduction technique class osgUtil::Simplifier to generate various detailed objects from an original model. You may also read low-polygon and high-polygon models from disk files.

1. Include the necessary headers:

```
#include <osg/LOD>
#include <osgDB/ReadFile>
#include <osgUtil/Simplifier>
#include <osgViewer/Viewer>
```

2. We would like to build three levels of model details. First, we need to create three copies of the original model. It is OK to read the Cessna from the file three times, but here a clone() method is called to duplicate the loaded model for immediate uses:

```
osg::ref_ptr<osg::Node> modelL3 = osgDB::readNodeFile("cessna.
osg");
osg::ref_ptr<osg::Node> modelL2 = dynamic_cast<osg::Node*>(
    modelL3->clone(osg::CopyOp::DEEP_COPY_ALL) );
osg::ref_ptr<osg::Node> modelL1 = dynamic_cast<osg::Node*>(
    modelL3->clone(osg::CopyOp::DEEP_COPY_ALL) );
```

3. We hope that level three will be the original Cessna, which has the maximum number of polygons for close-up viewing. Level two has fewer polygons to show, and level one will be the least detailed, which is displayed only at a very far distance. The osgUtil::Simplifier class is used here to reduce the vertices and faces. We apply the setSampleRatio() method to the level 1 and level 2 models with different values, which results in different simplifying rates:

```
osgUtil::Simplifier simplifier;
simplifier.setSampleRatio( 0.5 );
modelL2->accept( simplifier );

simplifier.setSampleRatio( 0.1 );
modelL1->accept( simplifier );
```

4. Add level models to the LOD node and set their visible range in descending order. Don't make overlapping ranges when you are configuring minimum and maximum range values with the addChild() or setRange() method, otherwise there will be more than one level of model shown at the same position, which results in incorrect behaviors:

```
osg::ref_ptr<osg::LOD> root = new osg::LOD;
root->addChild( modelL1.get(), 200.0f, FLT_MAX );
root->addChild( modelL2.get(), 50.0f, 200.0f );
root->addChild( modelL3.get(), 0.0f, 50.0f );
```

5. Start the viewer. The application will need a little more time to compute and reduce model faces this time:

```
osgViewer::Viewer viewer;
viewer.setSceneData( root.get() );
return viewer.run();
```

6. The Cessna model comes out again. Try pressing and holding the right mouse button to zoom in and out. You will find that the model is still well-represented when looking close, as shown in the left part of the following image. However, the model is slightly simpler when viewing from far distances, as in the right two parts of the image. This difference will not affect the rendering result a lot, but will enhance the system's efficiency if properly used.

What just happened?

Have you noticed that the Cessna model should be copied twice to prepare for different level polygons? The modelL3 pointer can't be shared here, because the simplifier will directly work on the geometric data in application memory, which will affect all pointers sharing the same memory. In fact, this is called a **shallow copy**.

In this example, we introduce a clone() method, which can be used by all scene nodes, **drawables**, and objects. It is able to perform a **deep copy**, that is, to make copies of all dynamically-allocated memory used by the source object. The modelL2 and modelL1 pointers thus manage newly-allocated memories, which are filled with the same data as modelL3.

The osgUtil::Simplifier class then starts to simplify the model for decreasing the workload on the graphics pipeline. To apply the simplifier, we have to call the accept() method of a node. In the *Visiting scene graph structures* section, you will learn more of it and the **visitor pattern**.

Proxy and paging nodes

The proxy node osg::ProxyNode, and the paging node osg::PagedLOD are provided for scene load balancing. Both of them are derived from the osg::Group class directly or indirectly.

The osg::ProxyNode node will reduce the start time of the viewer if there are huge numbers of models to be loaded and displayed in the **scene graph**. It is able to function as the interface of external files, help applications to start up as soon as possible, and then read those waiting models by using an independent data thread. It uses setFileName() rather than addChild() to set a model file and dynamically load it as a child.

The osg::PagedLOD node also inherits methods of osg::LOD, but dynamically loads and unloads levels of detail in order to avoid overloading the graphics pipeline and keep the rendering process as smooth as possible.

Time for action – loading a model at runtime

We are going to demonstrate the loading of a model file by using the osg::ProxyNode. The proxy will record the filename of the original model, and defer loading it until the viewer is running and sending corresponding requests.

1. Include the necessary headers:

```
#include <osg/ProxyNode>
#include <osgViewer/Viewer>
```

2. Instead of just loading model files as child nodes, we will set a filename to the specified index of children. This is similar to the insertChild() method, which puts a node into the specified position of the children list, but the list will not be filled until the dynamic loading process has finished.

```
osg::ref_ptr<osg::ProxyNode> root = new osg::ProxyNode;
root->setFileName( 0, "cow.osg" );
```

3. Start the viewer:

```
osgViewer::Viewer viewer;
viewer.setSceneData( root.get() );
return viewer.run();
```

4. The model seems to be loaded as usual, but you may have noticed that it came out a little suddenly, and the view point is not adjusted to a better position. That is because the proxy node, which is invisible, is used as if it contains no child at the start of rendering. Then the cow model will be loaded from the presetting file at runtime, and automatically added and rendered as the child node of the proxy then:

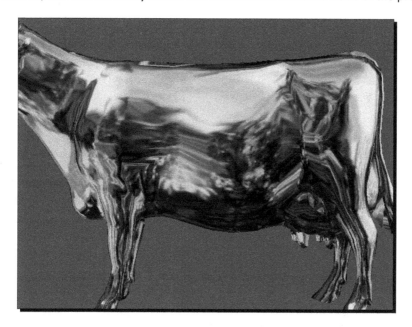

What just happened?

The `osg::ProxyNode` and `osg::PagedLOD` are pretty tiny themselves; they mainly just work as containers. OSG's internal data loading manager `osgDB::DatabasePager` will actually do the work of sending requests and loading the scene graph when new filenames or levels of detail are available, or falling back to the next available children.

The database pager works in several background threads and drives the loading of both static database (data generated files organized by proxy and paged nodes) and dynamic database data (paged nodes generated and added at runtime).

The database pager automatically recycles paged nodes that don't appear in the current view port, and removes them from the scene graph when the rendering backend is nearly overloaded, which is when it needs to support multi-threaded paging of massive rendering data. However, this doesn't affect `osg::ProxyNode` nodes.

Have a go hero – working with the PagedLOD class

Like the proxy node, the osg::PagedLOD class also has a setFileName() method to set the filename to load to the specified child position. However, as a **LOD** node, it should also set the minimum and maximum visible ranges of each dynamic loading child. Assuming that we have the cessna.osg file and a low-polygon version modelL1, we can organize a paged node like this:

```
osg::ref_ptr<osg::PagedLOD> pagedLOD = new osg::PagedLOD;
pagedLOD->addChild( modelL1, 200.0f, FLT_MAX );
pagedLOD->setFileName( 1, "cessna.osg" );
pagedLOD->setRange( 1, 0.0f, 200.0f );
```

Note that the modelL1 pointer will never be unloaded from memory, because it is a direct child and not a proxy to a file.

You will see no difference between using osg::LOD and osg::PagedLOD if displaying only one **level-of-detail** model. A better idea is to try using osg::MatrixTransform to construct a huge cluster of Cessnas. For example, you may use an independent function to build a transformable **LOD** Cessna:

```
osg::Node* createLODNode( const osg::Vec3& pos )
{
    osg::ref_ptr<osg::PagedLOD> pagedLOD = new osg::PagedLOD;
    ...
    osg::ref_ptr<osg::MatrixTransform> mt = new osg::MatrixTransform;
    mt->setMatrix( osg::Matrix::translate(pos) );
    mt->addChild( pagedLOD.get() );
    return mt.release();
}
```

Set different position parameters and add multiple createLODNode() nodes to the scene root. See how paged nodes are rendered. Switch to use osg::LOD instead and have a look at the difference in performance and memory usage.

Customizing your own NodeKits

The most important step in customizing a node and extending new features is to override the virtual method traverse(). This method is called every frame by the OSG rendering backend. The traverse() method has an input parameter, osg::NodeVisitor&, which actually indicates the type of traversals (update, event, or cull). Most OSG **NodeKits** override traverse() to implement their own functionalities, along with some other exclusive attributes and methods.

Note that overriding the `traverse()` method is a bit dangerous sometimes, because it affects the traversing process and may lead to the incorrect rendering of results if developers are not careful enough. It is also a little awkward if you want to add the same new feature to multiple node types by extending each node type to a new customized class. In these cases, consider using node callbacks instead, which will be discussed in *Chapter 8, Animating Scene Objects*.

Time for action – animating the switch node

The `osg::Switch` class can display specified child nodes while hiding others. It could be used to represent the animation states of various objects, for instance, traffic lights. However, a typical `osg::Switch` node is not able to automatically switch between children at different times. Based on this idea, we will develop a new `AnimatingSwitch` node, which will display its children at one time, and reverse the switch states according to a user-defined internal counter.

1. Include the necessary headers:

```
#include <osg/Switch>
#include <osgDB/ReadFile>
#include <osgViewer/Viewer>
```

2. Declare the `AnimatingSwitch` class. This will be derived from the `osg::Switch` class to take advantage of the `setValue()` method. We also make use of an OSG macro definition, `META_Node`, which is a little similar to the `META_Object` introduced in the last chapter, to define basic properties (library and class name) of a node:

```
class AnimatingSwitch : public osg::Switch
{
public:
    AnimatingSwitch() : osg::Switch(), _count(0) {}
    AnimatingSwitch( const AnimatingSwitch& copy,
            const osg::CopyOp& copyop=osg::CopyOp::SHALLOW_COPY )
    : osg::Switch(copy, copyop), _count(copy._count) {}
    META_Node( osg, AnimatingSwitch );

    virtual void traverse( osg::NodeVisitor& nv );

protected:
    unsigned int _count;
};
```

3. In the `traverse()` implementation, we will increase the internal counter and see if it reaches a multiple of 60, and reverse the states of the first and second child nodes:

```
void AnimatingSwitch::traverse( osg::NodeVisitor& nv )
{
    if ( !((++_count)%60) )
    {
        setValue( 0, !getValue(0) );
        setValue( 1, !getValue(1) );
    }
    osg::Switch::traverse( nv );
}
```

4. Read the Cessna model and the afire model again and add them to the customized `AnimatingSwitch` instance:

```
osg::ref_ptr<osg::Node> model1= osgDB::readNodeFile("cessna.osg");
osg::ref_ptr<osg::Node> model2= osgDB::readNodeFile("cessnafire.
osg");

osg::ref_ptr<AnimatingSwitch> root = new AnimatingSwitch;
root->addChild( model1.get(), true );
root->addChild( model2.get(), false );
```

5. Start the viewer:

```
osgViewer::Viewer viewer;
viewer.setSceneData( root.get() );
return viewer.run();
```

6. Because the hardware refresh rate is often at 60 Hz, the `if` condition in `traverse()` will become true once per second, which achieves the animation. Then you will see the Cessna is intact in the first second, and afire and smoking in the next, acting in cycles:

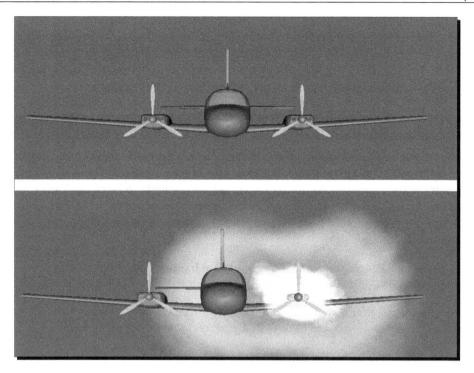

What just happened?

Because the `traverse()` method is widely re-implemented to extend different node types, it should involve a mechanism for reading transformation matrices and rendering states for actual use. For example, the `osg::LOD` node must calculate the distance from a child node's center to the viewer's eye point, which will be used as the visibility range for switching between levels.

The input parameter `osg::NodeVisitor&` is the key to various kinds of node operations. It indicates the type of traversals visiting this node, such as the update, the event, and the cull traversal. The first two are associated with **callbacks** and will be introduced in detail in *Chapter 8, Animating Scene Objects*.

The cull traversal, named `osgUtil::CullVisitor`, can be retrieved from the `osg::NodeVisitor&` parameter with following code snippet:

```
osgUtil::CullVisitor* cv = dynamic_cast<osgUtil::CullVisitor*>(&nv);
if ( cv )
{
    // Do something
}
```

You should include the `<osgUtil/CullVisitor>` header at the beginning of your program. The cull visitor class is able to obtain lots of scene states with different methods, and even change the structure and order of the internal rendering list. The concept and usage of `osgUtil::CullVisitor` is beyond the scope of this beginner's book, but is still worth understanding and learning from the source code of OSG **NodeKits**.

Have a go hero – creating a tracker node

Have you ever thought of implementing a tracker node, which will follow up the position of another node at all times? The trailer had better be an `osg::MatrixTransform` derived subclass. It can use a **smart pointer** member to record the node to be tracked and obtain the position in the 3D world in the `traverse()` override method. Then the tracker will use the `setMatrix()` method to set itself to a relative position, in order to realize the tracking operation.

You can compute a vertex in the absolute coordinate frame by using the `osg::computeLocalToWorld()` function:

```
osg::Vec3 posInWorld = node->getBound().center() *
            osg::computeLocalToWorld(node->getParentalNodePaths()[0]);
```

The `getBound()` method here will return an `osg::BoundingSphere` object. The `osg::BoundingSphere` class represents the bounding sphere of a node, which is used to decide if the node is invisible and cullable in the view frustum culling process. It has two main methods: the `center()` method simply reads the center point of the bounding sphere in the local coordinate; and the `radius()` method returns the radius.

Using the `getParentalNodePaths()` method mentioned in the *Managing parent nodes* section, we can get the parent node path and compute the transformation matrix from the node's relative reference frame to the world reference frame.

The visitor design pattern

The **visitor pattern** is used to represent a user operation to be performed on elements of a graph structure, without modifying classes of these elements. The visitor class implements all of the appropriate virtual functions to be applied to various element types, and archive the goal through the mechanism of **double dispatch**, that is, the dispatch of certain virtual function calls, depending on the runtime types of both the receiver element and the visitor itself.

Based on the theory of **double dispatch**, developers can customize their visitors with special operation requests, and bind the visitor to different types of elements at runtime without changing the element interfaces. This is a great way to extend element functionalities without defining many new element subclasses.

OSG supports `osg::NodeVisitor` class to implement the **visitor pattern**. In essence, an `osg::NodeVisitor` derived class traverses a **scene graph**, visits each node, and applies user-defined operations to them. It is the basic class of implementations of the update, event, and cull traversals (for example, `osgUtil::CullVisitor`), as well as some other scene graph utilities, including `osgUtil::SmoothingVisitor`, `osgUtil::Simplifier`, and `osgUtil::TriStripVisitor`, all of which will traverse the given sub-**scene graph** and apply polygon modifications to geometries found in `osg::Geode` nodes.

Visiting scene graph structures

To create a visitor subclass, we have to re-implement one or several `apply()` virtual overloaded methods declared in the `osg::NodeVisitor` base class. These methods are designed for most major OSG node types. The visitor will automatically call the appropriate `apply()` method for each node it visits during the traversal. User customized visitor classes should override only the `apply()` methods for required node types.

In the implementation of an `apply()` method, developers have to call the `traverse()` method of `osg::NodeVisitor` at the appropriate time. It will instruct the visitor to traverse to the next node, maybe a child, or a sibling node if the current node has no children to visit. Not calling the `traverse()` method means to stop the traversal at once, and the rest of the scene graph is ignored without performing any operations.

The `apply()` methods have the unified formats of:

```
virtual void apply( osg::Node& );
virtual void apply( osg::Geode& );
virtual void apply( osg::Group& );
virtual void apply( osg::Transform& );
```

To traverse a specified node's sub-**scene graph** and call these methods, we first need to select a traversal mode for the visitor object. Take an assumed `ExampleVisitor` class as an example; there are two steps to initialize and start this visitor on a certain node:

```
ExampleVisitor visitor;
visitor->setTraversalMode( osg::NodeVisitor::TRAVERSE_ALL_CHILDREN );
node->accept( visitor );
```

The enumerate or `TRAVERSE_ALL_CHILDREN` means to traverse all of the node's children. There are two other options: `TRAVERSE_PARENTS`, which backtracks from current node until arriving at the root node, and `TRAVERSE_ACTIVE_CHILDREN` , which only visits active child nodes, for instance, the visible children of an `osg::Switch` node.

Time for action – analyzing the Cessna structure

User applications may always search the loaded scene graph for nodes of interest after loading a model file. For example, we might like to take charge of the transformation or visibility of the loaded model if the root node is osg::Transform or osg::Switch. We might also be interested in collecting all transformation nodes at the joints of a skeleton, which can be used to perform character animations later.

The analysis of the loaded model structure is important in that case. We will implement an information printing visitor here, which prints the basic information of visited nodes and arranges them in a tree structure.

1. Include the necessary headers:

```
#include <osgDB/ReadFile>
#include <osgViewer/Viewer>
#include <iostream>
```

2. Declare the InfoVisitor class, and define the necessary virtual methods. We only handle leaf nodes and common osg::Node objects. The inline function spaces() is used for printing spaces before node information, to indicate its level in the tree structure:

```
class InfoVisitor : public osg::NodeVisitor
{
public:
    InfoVisitor() : _level(0)
    { setTraversalMode(osg::NodeVisitor::TRAVERSE_ALL_CHILDREN); }

    std::string spaces()
    { return std::string(_level*2, ' '); }

    Virtual void apply( osg::Node& node );
    virtual void apply( osg::Geode& geode );

protected:
    unsigned int _level;
};
```

3. We will introduce two methods className() and libraryName(), both of which return const char* values, for instance, "Node" as the class name and "osg" as the library name. There is no trick in re-implementing these two methods for different classes. The META_Object and META_Node macro definitions will do the work internally:

```
void InfoVisitor::apply( osg::Node& node )
{
    std::cout << spaces() << node.libraryName() << "::"
      << node.className() << std::endl;

    _level++;
    traverse( node );
    _level--;
}
```

4. The implementation of the `apply()` overloaded method with the `osg::Geode&` parameter is slightly different from the previous one. It iterates all attached drawables of the `osg::Geode` node and prints their information, too. Be aware of the calling time of `traverse()` here, which ensures that the level of each node in the tree is correct.

```
void apply( osg::Geode& geode )
{
    std::cout << spaces() << geode.libraryName() << "::"
      << geode.className() << std::endl;

    _level++;
    for ( unsigned int i=0; i<geode.getNumDrawables(); ++i )
    {
        osg::Drawable* drawable = geode.getDrawable(i);
        std::cout << spaces() << drawable->libraryName() << "::"
          << drawable->className() << std::endl;
    }

    traverse( geode );
    _level--;
}
```

5. In the main function, use `osgDB::readNodeFiles()` to read a file from command line arguments:

```
osg::ArgumentParser arguments( &argc, argv );
osg::ref_ptr<osg::Node> root = osgDB::readNodeFiles( arguments );
if ( !root )
{
    OSG_FATAL << arguments.getApplicationName() <<": No data
      loaded." << std::endl;
    return -1;
}
```

6. Use the customized `InfoVisitor` to visit the loaded model now. You will have noticed that the `setTraversalMode()` method is called in the constructor of the visitor in order to enable the traversal of all of its children:

```
InfoVisitor infoVisitor;
root->accept( infoVisitor );
```

7. Start the viewer or not. This depends on your opinion, because our visitor has already finished its mission:

```
osgViewer::Viewer viewer;
viewer.setSceneData( root.get() );
return viewer.run();
```

8. Assuming that your executable file is `MyProject.exe`, in the prompt, type:

```
# MyProject.exe cessnafire.osg
```

9. You may get following information on the console:

```
osg::Group
  osg::MatrixTransform
    osg::Geode
      osg::Geometry
    osg::MatrixTransform
      osgParticle::ModularEmitter
      osgParticle::ModularEmitter
  osgParticle::ParticleSystemUpdater
  osg::Geode
    osgParticle::ParticleSystem
    osgParticle::ParticleSystem
```

What just happened?

You can easily draw the structure of the input afire Cessna model now. It explicitly includes an `osg::Geode` node with a geometry object, which contains the geometric data of the Cessna. The geometry node can be transformed by its parent `osg::MatrixTransform` node. The whole model is managed under an `osg::Group` node, which is returned by the `osgDB::readNodeFile()` or `osgDB::readNodeFiles()` functions.

Other classes with the prefix `osgParticle` may still seem confusing at present. They actually represent the smoke and fire particle effects of the Cessna, which will be introduced in *Chapter 8, Animating Scene Objects*.

Now we are able to modify the primitive sets of the model, or control the particle system, based on the results of visiting the **scene graph**. To archive this purpose, now let's just save the specified node pointer to a member variable of your own visitor class, and reuse it in future code.

Summary

This chapters taught how to implement a typical **scene graph** by using OSG, which shows the usage of various types of **scene graph** nodes, with a special focus on the assembly of the graph tree and how to add state objects like the commonly used `osg::Transform`, `osg::Switch`, `osg::LOD`, and `osg::ProxyNode` classes. We specifically covered:

- How to utilize various `osg::Group` and `osg::Geode` nodes to assemble a basic hierarchy graph and handle parent and children nodes

- How to realize the spatial transform by using `osg::Transform`, based on the understanding of the concept of matrix and its implementation—the `osg::Matrix` variables

- How to use the `osg::Switch` node to shift the rendering status of scene nodes

- How to decide upon the detail of rendering complexity for scene nodes, by using the `osg::LOD` class

- Using the `osg::ProxyNode` and `osg::PagedLOD` classes to balance the runtime scene load

- How to customize a node and enhance its features

- The basic concept of the **visitor design pattern** and its implementation in OSG

- Traversing a node and its sub-scene graph with the `osg::NodeVisitor` derived classes

6
Creating Realistic Rendering Effects

*Any geometry model in a 3D scene is composed of vertices, texture, lighting,
and shading information. Rendering is, in the graphics pipeline, the last major
step, generating the image from the defined model with a number of visible
features, for example, the brightness, color, and detail of the surface that
the viewer sees. OSG has encapsulated almost all of the OpenGL's rendering
interfaces, including lighting, material, texture, alpha test, image blending,
fog effect, as well as the implementation of vertex, geometry, and fragment
shaders in OpenGL Shading Language.*

This chapter will give a detailed introduction to

- ◆ Understanding the concept of a state machine and the encapsulation of it in OSG
- ◆ How to set up different rendering attributes and modes for scene objects
- ◆ How to inherit rendering states in the scene graph
- ◆ Realizing various fixed-function rendering effects in OSG
- ◆ How to control the scene lights, which is a positional state
- ◆ How to add in textures and set texture coordinates of geometries
- ◆ Controlling the rendering order for drawing transparent and translucent objects
- ◆ Working with the vertex, geometry, and fragment shaders, with uniform variables

Encapsulating the OpenGL state machine

Typically, OpenGL employs a **state machine** to keep track of all rendering related states. The **rendering states** are collections of state attributes like scene lights, materials, textures and texture environments, and state modes, which can be switched on or off using the OpenGL functions `glEnable()` or `glDisable()`.

When a rendering state is set, it will remain in effect until some other function changes it. The OpenGL pipeline internally maintains a state stack to save or restore **rendering states** at any time.

The **state machine** gives developers exact control over current and saved **rendering states**. However, it may not be suitable for direct use in a **scene graph** structure. For this reason, OSG uses the `osg::StateSet` class to encapsulate the OpenGL **state machine**, and manages the push and pop operations of various rendering state sets in the culling and rendering traversals of a **scene graph**.

An `osg::StateSet` instance contains a subset of different OpenGL states, and can be applied to an `osg::Node` or `osg::Drawable` object by using the `setStateSet()` method. For example, you may add a newly-allocated **state set** to a *node* variable:

```
osg::StateSet* stateset = new osg::StateSet;
node->setStateSet( stateset );
```

A safer way is to use the `getOrCreateStateSet()` method, which ensures that a valid **state set** is always returned and automatically attached to the node or drawable object if necessary:

```
osg::StateSet* stateset = node->getOrCreateStateSet();
```

The `osg::Node` or `osg::Drawable` class manages the `osg::StateSet` member variable with the **smart pointer** `osg::ref_ptr<>`. It means that the **state set** can be shared by multiple scene objects, and will be destroyed when no longer used by any of them.

Attributes and modes

OSG defines an `osg::StateAttribute` class for recording rendering state attributes. It is a virtual base class which can be inherited to implement different **rendering attributes** such as lights, materials, and fogs.

Rendering modes perform like switches that can be enabled or disabled. Besides, it contains an enumeration parameter that is used to indicate the type of the OpenGL mode. Because of the simplicity, it is unnecessary to design a `StateMode` base class for **rendering modes**. Note that sometimes a rendering mode is associated with an attribute, for instance, the mode `GL_LIGHTING` enables light variables to be sent to the OpenGL pipeline when set to on, and disables scene lighting contrariwise.

The `osg::StateSet` class divides attributes and modes into two groups: texture and non-texture. It has several member methods to add non-texture attributes and modes to the **state set** itself:

1. The public method `setAttribute()` adds an `osg::StateAttribute` derived object to the **state set**. Attributes of the same type cannot coexist in one **state set**. The previous set one will just be overwritten by the new one.

2. The public method `setMode()` attaches a mode enumeration to the **state set** and sets its value to `osg::StateAttribute::ON` or `osg::StateAttribute::OFF`, which means to enable or disable the mode.

3. The public method `setAttributeAndModes()` attaches a rendering attribute and its associated mode to the **state set**, and sets the switch value (`ON` by default) at the same time. Be aware that not every attribute has a corresponding mode, but you can always make use of this method without being indecisive.

To attach an attribute `attr` and its associated mode to the `stateset` variable, type the following code:

```
stateset->setAttributeAndModes( attr, osg::StateAttribute::ON );
```

Texture attributes and modes have to assign an extra unit parameter to specify the **texture mapping unit** to be applied to, so `osg::StateSet` provides a few more public methods, each with a *Texture* infix, including `setTextureAttribute()`, `setTextureMode()`, and `setTextureAttributeAndModes()`. In order to attach a texture attribute `texattr` and its associated mode to the `stateset` variable, and specify the texture unit 0, just type:

```
stateset->setTextureAttributeAndModes(
    0, texattr, osg::StateAttribute::ON );
```

Time for action – setting polygon modes of different nodes

We are going to select the polygon rasterization mode of a loaded model. The `osg::PolygonMode` class, which is derived from the `osg::StateAttribute` base class, will be used to achieve this goal. It simply encapsulates OpenGL's `glPolygonMode()` function and implements interfaces for specifying face and drawing mode parameters, and thus changes the final rasterization of the attached node.

1. Include the necessary headers:

```
#include <osg/PolygonMode>
#include <osg/MatrixTransform>
#include <osgDB/ReadFile>
#include <osgViewer/Viewer>
```

2. We will work on the basis of the transformation example in the last chapter. We create two `osg::MatrixTransform` nodes and make them share the same loaded Cessna model. The two transformation nodes are placed at different positions in the 3D world, which will display two Cessna models as the result:

```
osg::ref_ptr<osg::Node> model = osgDB::readNodeFile(
    "cessna.osg" );

osg::ref_ptr<osg::MatrixTransform> transformation1 = new
osg::MatrixTransform;
transformation1->setMatrix(osg::Matrix::translate(-
25.0f,0.0f,0.0f));
transformation1->addChild( model.get() );

osg::ref_ptr<osg::MatrixTransform> transformation2 = new
osg::MatrixTransform;
transformation2->setMatrix(osg::Matrix::translate(25.0f,0.0f,0.
0f));
transformation2->addChild( model.get() );
```

3. Now, we will add an `osg::PolygonMode` rendering attribute to the associated **state set** of the node `transformation1`. It has a `setMode()` method which accepts two parameters: the face that the mode applied to, and the mode should be in which polygons will be rasterized:

```
osg::ref_ptr<osg::PolygonMode> pm = new osg::PolygonMode;
pm->setMode(osg::PolygonMode::FRONT_AND_BACK,
osg::PolygonMode::LINE);
transformation1->getOrCreateStateSet()->setAttribute( pm.get() );
```

4. The next step is familiar. Now we can add the nodes to a root node, and start the viewer to see if anything has changed:

```
osg::ref_ptr<osg::Group> root = new osg::Group;
root->addChild( transformation1.get() );
root->addChild( transformation2.get() );

osgViewer::Viewer viewer;
viewer.setSceneData( root.get() );
return viewer.run();
```

5. The Cessna model at the position (-25.09, 0.0, 0.0), or on the left of the initial display window, is drawn with outlined front and back facing polygons. On the contrary, the model on the right is still fully filled as usual:

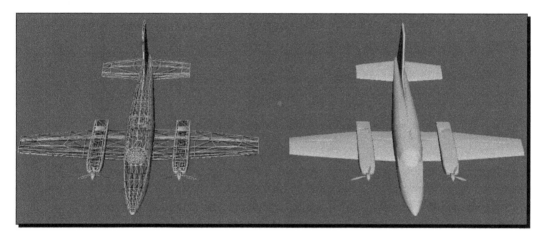

What just happened?

With prior knowledge of the OpenGL polygon mode, we can easily imagine the parameters required by the setMode() method of the osg::PolygonMode class. The first parameter can be one of osg::PolygonMode::FRONT, BACK, and FRONT_AND_BACK, corresponding to the OpenGL enumerations GL_FRONT, GL_BACK, and GL_FRONT_AND_BACK. The second parameter can be one of osg::PolygonMode::POINT, LINE, and FILL, which correspond to GL_POINT, GL_LINE, and GL_FILL. OSG needs no more tricks when encapsulating OpenGL rendering states!

The polygon mode doesn't have an associated mode, that is, it doesn't require calling the OpenGL glEnable()/glDisable() functions, nor making use of OSG state set's setMode() method.

The setAttributeAndModes() method can also work properly here, but the switch value (ON/OFF) is of no avail in this case.

Inheriting render states

The **state set** of a node will affect the current node and its children. For example, the `osg::PolygonMode` attribute set to node `transformation1` will make all of its children display as outlined. However, a child node's **state set** can override its parent's, that is, the rendering states will be inherited from the **parent node** unless a **child node** changes the behavior. The following image shows how different polygon mode states are traversed an imaginary **scene graph**:

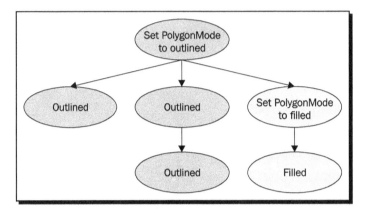

Sometimes you may want different behaviors. For example, in common 3D editor software, users can load multiple models from files and render all of them as textured, wireframe, or solid, no matter what the previous state of each model is. In other word, all children models in the editor should inherit a unified attribute regardless of what they have set before. This can be implemented in OSG by using an `osg::StateAttribute::OVERRIDE` flag, such as:

```
stateset->setAttribute( attr, osg::StateAttribute::OVERRIDE );
```

For setting rendering modes, or attribute and modes, use the bitwise OR operator:

```
stateset->setAttributeAndModes( attr,
    osg::StateAttribute::ON|osg::StateAttribute::OVERRIDE );
```

Returning to the topic of 3D editor software. Imagine that you select a model by using the mouse pointer; there will be a wireframe bounding box displayed to indicate that the model is selected. The selection box will never be affected by the textured/wireframe/solid states, that is, the attribute or mode is immune from it's parent's override. OSG uses an `osg::StateAttribute::PROTECTED` flag to support this.

OSG has a third flag, `osg::StateAttribute::INHERIT`, which is used to indicate that the current attribute or mode should be inherited from the parent node's **state set**. The applied attribute or mode will not actually be used in this situation.

Time for action – lighting the glider or not

We will show the usage of the `OVERRIDE` and `PROTECTED` flags in the following short example. The **root node** will be set to `OVERRIDE`, in order to force all children to inherit its attribute or mode. Meanwhile, the children will try to change their inheritance with or without a `PROTECTED` flag, which will lead to different results.

1. Include the necessary headers:

```
#include <osg/PolygonMode>
#include <osg/MatrixTransform>
#include <osgDB/ReadFile>
#include <osgViewer/Viewer>
```

2. Create two `osg::MatrixTransform` nodes and make them both share a glider model. After all, we don't want to use the well-known Cessna all the time. The glider is small in size, so only a small distance is required for the `setMatrix()` method:

```
osg::ref_ptr<osg::Node> model = osgDB::readNodeFile(
  "glider.osg" );

osg::ref_ptr<osg::MatrixTransform> transformation1 = new
osg::MatrixTransform;
transformation1->setMatrix(osg::Matrix::translate(
  -0.5f, 0.0f, 0.0f));
transformation1->addChild( model.get() );

osg::ref_ptr<osg::MatrixTransform> transformation2 = new
  osg::MatrixTransform;
transformation2->setMatrix(osg::Matrix::translate(
  0.5f, 0.0f, 0.0f));
transformation2->addChild( model.get() );
```

3. Add the two transformation nodes to the root:

```
osg::ref_ptr<osg::Group> root = new osg::Group;
root->addChild( transformation1.get() );
root->addChild( transformation2.get() );
```

4. Now we are going to set the rendering mode of each node's **state set**. The GL_LIGHTING mode is a famous OpenGL enumeration which can be used to enable or disable global lighting of the scene. Note that the OVERRIDE and PROTECTED flags are set to root and transformation2 separately, along with an ON or OFF switch value:

```
transformation1->getOrCreateStateSet()->setMode( GL_LIGHTING,
    osg::StateAttribute::OFF );
transformation2->getOrCreateStateSet()->setMode( GL_LIGHTING,
    osg::StateAttribute::OFF|osg::StateAttribute::PROTECTED);
root->getOrCreateStateSet()->setMode( GL_LIGHTING,
    osg::StateAttribute::ON|osg::StateAttribute::OVERRIDE );
```

5. Start the viewer:

```
osgViewer::Viewer viewer;
viewer.setSceneData( root.get() );
return viewer.run();
```

6. The node transformation1 is placed on the left side of the screen, without any obvious changes. However, transformation2 is completely different, even though it shares the same loaded model with transformation1:

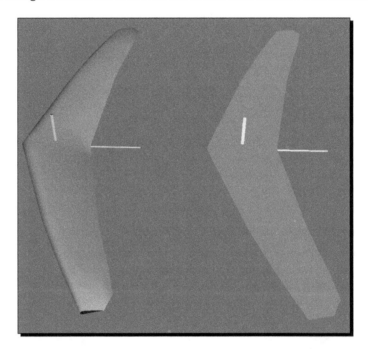

What just happened?

You can first find out what a normal lighted glider looks like with the following command:

```
# osgviewer glider.osg
```

In this example, we are trying to change the GL_LIGHTING modes of transformation1 and transformation2 to disable lights on them. Meanwhile, we have turned on the lighting mode for the **root node**, and used an OVERRIDE flag for all children to follow to retain their lighting states.

The node transformation1, as shown in the previous image, remains lighted in spite of its own setting. However, transformation2 uses a PROTECTED flag to prevent itself from being affected by the root. It becomes a little brighter as a result of "turning off" the light on its surfaces. This is simply because the geometries are now directly colored according to the original color arrays, without any more reaction to the lights.

Changing the filename of osgDB::readNodeFile() to cessna.osg will produce two lighted models in this example, because the Cessna model turns on the GL_LIGHTING mode inside its sub-scene graph, in order to override any previous states. Can you figure out how to disable the lights of transformation2 node this time?

Playing with fixed-function effects

OSG supports almost all kinds of OpenGL rendering attributes and modes by using the osg::StateAttribute derived classes. The following table is part of over 40 OSG components that encapsulate major OpenGL fixed-function states:

Type ID	Class name	Associated mode	Related OpenGL functions
ALPHAFUNC	osg::AlphaFunc	GL_ ALPHA_ TEST	glAlphaFunc()
BLENDFUNC	osg::BlendFunc	GL_BLEND	glBlendFunc() and glBlendFuncSeparate()
CLIPPLANE	osg::ClipPlane	GL_CLIP_ PLANEi (i ranges from 0 to 5)	glClipPlane()
COLORMASK	osg::ColorMask	-	glColorMask()

Type ID	Class name	Associated mode	Related OpenGL functions
CULLFACE	osg::CullFace	GL_CULLFACE	glCullFace()
DEPTH	osg::Depth	GL_DEPTH_TEST	glDepthFunc(), glDepthRange(), and glDepthMask()
FOG	osg::Fog	GL_FOG	glFog()
FRONTFACE	osg::FrontFace	-	glFrontFace()
LIGHT	osg::Light	GL_LIGHTi (i ranges from 0 to 7)	glLight()
LIGHTMODEL	osg::LightModel	-	glLightModel()
LINESTIPPLE	osg::LineStipple	GL_LINE_STIPPLE	glLineStipple()
LINEWIDTH	osg::LineWidth	-	glLineWidth()
LOGICOP	osg::LogicOp	GL_COLOR_LOGIC_OP	glLogicOp()
MATERIAL	osg::Material	-	glMaterial() and glColorMaterial()
POINT	osg::Point	GL_POINT_SMOOTH	glPointParameter()
POINTSPRITE	osg::PointSprite	GL_POINT_SPRITE_ARB	OpenGL point sprite functions
POLYGONMODE	osg::PolygonMode	-	glPolygonMode()
POLYGONOFFSET	osg::PolygonOffset	GL_POLYGON_OFFSET_POINT, and so on	glPolygonOffset()
POLYGONS TIPPLE	osg::PolygonStipple	GL_POLYGON_STIPPLE	glPolygonStipple()
SCISSOR	osg::Scissor	GL_SCISSOR_TEST	glScissor()

Type ID	Class name	Associated mode	Related OpenGL functions
SHADEMODEL	osg::ShadeModel	-	glShadeModel()
STENCIL	osg::Stencil	GL_STENCIL_TEST	glStencilFunc(), glStencilOp(), and glStencilMask()
TEXENV	osg::TexEnv	-	glTexEnv()
TEXGEN	osg::TexGen	GL_TEXTURE_GEN_S, and so on	glTexGen()

The *Type ID* column will retrieve specific attributes from a **state set**. It is used as the parameter of the method `getAttribute()`, for instance:

```
osg::PolygonMode* pm = dynamic_cast<osg::PolygonMode*>(
    stateset->getAttribute(osg::StateAttribute::POLYGONMODE) );
```

A valid pointer will be retrieved if you have set the polygon mode attribute to the `stateset` variable before. Otherwise, `getAttribute()` will return NULL.

The *Associated mode* column of the table shows how OSG calls OpenGL modes when using `setAttributeAndModes()`. You may also check to see if a mode is turned on or off by using the `getMode()` method:

```
osg::StateAttribute::GLModeValue value =
    stateset->getMode( GL_LIGHTING );
```

Here the enumeration `GL_LIGHTING` is used to enable or disable lighting in the whole scene.

The *Related OpenGL functions* column identifies which OpenGL functions are encapsulated in an OSG attribute class. An OSG attribute class will always have a series of methods to specify related function parameters—OpenGL developers can thus migrate from their applications to OSG without too many modifications.

Time for action – applying simple fog to models

We will take the fog effect as an ideal example of working with various rendering attributes and modes. OpenGL accepts one linear and two exponential fog equations, which are supported by the osg::Fog class as well.

1. Include the necessary headers:

```
#include <osg/Fog>
#include <osgDB/ReadFile>
#include <osgViewer/Viewer>
```

2. We would like to first create the fog attribute. Using the linear mode, we have to set the near and far distances by using setStart() and setEnd() methods. We will also set the fog color, in order to generate a dust fog-like effect:

```
osg::ref_ptr<osg::Fog> fog = new osg::Fog;
fog->setMode( osg::Fog::LINEAR );
fog->setStart( 500.0f );
fog->setEnd( 2500.0f );
fog->setColor( osg::Vec4(1.0f, 1.0f, 0.0f, 1.0f) );
```

3. We are going to load an example terrain model named lz.osg, which can be located in the data directory indicated by the environment variable OSG_FILE_PATH. The only work to do is to set the fog attribute and the associated mode to the node's **state set**.

```
osg::ref_ptr<osg::Node> model = osgDB::readNodeFile( "lz.osg" );
model->getOrCreateStateSet()->setAttributeAndModes( fog.get() );
```

4. Start the viewer and manipulate the scene, in order to make the terrain and the fog have a better appearance:

```
osgViewer::Viewer viewer;
viewer.setSceneData( model.get() );
return viewer.run();
```

5. As you scale the scene by using the right mouse button, the terrain model will fade in and out of the fog in a smooth progression. This is a very basic environment effect, but the result can still be fantastic sometimes:

What just happened?

The OpenGL `glFog()` function supports the setting of parameters of various modes such as `GL_FOG_MODE`, `GL_FOG_DENSITY`, `GL_FOG_START`, and `GL_FOG_END`. These are redefined in OSG as the `setMode()`, `setDensity()`, `setStart()`, and `setEnd()` methods, each of which has a paired `get*()` method.

Here is an additional trick about implementing the fog effect: developers may set the fog coordinate of each vertex of geometry and use it as a distance value in the computation. This can be done by using the `setFogCoordArray()` and `setFogCoordBinding()` methods of the `osg::Geometry` class, in addition to specifying the fog coordinate source:

```
fog->setFogCoordinateSource( GL_FOG_COORD );
```

The current fragment depth will be used in the fog color computation instead, if the method's parameter is set to `GL_FRAGMENT_DEPTH`.

Have a go hero – searching for more effects

There are more OSG rendering attribute classes that have encapsulated OpenGL functions and parameters into public class methods. For details, you may read the API documentation included in the prebuilt packages, or look for declarations in the header files in order to learn how to make use of them.

Some easy-to-read and easy-to-use **rendering attributes** are `osg::ColorMask`, `osg::LineWidth`, and `osg::ShadeModel`. They have intuitive methods for setting mask, width, and mode parameters, and can immediately make effects when attaching to state sets of nodes and **drawables**. Have a try of these rendering attributes and see if you can master them with only the API manuals and class declarations.

Lights and light sources

Like OpenGL, OSG only supports up to eight fixed-function light sources for directly illuminating the 3D scene, and won't be able to automatically generate and cast shadows are on objects. Light rays commonly originate from certain light sources, travel in straight lines, reflected on or scattered off scene objects, and are finally perceived by the viewer's eye. The light source properties, the surface material properties, and normals of geometries are all necessary to implement complete lighting effects.

The `osg::Light` class provides neat methods for operating on properties of a light source, including `setLightNum()` and `getLightNum()` for handling the OpenGL light number, `setAmbient()` and `getAmbient()` for the ambient component, `setDiffuse()` and `getDiffuse()` for the diffuse component of the light, and so on.

OSG also provides an `osg::LightSource` class for adding lights to the scene graph. It has a `setLight()` method and should be used as a leaf node with a single light attribute. All other nodes in the scene graph will be affected by the light source node if the corresponding `GL_LIGHTi` mode is set. For instance:

```
osg::ref_ptr<osg::Light> light = new osg::Light;
light->setLightNum( 1 );  // Specify light number 1
...
osg::ref_ptr<osg::LightSource> lightSource = new osg::LightSource;
lightSource->setLight( light.get() );  // Add to a light source node
...
// Add the source node to the scene root and enable rendering mode GL_
LIGHT1 to fit the light's set!
root->addChild( lightSource.get() );
root->getOrCreateStateSet()->setMode( GL_LIGHT1,
    osg::StateAttribute::ON );
```

Another more convenient solution for enabling specified light is the `setStateSetModes()` method, with which the light source will automatically attach the light number with the scene root:

```
root->addChild( lightSource.get() );
lightSource->setStateSetModes( root->getOrCreateStateSet(),
osg::StateAttribute::ON );
```

Sometimes you may add children to an `osg::LightSource` node, but this doesn't mean that you will light sub-graphs based on the hierarchical relationship to the node. It can be treated as a geometry representing the physical shape of the light source.

The osg::LightSource nodes can be placed under an osg::Transform node. Then a point light can be translated according to the current transformation matrix. You may disable this feature by setting the reference frame of osg::LightSource, such as:

```
lightSource->setReferenceFrame( osg::LightSource::ABSOLUTE_RF );
```

Its meaning is similar to the setReferenceFrame() method of the osg::Transform class.

Time for action – creating light sources in the scene

By default, OSG automatically turns on the first light (GL_LIGHT0) and gives the scene a soft, directional light. However, this time we will create multiple lights by ourselves, and move them with transformation parent nodes. Be aware: only positional lights can be translated. A directional light has no origin and cannot be placed anywhere.

OpenGL and OSG both use the fourth component of the position parameter to decide if a light is a point light. That is to say, if the fourth component is 0, the light is treated as a directional source; otherwise it is positional.

1. Include the necessary headers:

```
#include <osg/MatrixTransform>
#include <osg/LightSource>
#include <osgDB/ReadFile>
#include <osgViewer/Viewer>
```

2. We create a function to create light sources for the **scene graph**. A light source should have a number (ranging from 0 to 7), a translation position, and a color parameter. A point light is created because the fourth part of the position vector is 1.0. After that, we assign the light to a newly-created osg::LightSource node, and add the light source to a translated osg::MatrixTransform node, which is then returned:

```
osg::Node* createLightSource( unsigned int num,
                              const osg::Vec3& trans,
                              const osg::Vec4& color )
{
    osg::ref_ptr<osg::Light> light = new osg::Light;
    light->setLightNum( num );
    light->setDiffuse( color );
    light->setPosition( osg::Vec4(0.0f, 0.0f, 0.0f, 1.0f) );

    osg::ref_ptr<osg::LightSource> lightSource = new
        osg::LightSource;
    lightSource->setLight( light );
```

```
osg::ref_ptr<osg::MatrixTransform> sourceTrans =
    new osg::MatrixTransform;
sourceTrans->setMatrix( osg::Matrix::translate(trans) );
sourceTrans->addChild( lightSource.get() );
return sourceTrans.release();
}
```

3. The Cessna model is going to be lighted by our customized lights. We will load it from file before creating the light sources:

```
osg::ref_ptr<osg::Node> model = osgDB::readNodeFile(
    "cessna.osg" );

osg::ref_ptr<osg::Group> root = new osg::Group;
root->addChild( model.get() );
```

4. Now it's time to construct two light source nodes and put them at different positions in the scene:

```
osg::Node* light0 = createLightSource(
    0, osg::Vec3(-20.0f,0.0f,0.0f), osg::Vec4(
    1.0f,1.0f,0.0f,1.0f) );
osg::Node* light1 = createLightSource(
    1, osg::Vec3(0.0f,-20.0f,0.0f), osg::Vec4(0.0f,1.0f,1.0f,1.0f)
);
```

5. The light numbers 0 and 1 are used here. So we will turn on modes GL_LIGHT0 and GL_LIGHT1 of the root node, which means that all nodes in the scene graph could benefit from the two warm light sources:

```
root->getOrCreateStateSet()->setMode( GL_LIGHT0,
    osg::StateAttribute::ON );
root->getOrCreateStateSet()->setMode( GL_LIGHT1,
    osg::StateAttribute::ON );
root->addChild( light0 );
root->addChild( light1 );
```

6. Now let's start the viewer:

```
osgViewer::Viewer viewer;
viewer.setSceneData( root.get() );
return viewer.run();
```

7. You will figure out that one side of the Cessna is lighted in yellow, and its front is caught by a cyan light. That is exactly what we want in the example source code!

What just happened?

The osg::LightSource class is a node of special kind, which affects all nodes that enable its associated rendering mode, no matter whether these nodes are placed as children of the light source or not. This is sometimes confusing, but can be explained through the concept of **positional states**. That is, **rendering states** using the current **model-view matrix** to position themselves.

Typical **positional states** in OpenGL include the glLight() function (point light), glClipPlane() function, and glTexGen() function (GL_EYE_LINEAR mode). These states should be anchored during the space transformation; otherwise their appearances will vary widely according to different model-view matrices applied every time.

OSG uses three osg::Group derived nodes: osg::LightSource, osg::ClipNode, and osg::TexGenNode, to bind these special states. They all have a setReferenceFrame() method to use the absolute reference frame, and can be added to the transformation node to be located in space. The only difference is that osg::LightSource and osg::TexGenNode have influence over all nodes enabling related modes, but osg::ClipNode only clips children with specific clipping planes.

Pop quiz – lights without sources

We can treat `osg::Light` as a normal rendering attribute, too. For example, applying a light object to the **root node** will also affect its sub-graph. However, there will be an obvious difference if we don't make use of light sources. What do you think is the difference? When will the light act like a headlight (or skylight)?

The Image class

In the last chapter, we have already learnt how to create a quad and fill it with color. However, another idea is to apply it with a texture map (often a bitmap or raster image). This does not affect the vertices of a surface, but only changes final **pixel data**, which is more efficient and suitable for representing object details in most cases.

OSG provides several texture attributes and modes for **texture mapping** operations, which will be introduced in the next section. Before that, we will have to discuss the `osg::Image` class, which stores image data for OpenGL texture objects to upload and use.

The best way to load an image from a disk file is to use the `osgDB::readImageFile()` function. This is very similar to the `osgDB::readNodeFile()` function, which loads models as scene nodes. Assuming we have a bitmap file named `picture.bmp`, the following code will load it as an image object for **texture mapping** usage:

```
osg::ref_ptr<osg::Image> image =
    osgDB::readImageFile( "picture.bmp" );
```

If the image is loaded correctly, that is, the image pointer is valid, then we are able to read the image's properties by using some public methods:

- The public methods `s()`, `t()`, and `r()` return the width, height, and depth of the image.

- The public method `data()` returns the raw image data as an `unsigned char*` pointer. You may operate on the pointer directly in order to read or modify image **pixel data**.

  The meaning of each unsigned char element in the `data()` pointer is associated with the image's **pixel format** and **data type**, which can be read from `getPixelFormat()` and `getDataType()`. These two values have the same significance as the format and type parameters of the OpenGL `glTexImage*()` functions. For example, an image object with the **pixel format** `GL_RGB` and the **data type** `GL_UNSIGNED_BYTE` will use three separated unsigned char elements to represent each of the RGB components, which form a complete pixel, as the following image shows:

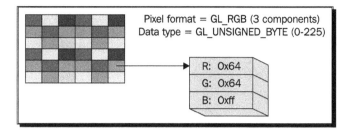

You may also allocate a new image object and put your own image data into this object:

```
osg::ref_ptr<osg::Image> image = new osg::Image;
image->allocateImage( s, t, r, GL_RGB, GL_UNSIGNED_BYTE );
unsigned char* ptr = image->data();
...   // Operate on the ptr variable directly!
```

Here s, t, and r indicate the size of the image, and GL_RGB and GL_UNSIGNED_BYTE are used as example settings of **pixel format** and **data type**. The internal buffer data will be allocated after calling the allocateImage() method, and automatically destroyed when the image is no longer referenced by any texture objects.

You can try a few more image files, such as .jpg, .png, .tif, and so on. OSG manages to handle most image formats via file I/O plugins, but some of them require third-party libraries as dependencies, and thus are unusable if you are building OSG from source code with the default settings. You may learn more about building and using file reader/writer plugins in detail in *Chapter 10, Saving and Loading Files*.

The basis of texture mapping

To perform basic **texture mapping** in your applications, you have to follow these steps:

1. Set the texture coordinates of specified geometries

2. Create a texture attribute object for a 1D, 2D, 3D or cube map **texture mapping** operation

3. Specify one or more images for the texture attribute

4. Attach the appropriate texture attribute and modes to a **state set**, which will be applied to related nodes and **drawables**

OSG defines the `osg::Texture` class to encapsulate all kinds of textures. It has subclasses `osg::Texture1D`, `osg::Texture2D`, `osg::Texture3D`, and `osg::TextureCubeMap`, which can represent different OpenGL **texture mapping** techniques.

The most common method of the `osg::Texture` class is `setImage()`. This simply sets an allocated image to the texture object. For instance:

```
osg::ref_ptr<osg::Image> image =
    osgDB::readImageFile( "picture.bmp" );
osg::ref_ptr<osg::Texture2D> texture = new osg::Texture2D;
texture->setImage( image.get() );
```

Otherwise, you may pass the image object to the constructor directly:

```
osg::ref_ptr<osg::Image> image =
    osgDB::readImageFile( "picture.bmp" );
osg::ref_ptr<osg::Texture2D> texture =
    new osg::Texture2D( image.get() );
```

The image variable is managed by the **smart pointer** inside the texture object. You may read it back from the texture object by using the `getImage()` method.

Another important thing is to set the texture coordinates for each vertex of `osg::Geometry` objects. You should apply an `osg::Vec2Array` or `osg::Vec3Array` to the geometry by using the `setTexCoordArray()` method, in order to make up all fragments with the corresponding texels in current 2D or a volume texture.

When specifying texture coordinates, we must also set a **texture mapping** unit for **multi-texture** implementation. To use a single texture on a model, we can simply specify the texture unit 0. For instance, the following code sets the texture coordinates array in unit 0 of the geometry variable `geom`:

```
osg::ref_ptr<osg::Vec2Array> texcoord = new osg::Vec2Array;
texcoord->push_back( osg::Vec2(...) );
...
geom->setTexCoordArray( 0, texcoord.get() );
```

After that, we can add the texture attribute to a **state set**, automatically switch on the related mode (`GL_TEXTURE_2D`), and apply the attribute to the geometry itself, or a node containing it:

```
geom->getOrCreateStateSet()->setTextureAttributeAndModes(
    texture.get() );
```

Note that OpenGL manages image data in the **graphics memory** (video card memory), but an `osg::Image` object will save loaded data in the **system memory**. The result will be two copies of the same image data, one owned by OpenGL and one stored in the `osg::Image` object. If the image is not shared among multiple texture attributes, it is possible to delete the image object and the **system memory** it occupies after applying it to the OpenGL pipeline. The `osg::Texture` class provides a `setUnRefImageDataAfterApply()` method to do this:

```
texture->setUnRefImageDataAfterApply( true );
```

Once the OpenGL texture object is created, the internally managed image will be released and `getImage()` will return an invalid pointer. This will make the viewer run more efficiently.

Time for action – loading and applying 2D textures

The most common **texture mapping** technique is 2D texture mapping. This accepts a 2D image as the texture and maps it onto one or more geometry surfaces. The `osg::Texture2D` class is used here as a texture attribute of a specific **texture mapping unit**.

1. Include the necessary headers:

```
#include <osg/Texture2D>
#include <osg/Geometry>
#include <osgDB/ReadFile>
#include <osgViewer/Viewer>
```

2. We will quickly create a quad and call the `setTexCoordArray()` method to bind texture coordinates per vertex. The texture coordinate array only affects the texture unit 0 in this example, but it is always possible to share arrays among units:

```
osg::ref_ptr<osg::Vec3Array> vertices = new osg::Vec3Array;
vertices->push_back( osg::Vec3(-0.5f, 0.0f,-0.5f) );
vertices->push_back( osg::Vec3( 0.5f, 0.0f,-0.5f) );
vertices->push_back( osg::Vec3( 0.5f, 0.0f, 0.5f) );
vertices->push_back( osg::Vec3(-0.5f, 0.0f, 0.5f) );

osg::ref_ptr<osg::Vec3Array> normals = new osg::Vec3Array;
normals->push_back( osg::Vec3(0.0f,-1.0f, 0.0f) );

osg::ref_ptr<osg::Vec2Array> texcoords = new osg::Vec2Array;
texcoords->push_back( osg::Vec2(0.0f, 0.0f) );
texcoords->push_back( osg::Vec2(0.0f, 1.0f) );
texcoords->push_back( osg::Vec2(1.0f, 1.0f) );
texcoords->push_back( osg::Vec2(1.0f, 0.0f) );
```

```
osg::ref_ptr<osg::Geometry> quad = new osg::Geometry;
quad->setVertexArray( vertices.get() );
quad->setNormalArray( normals.get() );
quad->setNormalBinding( osg::Geometry::BIND_OVERALL );
quad->setTexCoordArray( 0, texcoords.get() );
quad->addPrimitiveSet( new osg::DrawArrays(GL_QUADS, 0, 4) );
```

3. We will load an image from the disk and assign it to the 2D texture object. The file format .rgb is developed by SGI and is commonly used for storing 2D textures:

```
osg::ref_ptr<osg::Texture2D> texture = new osg::Texture2D;
osg::ref_ptr<osg::Image> image =
    osgDB::readImageFile( "Images/lz.rgb" );
texture->setImage( image.get() );
```

4. Add the quad to an osg::Geode node, and then add the texture attribute to the state set. Be careful to set the attribute to the same **texture mapping unit** as the texture coordinate array:

```
osg::ref_ptr<osg::Geode> root = new osg::Geode;
root->addDrawable( quad.get() );
root->getOrCreateStateSet()->setTextureAttributeAndModes(
    0, texture.get() );
```

5. Start the viewer and see what happened:

```
osgViewer::Viewer viewer;
viewer.setSceneData( root.get() );
return viewer.run();
```

6. Now we have a quad geometry with a regular texture applied to it. Try using another image file to see if we could build a more colorful world in the 3D space:

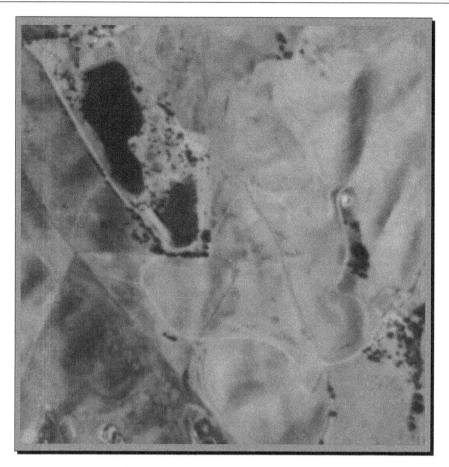

What just happened?

A 2D texture is a two-dimensional array of color values. Each value is called a **texel** (texture element), which has a unique address formed by a column and a row number. The row is labeled as the *s* axis and the column as the *t* axis, relative to the location (0,0) in the texture. The address, named a texture coordinate, should be mapped into object coordinates according to a unique vertex it is assigned to. That is why we should set the texture coordinate array of geometry and ensure that it has the same size as the vertex array.

The `osg::Geometry` class can have multiple texture coordinate arrays in different **texture mapping units**. To make all of them available, you have to set `osg::Texture` attributes for each unit by using the `setTextureAttributeAndModes()` method.

The osg::Texture2D class requires the texture coordinates normalized to [0, 1], otherwise it uses texture wrapping to handle extra parts. It checks if the dimensions of a texture are both power-of-two in size, for instance, 64x64 or 256x512, and will automatically scale non power-of-two images by default, using the OpenGL's gluScaleImage() function internally, which is convenient for reading arbitrary images, but spends more system time and leads to larger result size in graphics memory. There is also a setResizeNonPowerOfTwoHint() method that defines whether we have to force the resizing of images. Note that non power-of-two images are directly supported by some graphics cards.

The osg::TextureRectangle class supports 2D textures without requiring power-of-two dimensions. Re-sampling is thus avoided, and less graphics memory will be used to store image data. However, it doesn't have **mipmaps** for texture filtering, and texture coordinates must be dimension-dependent.

Have a go hero – making use of filters and wrapping modes

OpenGL has already designed perfect mechanisms for handling texture wrapping and filtering. The osg::Texture class also includes methods to encapsulate them.

The setWrap() method requires two parameters: the texture coordinate axis to apply and the wrap mode to use. We can then define the texture's wrapping behavior, such as:

```
texture->setWrap( osg::Texture::WRAP_S, osg::Texture::REPEAT );
texture->setWrap( osg::Texture::WRAP_R, osg::Texture::REPEAT );
```

This will cause the texture to be tiled if the texture coordinate on axes *s* and *t* is out of range [0, 1].

Similarly, the setFilter() method is used to define the minification and magnification filters of a texture object. Now, can you find out the usage and appearance of the setWrap() and setFilter() methods in comparison with same functionalities in OpenGL? The OpenGL online documentation and the red-book (*The OpenGL Programming Guide*) would be nice for understanding these topics.

Handling rendering order

Before starting to explain how to handle rendering order in OSG, we'd better understand what **rendering order** is and how it works in OpenGL.

OpenGL stores vertex and primitive data in various buffers, such as the **color buffer**, **depth buffer**, **stencil buffer**, and so on. Apart from this, it doesn't record vertices and triangles already sent to it in any other form. Therefore, OpenGL always renders new geometry primitives regardless of tracing old ones, which means that the order in which these primitives are rendered is significant.

With the help of **depth buffer**, opaque objects can be rendered correctly and the **rendering order** of these objects doesn't matter in simple cases, because the default depth test passes the incoming data if this is less than the stored one.

However, when using the OpenGL blending mechanism, for instance, to implement transparent and translucent effects, a special operation will be performed in order to update the **color buffer**. Instead of just overriding, the new and old pixels are mixed, taking into account the alpha value (which is always the fourth component of the color vector) or other factors. This leads to the problem that **rendering order** will affect the final results, as shown in the following diagram:

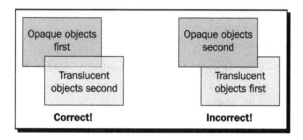

The `setRenderingHint()` method of the `osg::StateSet` class will tell OSG to control the rendering order of nodes and **drawables** if necessary. It simply indicates whether a state set is opaque or transparent, and ensures that objects associated with transparent states should be rendered after opaque ones, and these transparent objects should be sorted by the length from every object's center to the eye position (that is, from a distance to nearby).

In order to hint that a node or **drawable** is opaque (this is actually the default), just type:

```
node->getOrCreateStateSet()->setRenderingHint(

    osg::StateSet::OPAQUE_BIN );
```

And for a transparent node or **drawable**:

```
node->getOrCreateStateSet()->setRenderingHint(

    osg::StateSet::TRANSPARENT_BIN );
```

Time for action – achieving the translucent effect

We are going to implement a common translucent effect that treats a model as glass. Any other scene objects can be displayed through the `glass` object. This can be done with the OpenGL blending mechanism, but it is important to calculate the correct rendering order of scene objects in this case.

1. Include the necessary headers:

```
#include <osg/BlendFunc>
#include <osg/Texture2D>
#include <osg/Geometry>
#include <osgDB/ReadFile>
#include <osgViewer/Viewer>
```

2. We will continue using the quad geometry with a predefined texture coordinate array. It should be treated as a translucent object and the blending attribute and modes should be applied later:

```
osg::ref_ptr<osg::Vec3Array> vertices = new osg::Vec3Array;
vertices->push_back( osg::Vec3(-0.5f, 0.0f,-0.5f) );
vertices->push_back( osg::Vec3( 0.5f, 0.0f,-0.5f) );
vertices->push_back( osg::Vec3( 0.5f, 0.0f, 0.5f) );
vertices->push_back( osg::Vec3(-0.5f, 0.0f, 0.5f) );

osg::ref_ptr<osg::Vec3Array> normals = new osg::Vec3Array;
normals->push_back( osg::Vec3(0.0f,-1.0f, 0.0f) );

osg::ref_ptr<osg::Vec2Array> texcoords = new osg::Vec2Array;
texcoords->push_back( osg::Vec2(0.0f, 0.0f) );
texcoords->push_back( osg::Vec2(0.0f, 1.0f) );
texcoords->push_back( osg::Vec2(1.0f, 1.0f) );
texcoords->push_back( osg::Vec2(1.0f, 0.0f) );
```

3. Be careful to set the color array of the quad. To blend it with other scene objects, we have to set the alpha component to a value of less than 1.0 here:

```
osg::ref_ptr<osg::Vec4Array> colors = new osg::Vec4Array;
colors->push_back( osg::Vec4(1.0f, 1.0f, 1.0f, 0.5f) );
```

4. Create the quad geometry again:

```
osg::ref_ptr<osg::Geometry> quad = new osg::Geometry;
quad->setVertexArray( vertices.get() );
quad->setNormalArray( normals.get() );
quad->setNormalBinding( osg::Geometry::BIND_OVERALL );
quad->setColorArray( colors.get() );
quad->setColorBinding( osg::Geometry::BIND_OVERALL );
```

```
quad->setTexCoordArray( 0, texcoords.get() );
quad->addPrimitiveSet( new osg::DrawArrays(GL_QUADS, 0, 4) );

osg::ref_ptr<osg::Geode> geode = new osg::Geode;
geode->addDrawable( quad.get() );
```

6. Apply a texture to the quad, as we have already done in the last example:

```
osg::ref_ptr<osg::Texture2D> texture = new osg::Texture2D;
osg::ref_ptr<osg::Image> image =
    osgDB::readImageFile( "Images/lz.rgb" );
texture->setImage( image.get() );
```

7. Use the osg::BlendFunc class to implement the blending effect. It works exactly the same as OpenGL's glBlendFunc():

```
osg::ref_ptr<osg::BlendFunc> blendFunc = new osg::BlendFunc;
blendFunc->setFunction( GL_SRC_ALPHA, GL_ONE_MINUS_SRC_ALPHA );
```

8. Add the blend function attribute and the texture attribute to the **state set**:

```
osg::StateSet* stateset = geode->getOrCreateStateSet();
stateset->setTextureAttributeAndModes( 0, texture.get() );
stateset->setAttributeAndModes( blendFunc );
```

9. Now we can't wait to see if the scene is rendering correctly. Try adding the geometry node and a loaded glider model to the **scene graph,** and see what will happen in the next second.

```
osg::ref_ptr<osg::Group> root = new osg::Group;
root->addChild( geode.get() );
root->addChild( osgDB::readNodeFile("glider.osg") );

osgViewer::Viewer viewer;
viewer.setSceneData( root.get() );
return viewer.run();
```

10. The quad is of course translucent now, in comparison with its appearance in the last example. However, there is something unreasonable in the scene view. The glider, which is cut into half by the quad, lost one of its wings behind the translucent face! This is because of wrong rendering order of the quad and the glider. The latter is hence rendered incorrectly because of the depth test in OpenGL:

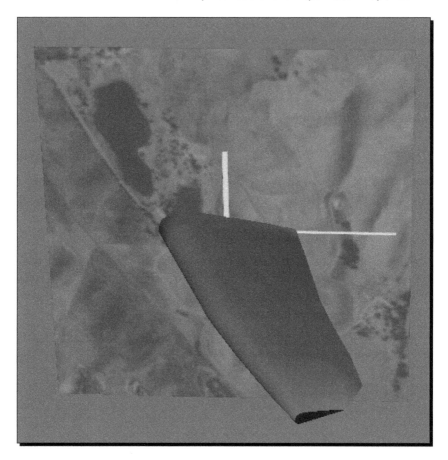

11. Have you remembered the `setRenderingHint()` method, which could solve this wacky problem? Now let's add a line in step 7 to indicate that the quad geometry is transparent, and allow OSG to sort and render it in a proper way:

```
stateset->setRenderingHint( osg::StateSet::TRANSPARENT_BIN );
```

12. Everything works fine now:

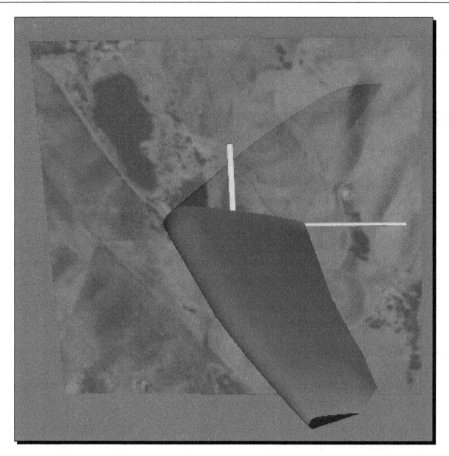

What just happened?

During the drawing traversal, the GL_SRC_ALPHA and GL_ONE_MINUS_SRC_ALPHA enumerations determine the blended color values by using the following equations:

```
R = srcR * srcA + dstR * (1 - srcA)
G = srcG * srcA + dstG * (1 - srcA)
B = srcB * srcA + dstB * (1 - srcA)
```

Here, [srcR, srcG, srcB] is a color value of the translucent quad being rendered, and [dstR, dstG, dstB] is the screen color value to be overridden, which was actually filled by the opaque glider model just now. The resultant color [R, G, B] is computed according to the alpha factor srcA of the quad's color vector, and hence mixed by the incoming and previous color values to generate the translucent effect.

The `setRenderingHint()` method controls the rendering order nicely, but it is not efficient to overuse it. Sorting all transparent objects by depth in each frame requires more system time, and will cause huge resource consumption if there is massive data to be sorted. It is the developers who should consider keeping the balance at any time.

Understanding graphics shaders

The **OpenGL shading language (GLSL)** was originally introduced as an extension to OpenGL 1.4, to allow for programmability in the rendering pipeline at the vertex and fragment level. Now the GLSL is formally included into the OpenGL 2.0, which provides developers the ability to develop **graphics shaders** (blocks of graphics software instructions) to calculate more realistic rendering effects, rather than only using the fixed-function states.

It is impossible to introduce the details of GLSL and its implementations in OpenGL in this book. However, there are a few steps to follow if you have an interest in designing different shaders and applying them to the **scene graph**.

First, write your own shaders, like C programs. These are treated as a set of strings passed to the hardware, so just create them on the fly, or read them as text files.

You may specify no more than a vertex shader, a geometry shader, and a fragment shader (each stage has only one `main()` function) to be processed in the OpenGL pipeline. These will totally replace fixed functionalities such as the fog, lighting, and texture mapping, which have to be re-implemented in your shader source code.

Shaders require the OpenGL API to compile and execute them. **Vertex shaders** can apply transformations to each vertex; **fragment shaders** calculate the color of individual pixels coming from the rasterizer; and **geometry shaders** re-generate geometries from existing vertices and primitive data.

OSG uses the `osg::Shader` class to define a shader object containing source code strings. The method `setShaderSource()` is used to specify the source code text from a `std::string` variable, and `loadShaderSourceFromFile()` will read a source file from the disk. Besides that, developers can directly construct a shader object from an existing string *vertText* as follows:

```
osg::ref_ptr<osg::Shader> vertShader =
    new osg::Shader( osg::Shader::VERTEX, vertText );
```

The input parameter `osg::Shader::VERTEX` represents the **vertex shader**. You may also use the enumerations `GEOMETRY` or `FRAGMENT` instead, in order to specify a **geometry shader** or **fragment shader**. For example:

```
osg::ref_ptr<osg::Shader> fragShader = new osg::Shader(
osg::Shader::FRAGMENT, fragText );
```

```
osg::ref_ptr<osg::Shader> geomShader = new osg::Shader(
    osg::Shader::GEOMETRY );
geomShader->loadShaderSourceFromFile( "source.geom" );
```

Here we assume that the file `source.geom` is loaded and contains our **geometry shader**.

The `osgDB::readShaderFile()` function may be even better for reading from files, because it can automatically check shader types according to file extensions (`.vert`, `.frag`, or `.geom`). It will return a completely formed `osg::Shader` instance of the correct type and data, for instance:

```
osg::Shader* fragShader =  osgDB::readShaderFile("source.frag");
```

After all shaders are set and are ready to be used, we can use the `osg::Program` class and `addShader()` method to include them and set the GLSL rendering attribute and modes to a **state set**. Note that most other fixed-function states will become invalid after the shaders make effects, including the lights, materials, fog, texture mapping, texture coordinate generation, and texture environment.

The following code snippet adds all of the above shaders to an `osg::Program` object and attaches it to the **state set** of an existing node:

```
osg::ref_ptr<osg::Program> program = new osg::Program;
program->addShader( vertShader.get() );
program->addShader( fragShader.get() );
program->addShader( geomShader.get() );
node->getOrCreateStateSet()->setAttributeAndModes( program.get() );
```

Using uniforms

There are three types of inputs and outputs in a typical shader: **uniforms**, **vertex attributes**, and **varyings**. **Uniforms** and **vertex attributes** are read-only during the shader's execution, but can be set by host OpenGL or OSG applications. They are actually global GLSL variables used for interactions between shaders and user applications.

Varyings are used for passing data from one shader to the next one. They are invisible to external programs.

OSG uses the `osg::Uniform` class to define a GLSL uniform variable. Its constructor has a name and an initial value parameter, which should match the definition in the shader source code, for instance:

```
float length = 1.0f;
osg::ref_ptr<osg::Uniform> uniform =
    new osg::Uniform( "length", length );
```

You may add this uniform object to the **state set**, which has already attached an osg::Program object by using the addUniform() method:

```
stateset->addUniform( uniform.get() );
```

Meanwhile, there should be a variable defined in one of the shader sources, such as:

```
uniform float length;
```

Otherwise, the uniform variable will not be available in either OSG programs or shaders.

Uniforms can be any basic type, or any aggregation of types, such as Boolean, float, integer, 2D/3D/4D vector, matrix, and various **texture samplers**. The osg::Uniform class accepts all kinds of basic types with the constructor and the set() method. It also provides some more data types, such as osg::Matrix2 and osg::Matrix3 to support 2x2 and 3x3 matrices. In order to bind **texture samplers**, which are used in shaders to represent a particular texture, the only work for the osg::Uniform object is to specify the **texture mapping unit** by using an unsigned int value, such as:

```
osg::ref_ptr<osg::Uniform> uniform = new osg::Uniform(
    "texture", 0 );
```

Of course, you should have already had an osg::Texture object at unit 0, as well as a sampler uniform in the shader source:

```
uniform sampler2D texture;
```

Here we assume that it is a 2D texture that will be used to change the shader's executing behavior.

Time for action – implementing a cartoon cow

The cartoon shading is a simple non-photorealistic effect which changes abruptly between tones. To archive a cartoon shader, we only have to transform the vertex to built-in gl_Position variables in the **vertex shader**, and then calculate and select a tone by using the normal and light direction in the **fragment shader**. After that, we may apply it to a loaded model, for instance, a pretty cow.

1. Include the necessary headers:

```
#include <osg/Program>
#include <osgDB/ReadFile>
#include <osgViewer/Viewer>
```

2. We'd like to write the **vertex shader** source using strings. It passes a normal varying variable to the **fragment shader**, besides setting the gl_Position:

```
static const char* vertSource = {
    "varying vec3 normal;\n"
    "void main()\n"
    "{\n"
    "    normal = normalize(gl_NormalMatrix * gl_Normal);\n"
    "    gl_Position = ftransform();\n"
    "}\n"
};
```

3. The **fragment shader** uses four color **uniforms** to represent tones in cartoon shading. It calculates the cosine angle between the normal variation and the light position due to the geometric interpretation of **dot product**. Be aware that the fixed-function lighting state loses its effect when using the shaders, but light properties are still available and can be read from built-in GLSL uniforms:

```
static const char* fragSource = {
    "uniform vec4 color1;\n"
    "uniform vec4 color2;\n"
    "uniform vec4 color3;\n"
    "uniform vec4 color4;\n"
    "varying vec3 normal;\n"
    "void main()\n"
    "{\n"
    "    float intensity = dot(vec3(gl_LightSource[0].position),
        normal);\n"
    "    if (intensity > 0.95) gl_FragColor = color1;\n"
    "    else if (intensity > 0.5) gl_FragColor = color2;\n"
    "    else if (intensity > 0.25) gl_FragColor = color3;\n"
    "    else gl_FragColor = color4;\n"
    "}\n"
};
```

4. We will create two shader objects and add them to a program attribute:

```
osg::ref_ptr<osg::Shader> vertShader =
    new osg::Shader( osg::Shader::VERTEX, vertSource );
osg::ref_ptr<osg::Shader> fragShader =
    new osg::Shader( osg::Shader::FRAGMENT, fragSource );

osg::ref_ptr<osg::Program> program = new osg::Program;
program->addShader( vertShader.get() );
program->addShader( fragShader.get() );
```

4. Read a cow model, and apply the attribute and modes to its **state set**. There are four uniform variables to be defined in the user application, so we must use the `addUniform()` method four times in order to bind values to uniforms here:

```
osg::ref_ptr<osg::Node> model = osgDB::readNodeFile( "cow.osg" );

osg::StateSet* stateset = model->getOrCreateStateSet();
stateset->setAttributeAndModes( program.get() );
stateset->addUniform(
    new osg::Uniform("color1", osg::Vec4(
        1.0f, 0.5f, 0.5f, 1.0f)) );
stateset->addUniform(
    new osg::Uniform("color2", osg::Vec4(
        0.5f, 0.2f, 0.2f, 1.0f)) );
stateset->addUniform(
    new osg::Uniform("color3", osg::Vec4(
        0.2f, 0.1f, 0.1f, 1.0f)) );
stateset->addUniform(
    new osg::Uniform("color4", osg::Vec4(
        0.1f, 0.05f, 0.05f, 1.0f)) );
```

5. That is all! Start the viewer now:

```
osgViewer::Viewer viewer;
viewer.setSceneData( model.get() );
return viewer.run();
```

6. You will see a completely different cow model this time. It seems to be painted by a child or a comic artist. This technique is widely used in computer games and animation movies:

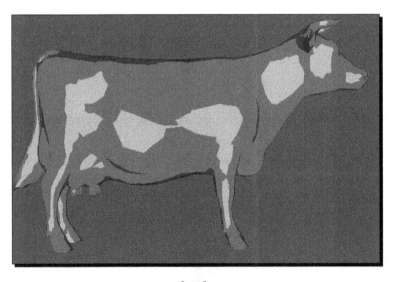

What just happened?

The basic algorithm for cartoon shading is: If we have a normal that is close to the light direction, the brightest tone (color1) is used. As the angle between the surface normal and the light direction is increasing, a number of darker tones (color2, color3, and color4) will be used, which in fact provides an intensity value for selecting tones.

The shader source code is adapted from a nice GLSL tutorial available on the following website: http://www.lighthouse3d.com.

All four tones are declared as uniform 4D vectors in the **fragment shader**, and passed to osg::Uniform objects as osg::Vec4 variables in the user application.

Pop quiz – replacements of built-in uniforms

From the OpenGL 3.x releases, built-in uniforms like gl_LightSource are not going to track states automatically, that is, they work like user-defined uniforms and will have no value unless the user sets them.

This situation will force us to replace all built-in variables with those managed by OSG someday. So why not have some tests before that day comes? For example, can you figure out how to replace gl_LightSource with user uniforms that record OSG light attributes?

Have a go hero – setting vertex attributes to shaders

The osg::Geometry class uses the setVertexAttribArray() and setVertexAttribBinding() methods to bind **vertex attributes** to shaders. They should be provided per vertex. GLSL's built-in **vertex attributes** include the gl_Position, gl_Normal, and gl_MultiTexCoord* variables. However, you may still specify your own **vertex attributes**, such as tangents or vertex weights.

Try declaring an attribute in the **vertex shader** and make use of the osg::Geometry's vertex attribute arrays. Another important task that you need to perform is to bind the external attribute array and the GLSL attribute, with the help of the addBindAttribLocation() method of osg::Program. It has a name and an index parameter, the first of which indicates the attribute name in the shader source code, and the second should correspond to the input index value of setVertexAttribArray().

Working with the geometry shader

The **geometry shader** is included into the OpenGL 3.2 core, and in lower versions it is used as an extension, `GL_EXT_geometry_shader4`, which should be declared in the shader source code.

The geometry shader introduces some new adjacency primitives, which can be used as arguments of `osg::PrimitiveSet` derived classes. It also requires setting a few more parameters in order to manipulate the operations of the shader, including:

1. `GL_GEOMETRY_VERTICES_OUT_EXT`: Number of vertices that the shader will emit

2. `GL_GEOMETRY_INPUT_TYPE_EXT`: The primitive type to be sent to the shader

3. `GL_GEOMETRY_OUTPUT_TYPE_EXT`: The primitive type to be emitted from the shader

The `osg::Program` class uses the `setParameter()` method to set values for these parameters. For example, to indicate that 100 vertices will be emitted from the shader to the primitive assembly processor in the rendering pipeline, we use:

```
program->setParameter( GL_GEOMETRY_VERTICES_OUT_EXT, 100 );
```

Time for action – generating a Bezier curve

OpenGL has provided functions to generate Bezier and NURBS curves and surfaces for years, but they are not as good as we wish. Today's **geometry shader** can do the same work in a more convenient and efficient way. Take the generation of a Cubic Bezier curve as an example. Given two endpoints, and two control points to the shader, it will then produce a smooth curve, with specific segments, that begins and ends at two different endpoints, and be *pulled away* towards the control points.

1. Include the necessary headers. We'd like to change the output line width, so the `osg::LineWidth` class is used here, too:

   ```
   #include <osg/Program>
   #include <osg/LineWidth>
   #include <osgDB/ReadFile>
   #include <osgViewer/Viewer>
   ```

2. The vertex shader is always required. But this time it only transforms vertices to successive shaders:

   ```
   static const char* vertSource = {
       "#version 120\n"
       "#extension GL_EXT_geometry_shader4 : enable\n"
       "void main()\n"
   ```

```
        "{ gl_Position = ftransform(); }\n"
};
```

3. The geometry shader source code is the key of this example. It reads endpoints and controls points from the built-in `gl_PositionIn` variable, reassembles them, and emits new vertices with the `EmitVertex()` function. A uniform variable `segments` is used to control the smoothness of the generated curve:

```
static const char* geomSource = {
    "#version 120\n"
    "#extension GL_EXT_geometry_shader4 : enable\n"
    "uniform int segments;\n"
    "void main(void)\n"
    "{\n"
    "    float delta = 1.0 / float(segments);\n"
    "    vec4 v;\n"
    "    for ( int i=0; i<=segments; ++i )\n"
    "    {\n"
    "        float t = delta * float(i);\n"
    "        float t2 = t * t;\n"
    "        float one_minus_t = 1.0 - t;\n"
    "        float one_minus_t2 = one_minus_t * one_minus_t;\n"
    "        v = gl_PositionIn[0] * one_minus_t2 * one_minus_t
        +\n"
    "            gl_PositionIn[1] * 3.0 * t * one_minus_t2 +\n"
    "            gl_PositionIn[2] * 3.0 * t2 * one_minus_t +\n"
    "            gl_PositionIn[3] * t2 * t;\n"
    "        gl_Position = v;\n"
    "        EmitVertex();\n"
    "    }\n"
    "    EndPrimitive();\n"
    "}\n"
};
```

4. We will create the input primitive of the **geometry shader** by using an `osg::Geometry` class. It contains a new type of primitive, named `GL_LINES_ADJACENCY_EXT`, which gives a dimension of four of the shader's `gl_PositionIn` variable:

```
osg::ref_ptr<osg::Vec3Array> vertices = new osg::Vec3Array;
vertices->push_back( osg::Vec3(0.0f, 0.0f, 0.0f) );
vertices->push_back( osg::Vec3(1.0f, 1.0f, 1.0f) );
vertices->push_back( osg::Vec3(2.0f, 1.0f,-1.0f) );
vertices->push_back( osg::Vec3(3.0f, 0.0f, 0.0f) );

osg::ref_ptr<osg::Geometry> controlPoints = new osg::Geometry;
```

```
controlPoints->setVertexArray( vertices.get() );
controlPoints->addPrimitiveSet(
    new osg::DrawArrays(GL_LINES_ADJACENCY_EXT, 0, 4) );

osg::ref_ptr<osg::Geode> geode = new osg::Geode;
geode->addDrawable( controlPoints.get() );
```

5. We are going to set parameters of the shader. It has `segments+1` vertices to emit, receives the `GL_LINES_ADJACENCY_EXT` type, and outputs the resulting curve as line strips, as shown in the following code:

```
int segments = 10;

osg::ref_ptr<osg::Program> program = new osg::Program;
program->addShader(
    new osg::Shader(osg::Shader::VERTEX, vertSource) );
program->addShader(
    new osg::Shader(osg::Shader::GEOMETRY, geomSource) );
program->setParameter( GL_GEOMETRY_VERTICES_OUT_EXT, segments+1 );
program->setParameter( GL_GEOMETRY_INPUT_TYPE_EXT,
                       GL_LINES_ADJACENCY_EXT );
program->setParameter( GL_GEOMETRY_OUTPUT_TYPE_EXT,
                       GL_LINE_STRIP );
```

6. The default line width is 1.0. Setting the line width can help us discern the output curve:

```
osg::ref_ptr<osg::LineWidth> lineWidth = new osg::LineWidth;
lineWidth->setWidth( 2.0f );
```

7. Set all **rendering attributes** to the **state set**, and don't forget to add the uniform for the shader's use:

```
osg::StateSet* stateset = geode->getOrCreateStateSet();
stateset->setAttributeAndModes( program.get() );
stateset->setAttribute( lineWidth.get() );
stateset->setMode( GL_LIGHTING, osg::StateAttribute::OFF );
stateset->addUniform( new osg::Uniform("segments", segments) );
```

8. Everything is ready. Now start the viewer:

```
osgViewer::Viewer viewer;
viewer.setSceneData( geode.get() );
return viewer.run();
```

9. You will see a Bezier curve displayed in the scene. Try changing the value of the uniform `segments`. A larger number will make the curve smoother and suppler, but may cause more resource consumption and thus lower rendering efficiency.

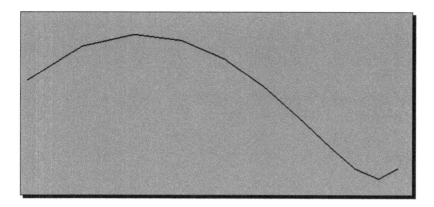

What just happened?

The **geometry shader** defines a new primitive type GL_LINE_STRIP_ADJACENCY_EXT which means a line strip with adjacency. The first and last vertices provide adjacency information but are not visible as line segments. Thus, we could use these two extra vertices as the endpoints of a Bezier curve, and the others as control points. That is actually what we have read from the GLSL variable gl_PositionIn[0] to gl_PositionIn[3].

The Cubic Bezier curve can then be calculated according to the following equation:

```
P(t) = (1-t)³ *P0 + 3*t*(1-t)²*P1 + 3*t²*(1-t)*P2 + t³*P3
```

The factor *t* can be set in the range from 0 to 1.

Have a go hero – having fun with shaders

Some may believe that shaders are omnipotent, and some not. But no one can deny that shaders make our development much more interesting. There are already successful implementations of realistic ocean, atmosphere, lighting, character animation, and so on, using **graphics shaders**. It is now really a critical task for replacing the use of the fixed-function pipeline with shaders, which always offers a considerable number of advantages to your applications.

OSG provides full support of the shading language, even those coming with OpenGL4. It also supports the **NVIDIA Cg** through a third-party project named **osgNV**. Can't wait to have fun with shaders? Besides your own adventures, there are several great open source projects that are making good use of shaders for your reference:

- The **osgCompute** and **osgCUDA** projects are used for computing with GPU parallel streaming processors: http://www.cg.informatik.uni-siegen.de/svt/osgcompute/

- The **osgNV** project can support the **NVIDIA Cg** language: `http://osgnv.sourceforge.net/`

- The **osgOcean** project is used for realistic ocean simulation: `http://code.google.com/p/osgocean/`

- The **osgPPU** project implements various effects using the post processing technique: `http://projects.tevs.eu/osgppu`

Summary

After a wireframed sketch is ready in the pipeline, as you may find out from this chapter, the graphic rendering is then applied to add lights, textures, bump mapping, or programmable effects to other objects, with the help of the `osg::StateSet` class and a set of `osg::StateAttribute` subclasses. In this chapter, we introduced in detail the techniques of manipulating rendering states and attributes, especially the two different ways to realize realistic rendering effects by using the fixed-function pipeline and with the OpenGL shading language.

In this chapter, we specifically covered:

- Controlling and inheriting the rendering attributes and modes stored in `osg::StateSet` objects of nodes and **drawables**.

- Realizing fixed-function rendering effects by using different OSG rendering state classes, such as `osg::PolygonMode`, `osg::Fog`, and `osg::BlendFunc`. The rendering order of state sets should be paid attention to when rendering transparent and translucent objects.

- How to create and control `osg::Light` objects by using the `osg::LightSource` nodes.

- How to realize texture mapping by using `osg::Image` images and associated `osg::Texture` subclasses, especially the `osg::Texture2D` class, which manages and renders 2D textures.

- The basic concept of **graphic shaders** and their implementer classes: `osg::Shader` and `osg::Program`.

7
Viewing the World

The viewer's observation of the scene graph is the result of transforming the 3D world into a 2D image, which is done by a rendering engine in real-time. Assuming that a virtual camera is employed for observing and recording the 3D world and its dynamic changes, then its movement, angle, focal distance variation, and a different lens type will change the rendering results and this is exactly the way that in which we change the view we can see on the screen.

This chapter will mainly focus on:

◆ Understanding the coordinate system defined in OpenGL

◆ Alternating the view point and orientation, projection frustum, and final viewport

◆ Changing and controlling the rendering order if there exists more than one camera.

◆ How to create single and composite viewers

◆ How to manage global display settings and generate easy-to-use stereo visualization effects

◆ How to apply the rendered scene as a texture object—so called rendering to textures (RTT)

From world to screen

When drawing a point, a line, or a complex polygon in the 3D world, our final goal is to display it on the screen. That is, the 3D object that we are going to represent will be converted to a set of pixels in a 2D window. In this process, three major matrices are used to determine the transformations between different coordinate systems. These are often called the model, view, and projection matrices.

The **model matrix** is used to describe the specific location of an object in the world. It can transform vertices from an object's **local coordinate system** into **world coordinate system**. Both coordinates are **right-handed**.

The next step is to transform the entire world into view space, by using the **view matrix**. Suppose we have a camera placed at a certain position in the world; the inverse of the camera's transformation matrix is actually used as the **view matrix**. In the **right-handed view coordinate system**, OpenGL defines that the camera is always located at the origin (0, 0, 0), and facing towards the negative Z axis. Hence, we can represent the world on our camera's screen.

Note that, there is no separate **model matrix** or **view matrix** in OpenGL. However, it defines a **model-view matrix** to transform from the object's local space to view space, which is a combination of both matrices. Thus, to transform the vertex V in local space to Ve in view space, we have:

```
Ve = V * modelViewMatrix
```

The next important work is to determine how 3D objects are projected onto the screen (perspective or orthogonal), and calculate the frustum from which objects get rendered. The **projection matrix** is used to specify the frustum in the **world coordinate system** with six clipping planes: the left, right, bottom, top, near, and far planes. OpenGL also provides an additional `gluPerspective()` function to determine a field of view with camera lens parameters.

The resulting coordinate system (called the **normalized device coordinate system**) ranges from -1 to +1 in each of the axes, and is changed to **left-handed** now. And as a final step, we project all result data onto the viewport (the window), define the window rectangle in which the final image is mapped, and the z value of the window coordinates. After that, the 3D scene is rendered to a rectangular area on your 2D screen. And finally, the screen coordinate Vs can represent the local vertex V in the 3D world by using the so called **MVPW** matrix, that is:

```
Vs = V * modelViewMatrix * projectionMatrix * windowMatrix
```

The `Vs` is still a 3D vector that represents a 2D pixel location with a depth value.

By reversing this mapping process, we can get a line in the 3D space from a 2D screen point (`Xs`, `Ys`). That's because the 2D point can actually be treated as two points: one on the near clipping plane (`Zs = 0`), and the other on the far plane (`Zs = 1`).

The inverse matrix of MVPW is used here to obtain the result of the "unproject" work:

```
V0 = (Xs, Ys, 0) * invMVPW
V1 = (Xs, Ys, 1) * invMVPW
```

The Camera class

OpenGL developers often love to use `glTranslate()` and `glRotate()` to *move* the scene, and `gluLookAt()` to *move* the camera, although they can all be replaced by the same `glMultMatrix()` function. In fact, these functions actually do the same thing—calculate the **model-view matrix** for transforming data from world space to view space. Similarly, OSG provides the `osg::Transform` class, which can add or set its own matrix to the current **model-view matrix** when placed in the scene graph, but we always intend to operate on **model matrix** by using the `osg::MatrixTransform` and `osg::PositionAttitudeTransform` subclasses, and handle **view matrix** with the `osg::Camera` subclass.

The `osg::Camera` class is one of the most important classes in the core OSG libraries. It can be used as a **group node** of the **scene graph**, but it is far more than a common node. Its main functionalities can be divided into four categories:

Firstly, the `osg::Camera` class handles the **view matrix**, **projection matrix**, and the viewport, which will affect all its children and project them onto the screen. Related methods include:

1. The public `setViewMatrix()` and `setViewMatrixAsLookAt()` methods set the **view matrix** by using the `osg::Matrix` variable or classic eye/center/up variables.

2. The public `setProjectionMatrix()` method accepts an `osg::Matrix` parameter in order to specify the **projection matrix**.

3. Other convenient methods, including `setProjectionMatrixAsFrustum()`, `setProjectionMatrixAsOrtho()`, `setProjectionMatrixAsOrtho2D()`, and `setProjectionMatrixAsPerspective()`, are used to set a perspective or orthographic **projection matrix** with different frustum parameters. They work just like the OpenGL projection functions (`glOrtho()`, `gluPerspective()`, and so on).

4. The public `setViewport()` method can define a rectangular window area with an `osg::Viewport` object.

The following code segments demonstrate how to set the view and projection matrix of a camera node, and set its viewport to (x, y) - (x+w, y+h):

```
camera->setViewMatrix( viewMatrix );
camera->setProjectionMatrix( projectionMatrix );
camera->setViewport( new osg::Viewport(x, y, w, h) );
```

You can obtain the current view and projection matrices and viewport of the osg::Camera object by using the corresponding get*() methods at any time. For example:

```
osg::Matrix viewMatrix = camera->getViewMatrix();
```

In order to get the position and orientation of the **view matrix**, use the following code:

```
osg::Vec3 eye, center, up;
camera->getViewMatrixAsLookAt( eye, center, up );
```

Secondly, the osg::Camera encapsulates the OpenGL functions, such as glClear(), glClearColor(), and glClearDepth(), and clears the frame buffers and presets their values when redrawing the scene to the window in every frame. Primary methods include:

1. The setClearMask() method sets the buffer to be cleared. The default is GL_COLOR_BUFFER_BIT|GL_DEPTH_BUFFER_BIT.

2. The setClearColor() method sets the clear color in RGBA format, by using an osg::Vec4 variable.

Similarly, there are setClearDepth(), setClearStencil(), and setClearAccum() methods, as well as corresponding get*() methods to obtain set values from the camera object.

The third category includes the management of OpenGL graphics context associated with this camera. We are going to discuss this in *Chapter 9, Interacting with Outside Elements*.

Finally, a camera can attach a texture object to internal buffer components (color buffer, depth buffer, and so on), and directly render the sub-scene graph into this texture. The resultant texture can then be mapped to surfaces of other scenes. This technique is named **render-to-textures**, or **texture baking**, which will be introduced later in this chapter.

Rendering order of cameras

There is at least one **main camera** node in any scene graphs. It is created and managed by the osgViewer::Viewer class, and can be read via the getCamera() method. It automatically adds the **root node** as its **child node** before starting the simulation. By default, all other cameras, whether directly or indirectly added to the **root node**, will share the graphics context associated with the **main camera**, and draw their own sub-scenes successively onto the same rendering window.

The osg::Camera class provides a setRenderOrder() method to precisely control the rendering order of cameras. It has an order enumeration and an optional order number parameter. The first enumeration can be PRE_RENDER or POST_RENDER, which indicates the general rendering order. The second is an integer number for sorting cameras of the same type in ascending order. It is set to 0 by default.

For example, the following code will force OSG to render camera1 first, and then camera2 (with a larger number), and camera3 after these two cameras and the **main camera** are all finished:

```
camera1->setRenderOrder( osg::Camera::PRE_RENDER );
camera2->setRenderOrder( osg::Camera::PRE_RENDER, 5 );
camera3->setRenderOrder( osg::Camera::POST_RENDER );
```

If a camera is rendered first (PRE_RENDER), its rendering result in the buffers will be cleared and covered by the next camera, and the viewer may not be able to see its sub-scene. This is especially useful in the case of the **render-to-textures** process, because we want the sub-scene to be hidden from the screen, and update the attached texture objects before starting the main scene.

In addition, if a camera is rendered afterwards (POST_RENDER), it may erase the current color and depth values in the buffers. We can avoid this by calling setClearMask() with fewer buffer masks. A typical example is the implementation of a head-up display (HUD).

Time for action – creating an HUD camera

A head-up display (HUD) can render data without requiring users to look away from their usual viewpoints. It is widely used in 3D scenes, for displaying important 2D texts, computer game statistics, and flight and cockpit instruments. This time, we are going to design an HUD camera, which contains a model that should be placed in front of other scene objects at any time.

1. Include the necessary headers:

```
#include <osg/Camera>
#include <osgDB/ReadFile>
#include <osgViewer/Viewer>
```

2. Two models are loaded from disk files. `lz.osg` is used as a demo terrain, and `glider.osg` will be put under an HUD camera. That is, it will always be visible to viewers who are looking ahead; no matter how other parts of the scene graph are changing:

```
osg::ref_ptr<osg::Node> model = osgDB::readNodeFile("lz.osg");
osg::ref_ptr<osg::Node> hud_model = osgDB::readNodeFile("glider.osg");
```

3. The HUD camera and its children must be rendered after the **regular scene** is finished being drawn on the screen. It will overwrite all present pixel data, regardless of its location and depth. That is why we use `GL_DEPTH_BUFFER_BIT` to clear the depth buffer. The `GL_COLOR_BUFFER_BIT` is not set here, to ensure that the color buffer is correctly reserved.

```
osg::ref_ptr<osg::Camera> camera = new osg::Camera;
camera->setClearMask( GL_DEPTH_BUFFER_BIT );
camera->setRenderOrder( osg::Camera::POST_RENDER );
```

4. The HUD camera should not be affected by the viewer or any other parent nodes, so it needs to be changed to the **absolute reference frame**, and be set as a custom fixed view matrix. The glider is also added to the camera node, used as the content to be displayed:

```
camera->setReferenceFrame( osg::Camera::ABSOLUTE_RF );
camera->setViewMatrixAsLookAt(
    osg::Vec3(0.0f,-5.0f,5.0f), osg::Vec3(),
osg::Vec3(0.0f,1.0f,1.0f)
);
camera->addChild( hud_model.get() );
```

5. We will add the HUD camera, along with a regular loaded model, to the root node:

```
osg::ref_ptr<osg::Group> root = new osg::Group;
root->addChild( model.get() );
root->addCh XE "render-to-textures technique:ild( camera.get() );
```

6. Now, start the viewer as usual:

```
osgViewer::Viewer viewer;
viewer.setSceneData( root.get() );
return viewer.run();
```

7. You will see that the demo terrain (**regular scene**) is rendered and manipulated under the user's control. However, the glider (**post-rendered scene**) always stays on top of all other scene objects, and its position and orientation will never be affected by the mouse or keyboard inputs.

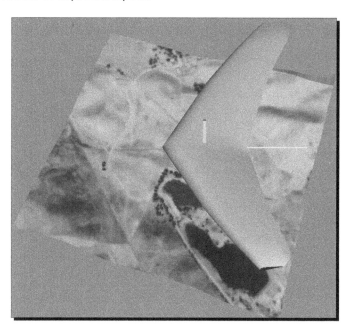

What just happened?

We have created an additional camera which contains a glider model that is to be rendered as the sub-scene graph. The render order is set to POST_RENDER, that is, this camera will come after the main camera has rendered its scene (the terrain). In other words, it will always draw its sub-scene graph on top of the rendering result (**color buffer** and **depth buffer**) of the main camera.

The additional camera's goal is to implement a HUD scene that overlays the main scene. It clears the **depth buffer** to ensure that all pixel data drawn by this camera can pass the depth test. However, the **color buffer** is not cleared, keeping the uncovered pixel data of the main scene on the screen. That is why we set it up like this:

```
camera->setClearMask(GL_DEPTH_BUFFER_BIT);  // No color buffer bit
```

Pop quiz – changing model positions in the HUD camera

The HUD camera we just created uses its own **view matrix** for configuring its sub-graph's position and orientation in the view coordinates, but it doesn't have a preset **projection matrix**. Do you know what its actual value is? Can you figure out how to fill the entire screen with the glider model by using the HUD camera's **projection matrix**? And how can you display an upside-down model?

Using a single viewer

OSG supports the single viewer class `osgViewer::Viewer` for holding a view on a single scene. It uses the `setSceneData()` method to manage the **scene graph**'s **root node**, and `run()` to start the **simulation loop**, in which the scene is rendered again and again. The frame buffer is therefore continuously updated by the result of every rendering cycle, so called a frame.

Besides that, the viewer also contains an `osg::Camera` object as the **main camera**, which we discussed before. The **view matrix** of the camera is controlled by the viewer's internal `osgGA::CameraManipulator` object. Meanwhile, user input events are also received and handled by the viewer, via a list of `osgGA::GUIEventHandler` handlers. The viewer can even be set up in full screen mode, in a window, and onto a spherical display. We will gradually begin to explain these concepts in this and the following chapters.

Digging into the simulation loop

The **simulation loop** defined by the `run()` method always has three types of tasks to perform: specify the main camera's manipulator, set up associated graphics contexts, and render frames in cycles.

The manipulator can read keyboard and mouse events and accordingly adjust the **main camera**'s **view matrix** to navigate the **scene graph**. It is set by using the `setCameraManipulator()` method, of which the parameter must be an `osgGA::CameraManipulator` subclass. For example:

```
viewer.setCameraManipulator( new osgGA::TrackballManipulator );
```

This adds a classic trackball (arc ball) manipulator to the viewer object, with free motion behaviors. Because the camera manipulator is kept as a smart pointer in the viewer, we can assign a new manipulator by using the `setCameraManipulator()` method at any time. Some in-built manipulators defined in the **osgGA** namespace can be found in the following table:

Manipulator class	Description	Basic usage
DriveManipulator	Drive-like simulator	Key space: reset the viewer position
		Mouse moving: changes the viewer's orientation
		Mouse dragging: the left button accelerates, the right decelerates, and the middle stops the navigation
FlightManipulator	Flight simulator	Key space: reset the viewer position
		Mouse moving: changes the viewer's position and orientation
KeySwitchMatrixManipulator	A decorator allowing different manipulators to be switched	Use `addMatrixManipulator()` to add a manipulator and switch to it by pressing the specified key on the fly, for instance:
		`addMatrixManipulator('1', "trackball", new osgGA:: TrackballManipulator);`
NodeTrackerManipulator	A manipulator tracking a node	Use `setTrackNode()` to select a node to track before starting
SphericalManipulator	A manipulator for browsing spherical objects	Key space: reset the viewer position
		Mouse dragging: the left mouse button rotates the viewer, the middle mouse button pans the world, and the right mouse button scales the world
TerrainManipulator	An enhanced trackball-like manipulator for viewing terrains	Key space: reset the viewer position.
		Mouse dragging: the left mouse button rotates the viewer, the middle mouse button pans the world, and the right mouse button scales the world
TrackballManipulator	The default trackball manipulator	Key space: reset the viewer position.
		Mouse dragging: the left mouse button rotates the viewer, the middle mouse button pans the world, and the right mouse button scales the world

Be aware here, that to declare and use a manipulator you should add the **osgGA** library as a dependence of your project. This can be done either in your own project properties or by using the CMake scripts.

The graphics contexts of a viewer, as well as possible threads and resources, are all initialized in the `realize()` method. It is automatically called before the first frame is rendered.

After that, the viewer enters the loop. Each time it uses the `frame()` method to render a frame, and checks if the rendering process should stop and exit with the `done()` method. The process can be described with just a few lines of code:

```
while ( !viewer.done() )
{
    viewer.frame();
}
```

This is the default rendering scheme used in the viewer class. The frame rate is synchronized to the monitor's refresh rate to avoid wasting system energy, if the *vsync* option of the graphics card is on. But OSG supports another **on-demand rendering** scheme. Configure the viewer variable as follows:

```
viewer.setRunFrameScheme( osgViewer::Viewer::ON_DEMAND );
```

Now, the `frame()` method will only be executed when there are scene graph modifications, updating processes, or user input events, until the scheme is changed back to the default value of `CONTINUOUS`.

As an addition, the `osgViewer::Viewer` class also contains a `setRunMaxFrameRate()` method which uses a frame rate number as the parameter. This can set a maximum frame rate to control the viewer running to force rendering frames without lots of consumption.

Time for action – customizing the simulation loop

We are already very familiar with the `run()` method of the `osgViewer::Viewer` class. It was used many times to start a default simulation loop that loads the **scene graph** into the viewer and performs update, cull, and draw traversals on each frame.

But what does the `run()` method actually do? Is it possible to add some pre- and post-frame events for certain purposes? In this example, we are going to customize the **simulation loop** with a C++ `while` statement, as well as display the frame number after advancing one frame at a time.

Note that, the customized **simulation loop** cannot benefit from the **on-demand rendering** scheme and the maximum frame rate setting. They are only available when using the `run()` method.

1. Include the necessary headers:

```
#include <osgDB/ReadFile>
#include <osgGA/TrackballManipulator>
#include <osgViewer/Viewer>
#include <iostream>
```

2. Load the model and set it as the scene data of the viewer:

```
osg::ref_ptr<osg::Node> model = osgDB::readNodeFile( "lz.osg" );

osgViewer::Viewer viewer;
viewer.setSceneData( model.get() );
```

3. We have to set a manipulator to the viewer; otherwise we will be unable to navigate the scene, including zoom, pan, orbit, and other controlling operations. Here, a new trackball manipulator is set to the viewer. It allows the user to click and drag a point on the screen, having the object rotate to follow it. The osgGA::TrackballManipulator is the default manipulator used internally in the run() method:

```
viewer.setCameraManipulator( new osgGA::TrackballManipulator );
```

4. We then run the viewer in a while loop. Its condition is tested every time to see if the viewer is finished, by using the done() method. The body of the loop includes the frame() method, which executes one frame to update, cull, and render the **scene graph**, and a std::cout statement to output the current frame number:

```
while ( !viewer.done() )
{
    viewer.frame();
    std::cout << "Frame number: " <<
        viewer.getFrameStamp()->getFrameNumber() << std::endl;
}
return 0;
```

5. Start the viewer and have a look at the console output. You will see an increasing list of strings that indicate the frame number, after executing each frame. Apart from this, there is no difference between using the run() method and the customized simulation loop!

```
Frame number: 327
Frame number: 328
Frame number: 329
Frame number: 330
Frame number: 331
Frame number: 332
Frame number: 333
Frame number: 334
Frame number: 335
Frame number: 336
Frame number: 337
Frame number: 338
Frame number: 339
Frame number: 340
Frame number: 341
Frame number: 342
Frame number: 343
Frame number: 344
Frame number: 345
Frame number: 346
Frame number: 347
Frame number: 348
Frame number: 349
Frame number: 350
```

What just happened?

Here we propose the concept of pre- and post-frame events, and simply think that they are sure to be executed before and after the frame() method. This definition is actually inaccurate.

OSG uses multiple threads to manage user updating, culling, and drawing of different cameras, especially in the presence of multiple screens, processors, and graphics devices. The frame() method only starts a new updating/culling/drawing traversal work, but does not take care of thread synchronization. In this case, the code before and after frame() will be considered unstable and unsafe, because they may conflict with other process threads when reading or writing the **scene graph**. Thus, the approach described here is not recommended for future development. We are going to introduce some more common used methods to dynamically modify scene data in the next chapter.

Another interesting question is when will `viewer.done()` return true? Of course, developers can programmatically set the `done` flag via the `setDone()` method of the viewer. The OSG system will check if all present graphics contexts (for example, the rendering window) have been closed, or if the `Esc` key is pressed, which will also change the `done` flag. The `setKeyEventSetsDone()` method can even set which key is going to carry out the duty, instead of the default `Esc` (or set this to `0` to turn off the feature).

Have a go hero – viewing in a non-full screen window

The `osgViewer::Viewer` class can be quickly configured to work in non-full screen mode. The default full screen display is in fact a window covering the whole screen. To produce a window with a specific top-left coordinate, width, and height, the `setUpViewInWindow()` method is convenient. Another opinion is the environment variable `OSG_WINDOW`, which can be defined as follows (under UNIX systems, please use the `export` command):

```
# set OSG_WINDOW=50 50 800 600
```

This can have four or five parameters: the first four are the top-left and size of the created window, and the last one defines the working screen in a multi-screen environment. The default screen number 0 indicates that the first screen is used to contain the rendering window. Try some other unsigned integers if you have more than one computer monitor.

Apart from this, the `setUpViewOnSingleScreen()` method sets up a full-screen window on other screens by using an integer number parameter. There is demonstrated spherical display support in OSG as well. Try the `setUpViewFor3DSphericalDisplay()` method with given arguments. More details can be found in the API documentation and the **osgVIewer** header files.

Using a composite viewer

While the `osgViewer::Viewer` class manages only one single view on one scene graph, there is also an `osgViewer::CompositeViewer` class, which supports multiple views and multiple scenes. This has the same methods such as `run()`, `frame()`, and `done()` to manage the rendering process, but also supports adding and removing independent scene views by using the `addView()` and `removeView()` methods, and obtaining a view object at a specific index by using the `getView()` method. The view object here is defined by the `osgViewer::View` class.

The `osgViewer::View` class is the **super class** of `osgViewer::Viewer`. It accepts setting a `root` node as the scene data, and adding a camera manipulator and event handlers to make use of user events as well. The main difference between `osgViewer::View` and `osgViewer::Viewer` is that the former cannot be used as a single viewer directly—that is, it doesn't have `run()` or `frame()` methods.

To add a created `view` object to the composite viewer, use the following code:

```
osgViewer::CompositeViewer multiviewer;
multiviewer.addView( view );
```

Time for action – rendering more scenes at one time

Multi-viewers are practical in representing complex scenes, for instance, to render a wide area with a main view and an eagle eye view, or to display the front, side, top, and perspective views of the same scene. Here we will create three separate windows, containing three different models, each of which can be independently manipulated.

1. Include the necessary headers:

   ```
   #include <osgDB/ReadFile>
   #include <osgViewer/CompositeViewer>
   ```

2. We design a function to create a new `osgViewer::View` object and apply an existing node to it. The `setUpViewInWindow()` method is used here to produce non-full screen views:

   ```
   osgViewer::View* createView( int x, int y, int w, int h,
                                osg::Node* scene )
   {
       osg::ref_ptr<osgViewer::View> view = new osgViewer::View;
       view->setSceneData( scene );
       view->setUpViewInWindow( x, y, w, h );
       return view.release();
   }
   ```

3. Next, read three models from disk files. These will be added to different views, and rendered in different windows:

   ```
   osg::ref_ptr<osg::Node> model1 = osgDB::readNodeFile("cessna.
   osg");
   osg::ref_ptr<osg::Node> model2 = osgDB::readNodeFile("cow.osg");
   osg::ref_ptr<osg::Node> model3 = osgDB::readNodeFile("glider.
   osg");
   ```

4. Three views are created within small 320x240 windows at specific positions:

```
osgViewer::View* view1 = createView(50, 50, 320, 240, model1);
osgViewer::View* view2 = createView(370, 50, 320, 240, model2);
osgViewer::View* view3 = createView(185, 310, 320, 240, model3);
```

5. The usage of a composite viewer is simple to understand: add all views to it and start the simulation as if it is a single viewer. Of course, the `while` loop is also usable in this case:

```
osgViewer::CompositeViewer viewer;
viewer.addView( view1 );
viewer.addView( view2 );
viewer.addView( view3 );
return viewer.run();
```

6. Now we have multiple windows with multiple scenes rendered at a time. Any of these windows can be closed by clicking the close button on the top-right corner. And you can also close all windows and quit the application by pressing the `Esc` key on the keyboard.

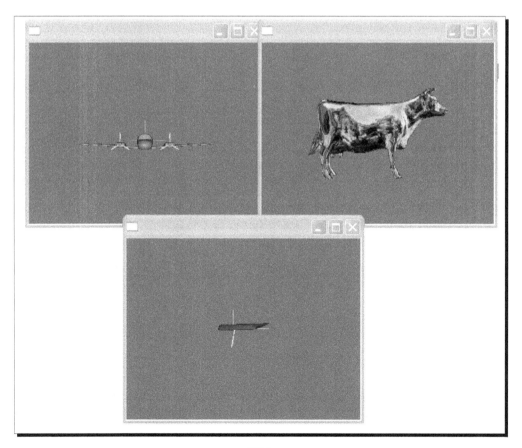

What just happened?

There are some similarities between the osgVIewer::CompositeViewer and multiple cameras. It is possible to create three osg::Camera nodes, add different sub-scenes to them, and attach them to different graphics contexts (rendering windows) in order to achieve the same result as the previous image. In a word, every osgViewer::View object has an osg::Camera node that can be used to manage its subscene and associated window. It actually works like a container.

However, the osgViewer::View class handles manipulator and user events, too. So in a composite viewer, each osgViewer::View object holds its own manipulator and event handlers (this will be discussed in *Chapter 9, Interacting with Outside Elements*). However, a set of cameras can hardly interact with user inputs separately. That is why we choose to use a composite viewer and a few view objects to represent multiple scenes in some cases.

Have a go hero – different views of the same scene

In the last example, we add three different loaded models to the view objects, and they render different scenes as results. However, it is also possible to add the same root node to all views in use. For example:

```
view1->setSceneData( root.get() );
view2->setSceneData( root.get() );
view3->setSceneData( root.get() );
...
```

After that, if you would like to design the front, side, and top views of the same scene, try adding a **view matrix** and a **projection matrix** to the **main camera** of each view, and ensure that the manipulator is disabled, because it will reset your matrices configurations according to user interface events:

```
view1->getCamera()->setViewMatrix( ... );
view1->getCamera()->setProjectionMatrix( ... );
view1->setCameraManipulator( NULL );  // Set the manipulator to null!

// Avoid using default manipulator, too!
view1->getCamera()->setAllowEventFocus( false );
```

Here, the setAllowEventFocus() method indicates whether the camera can receive user inputs and events, or not. This will be discussed again in *Chapter 9, Interacting with Outside Elements*.

Now, can you figure out what the view and projection matrices should be, when designing the front, side, and top views of the scene? As a reminder, the bounding sphere of the root node, acquired by the getBound() method, can help a lot in specifying the view point and projection range.

Pop quiz – another way to display the same scene in different views

A different way to display the same scene in three or more views is to use the `osg::Camera` node. By setting the `setViewport()` method to different areas, we can arrange the camera views in one rendering window without overlapping. Do you know how to design such a scene graph to achieve this goal?

Changing global display settings

OSG manages a set of global display settings that are required by cameras, viewers, and other scene elements. It uses the singleton pattern to declare a unique instance of the container of all of these settings, by using the `osg::DisplaySettings` class. We can thus obtain the display settings instance at any time in our applications:

```
osg::DisplaySettings* ds = osg::DisplaySettings::instance();
```

The `osg::DisplaySettings` instance sets up properties requested by all newly created rendering devices, mainly OpenGL graphics contexts of rendering windows. Its characteristics include:

1. Set double or single buffering with the `setDoubleBuffer()` method. The default is on.

2. Set whether to use the depth buffer or not, via the `setDepthBuffer()` method. Default is on.

3. Set bits for an OpenGL alpha buffer, a stencil buffer, and an accumulation buffer, by using a series of methods such as `setMinimumNumAlphaBits()`, and so on. The defaults are all 0.

4. Set using multisampling buffers and number of samples with the `setNumMultiSamples()` method. The defaults is 0.

5. Enable stereo rendering and configure stereo mode and eye mapping parameters.

In the following chapters, we will learn that some of these characteristics can be separately set for different graphics contexts, by using a specific traits structure. However, at this time, we will first focus on how to make use of the global display settings on our scene viewers.

Time for action – enabling global multisampling

Multisampling is a type of anti-aliasing technique. It can improve the final result's quality without much performance hit. User applications should set a sampling number for implementing multisample rasterization. Note that not all graphics cards support the multisampling extension, thus this example may fail on some systems and platforms.

1. Include the necessary headers:

```
#include <osgDB/ReadFile>
#include <osgViewer/Viewer>
```

2. Set the number of multisamples. Available values often include 2, 4, and 6, depending on specific graphics devices:

```
osg::DisplaySettings::instance()->setNumMultiSamples( 4 );
```

3. Load a model and render it with a standard viewer. The global multisampling attribute managed by the osg::DisplaySettings singleton has already come into effect now:

```
osg::ref_ptr<osg::Node> model = osgDB::readNodeFile(
    "cessna.osg" );

osgViewer::Viewer viewer;
viewer.setSceneData( model.get() );
return viewer.run();
```

4. A close-up shot of the standard Cessna model's propellers (without applying the setNumMultiSamples() method) is shown in the following screenshot. We can clearly see that there is an aliasing error at the edges of propellers:

5. The multisampling now obviously minimizes the distortion of the rendered model, and generates levels of smooth results according to the global display setting attribute. This will affect all viewers created in the current application:

What just happened?

The multisampling technique allows applications to create a frame buffer with a given number of samples per pixel, containing necessary color, depth, and stencil information. More video memory is required but a better rendering result will be produced. In WGL (the windowing interface to the Win32 implementation of OpenGL), it is essentially determined by two pixel format attributes: WGL_SAMPLE_BUFFERS_ARB and WGL_SAMPLES_ARB.

OSG has an internal graphics context manager osg::GraphicsContext. Its subclass osgViewer::GraphicsWindowWin32, which manages the configuration and creation of rendering windows under Windows, will apply these two attributes to the encapsulated wglChoosePixelFormatARB() function, and enable multisampling of the entire scene.

osg::DisplaySettings actually works like a default value set of various display attributes. If there is no separate setting for a specific object, the default one will take effect; otherwise the osg::DisplaySettings instance will not be put to use.

We are going to talk about the separate settings for creating graphics context and the osg::GraphicsContext class in *Chapter 9, Interacting with Outside Elements*.

Stereo visualization

We have already experienced the charm of stereoscopic 3D films and photographs. A good example is James Cameron's *Avatar*, which brings us a spectacular new world beyond imagination. The anaglyph image is the earliest and most popular method of presenting stereo visualization. Other implementations include NVIDIA's quad-buffering, horizontal or vertical split, horizontal or vertical interlace, and so on. Fortunately, OSG supports most of these common stereo techniques, and can immediately realize one of them in the viewer with just a few commands:

```
osg::DisplaySettings::instance()->setStereoMode( mode );
osg::DisplaySettings::instance()->setStereo( true );
```

The method setStereoMode() selects a stereo mode from a set of enumerations, and the setStereo() method enables or disables it. Available stereo modes in OSG are: ANAGLYPHIC, QUAD_BUFFER (NVIDIA's quad-buffering), HORIZONTAL_SPLIT, VERTICAL_SPLIT, HORIZONTAL_INTERLACE, VERTICAL_INTERLACE, and CHECKERBOARD (on a DLP projector). You may also use LEFT_EYE or RIGHT_EYE to indicate that the screen is used for left-eye or right-eye views.

There are additional methods of the osg::DisplaySettings class for specifying special stereo parameters, such as the eye separation. Have a look at the API documentation and header files for more details.

Time for action – rendering anaglyph stereo scenes

We are going to make use of OSG's internal anaglyph stereo mode to implement a simple and quick stereoscopic 3D effect. Before starting programming and rendering the scene, we have to prepare a pair of 3D red/cyan glasses to view the result correctly:

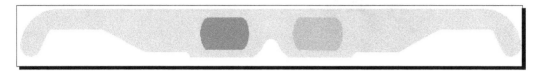

In most cases, the left eye of the glasses is red, and the right eye is cyan. This is the most commonly-used anaglyph effect, with limited color perception.

1. Include the necessary headers:

```
#include <osgDB/ReadFile>
#include <osgViewer/Viewer>
```

2. We will directly work on the global display settings. There are three steps to follow: switch the stereo mode to ANAGLYPHIC, set a suitable eye separation (distance from the left eye to the right) with the setEyeSeparation() method, and enable the stereo visualization:

```
osg::DisplaySettings::instance()->setStereoMode(
    osg::DisplaySettings::ANAGLYPHIC );
osg::DisplaySettings::instance()->setEyeSeparation( 0.05f );
osg::DisplaySettings::instance()->setStereo( true );
```

3. After that, we can construct and render our **scene graph** as usual. Here we will take the Cessna model as a simple enough example:

```
osg::ref_ptr<osg::Node> model = osgDB::readNodeFile(
    "cessna.osg" );

osgViewer::Viewer viewer;
viewer.setSceneData( model.get() );
return viewer.run();
```

4. The result is completely different from previous ones. Wear the glasses right now and see if there is a depth perception:

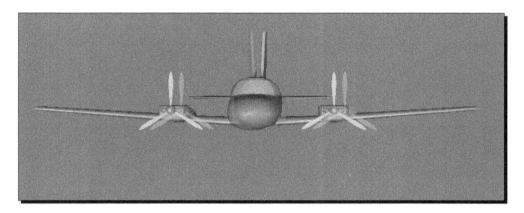

What just happened?

In the ANAGLYPHIC mode, the final rendering result is always made up of two color layers, with a small offset to produce a depth effect. Each eye of the glasses will see a slightly different picture, and their composition produces a stereograph image, which will be fused by our brain into a three dimensional scene.

OSG supports the anaglyphic stereo mode with a two-pass rendering scheme. The first pass renders the left eye image with a red channel color mask, and the second pass renders the right eye image with a cyan channel. The color mask is defined by the rendering attribute osg::ColorMask. It can be easily applied to state sets of nodes and drawables by using:

```
osg::ref_ptr<osg::ColorMask> colorMask = new osg::ColorMask;
colorMask->setMask( true, true, true, true );
stateset->setAttribute( colorMask.get() );
```

The stereo mode often causes the scene graph to be rendered multiple times, which slows down the frame rate as a side effect.

Rendering to textures

The **render-to-textures** technique allows developers to create textures based on a sub-scene's appearance in the rendered scene. These textures are then "baked" into objects of coming scene graphs via **texture mapping**. They can be used to create nice special effects on the fly, or can be stored for subsequent deferred shading, multi-pass rendering, and other advanced rendering algorithms.

To implement **texture baking** dynamically, there are generally three steps to follow:

1. Create the texture for rendering to.

2. Render the scene to the texture.

3. Use the texture as you want.

We have to create an empty texture object before putting it into use. OSG can create an empty `osg::Texture` object by specifying its size. The `setTextureSize()` method defines the width and height of a 2D texture, and an additional depth parameter of a 3D texture.

The key to rendering a **scene graph** to the newly created texture is the `attach()` method of the `osg::Camera` class. This accepts the texture object as an argument, as well as a buffer component parameter, which indicates which part of the frame buffer will be rendered to the texture. For example, to attach the **color buffer** of a camera's sub-scene to the texture, we use:

```
camera->attach( osg::Camera::COLOR_BUFFER, texture.get() );
```

Other usable buffer components include the `DEPTH_BUFFER`, `STENCIL_BUFFER`, and `COLOR_BUFFER0` to `COLOR_BUFFER15` (**multiple render target** outputs, depending on the graphics card).

Continue setting suitable view and projection matrices of this camera, and a viewport to meet the texture size, and set the texture as an attribute of nodes or **drawables**. The texture will be updated with the camera's rendering result in every frame, dynamically varying with the alteration of the **view matrix** and the **projection matrix**.

Be aware that the **main camera** of a viewer is not suitable for attaching a texture. Otherwise there will be no outputs to the actual window, which will make the screen pitch-dark. Of course, you may ignore this if you are doing off-screen rendering and don't care of any visual effects.

Frame buffer, pixel buffer, and FBO

A concern is how to get the rendered frame buffer image into the texture object. A direct approach is to use the `glReadPixels()` method to return pixel data from the frame buffer, and apply the result to a `glTexImage*()` method. This is easy to conceptualize and use, but will always copy data to the texture object, which is extremely slow.

The `glCopyTexSubImage()` method would be better in terms of improving the efficiency. However, we can still optimize the process. Rendering the scene directly to a target other than the frame buffer is a good idea. There are mainly two solutions for this:

1. The **pixel buffer** (**pbuffer** for short) extension can create an invisible rendering buffer with a pixel format descriptor, which is equivalent to a window. It should be destroyed after being used, as is done for the rendering window.

2. The **frame buffer object** (**FBO** for short), which is sometimes better than **pixel buffer** in saving the storage space, can add application-created frame buffers and redirect the rendering output to it. It can either output to a texture object or a **renderbuffer object**, which is simply a data storage object.

OSG supports making use of different render target implementations: directly copying from the frame buffer, **pixel buffer**, or **FBO**. It uses the method `setRenderTargetImplementation()` of the `osg::Camera` class to select a solution from them, for example:

```
camera->setRenderTargetImplementation( osg::Camera::FRAME_BUFFER );
```

This indicates that the rendering result of `Camera` will be rendered to the attached texture by using the `glCopyTexSubImage()` method internally. In fact, this is the default setting of all camera nodes.

Other major implementations include `PIXEL_BUFFER` and `FRAME_BUFFER_OBJECT`.

Time for action – drawing aircrafts on a loaded terrain

In this section, we are going to integrate what we learned before to create a slightly complex example, which identifies all texture objects in a **scene graph** by using the `osg::NodeVisitor` utility, replaces them with a newly created shared texture, and binds the new texture to a **render-to-textures** camera. The texture is expected to represent more than a static image, so a customized simulation loop will be used to animate the sub-scene graph before calling the `frame()` method.

1. Include the necessary headers:

```
#include <osg/Camera>
#include <osg/Texture2D>
#include <osgDB/ReadFile>
#include <osgGA/TrackballManipulator>
#include <osgViewer/Viewer>
```

2. The first task is to look for any textures applied to a loaded model. We have to derive a `FindTextureVisitor` from the `osg::NodeVisitor` base class. This manages a texture object, which will be used for **render-to-textures** operation later. Every time we find an existing texture in the **scene graph**, we replace it with the managed one. This is implemented in the `replaceTexture()` method:

```
class FindTextureVisitor : public osg::NodeVisitor
{
public:
    FindTextureVisitor( osg::Texture* tex ) : _texture(tex)
    {
        setTraversalMode(
    osg::NodeVisitor::TRAVERSE_ALL_CHILDREN );
    }

    virtual void apply( osg::Node& node );
    virtual void apply( osg::Geode& geode );
    void replaceTexture( osg::StateSet* ss );
protected:
    osg::ref_ptr<osg::Texture> _texture;
};
```

3. In the `apply()` method, call `replaceTexture()` on each node and drawable to see if there are any textures stored. Don't forget to call `traverse()` at the end of each method body to continue going through the **scene graph**:

```
void FindTextureVisitor::apply( osg::Node& node )
{
    replaceTexture( node.getStateSet() );
    traverse( node );
}

void FindTextureVisitor::apply( osg::Geode& geode )
{
    replaceTexture( geode.getStateSet() );
    for ( unsigned int i=0; i<geode.getNumDrawables(); ++i )
    {
        replaceTexture( geode.getDrawable(i)->getStateSet() );
    }
    traverse( geode );
}
```

4. This user method uses `getTextureAttribute()` to obtain the texture in unit `0` from the input state set, and replace it with the managed one. Because the state set is obtained via the `getStateSet()` method of node or drawable, not `getOrCreateStateSet()` which is sure to return an existing or new state set object, the input pointer may be null here:

```
void replaceTexture( osg::StateSet* ss )
{
    if ( ss )
    {
        osg::Texture* oldTexture = dynamic_cast<osg::Texture*>(
            ss->getTextureAttribute(0,osg::StateAttribute::TEXTURE)
        );
        if ( oldTexture ) ss->setTextureAttribute(
0,_texture.get() );
    }
}
```

5. Load two models as scene graphs. The `lz.osg` model is used as the main scene, and the glider will be treated as a sub-graph that will be rendered to a texture, and presented on the surfaces of models in the main scene:

```
osg::ref_ptr<osg::Node> model = osgDB::readNodeFile("lz.osg");
osg::ref_ptr<osg::Node> sub_model = osgDB::readNodeFile("glider.
osg");
```

6. Create a new texture object. This differs from the previous example that creates 2D textures and applies an image to it. This time we should specify the texture size, the internal format, and other attributes by ourselves:

```
int tex_width = 1024, tex_height = 1024;

osg::ref_ptr<osg::Texture2D> texture = new osg::Texture2D;
texture->setTextureSize( tex_width, tex_height );
texture->setInternalFormat( GL_RGBA );
texture->setFilter( osg::Texture2D::MIN_FILTER,
                    osg::Texture2D::LINEAR );
texture->setFilter( osg::Texture2D::MAG_FILTER,
                    osg::Texture2D::LINEAR );
```

7. Use the `FindTextureVisitor` to locate all textures used in the `lz.osg` model, and replace them with the new, empty texture object:

```
FindTextureVisitor ftv( texture.get() );
if ( model.valid() ) model->accept( ftv );
```

8. Now it's time to create the **render-to-textures** camera. We set it up to have the same viewport as the texture size specified, and clear the background color and buffer when starting to render the sub-scene:

```
osg::ref_ptr<osg::Camera> camera = new osg::Camera;
camera->setViewport( 0, 0, tex_width, tex_height );
camera->setClearColor( osg::Vec4(1.0f, 1.0f, 1.0f, 0.0f) );
camera->setClearMask( GL_COLOR_BUFFER_BIT|GL_DEPTH_BUFFER_BIT );
```

9. Force the camera to be rendered before the main scene, and use the high efficiency FBO to implement the **render-to-textures** technique. The key statement in this example is to bind the **color buffer** with the texture object, which leads to continuous updates of the texture object, redrawing the sub-scene graph again and again:

```
camera->setRenderOrder( osg::Camera::PRE_RENDER );
camera->setRenderTargetImplementation(
    osg::Camera::FRAME_BUFFER_OBJECT );
camera->attach( osg::Camera::COLOR_BUFFER, texture.get() );
```

10. Set the camera to be absolute, and set the loaded glider to be its sub-scene graph:

```
camera->setReferenceFrame( osg::Camera::ABSOLUTE_RF );
camera->addChild( sub_model.get() );
```

11. Initialize the viewer and set a default manipulator to it:

```
osgViewer::Viewer viewer;
viewer.setSceneData( root.get() );
viewer.setCameraManipulator( new osgGA::TrackballManipulator );
```

12. The last step is to animate the glider. We haven't learnt any animation functionalities in OSG, but we already known that the simulation loop can be customized to add some pre- and post-frame events. We will simply modify the view matrix of the **render-to-textures** camera during each frame, as if making the glider swing. This is done by altering the up direction of the "look-at" view matrix, as shown:

```
float delta = 0.1f, bias = 0.0f;
osg::Vec3 eye(0.0f,-5.0f, 5.0f);
while ( !viewer.done() )
{
    if ( bias<-1.0f ) delta = 0.1f;
    else if ( bias>1.0f ) delta = -0.1f;
    bias += delta;
    camera->setViewMatrixAsLookAt( eye, osg::Vec3(),
```

```
                                    osg::Vec3(bias, 1.0f, 1.0f) );

        viewer.frame();
    }
    return 0;
```

13. Now let's execute the program. A huge glider with black background is displayed on the terrain surface, along with a few small gliders growing like trees. All of the gliders are quickly rotating left and right, as the result of rendering the sub-scene graph of the parent `camera` node to a shared texture:

14. If you forget what the original scene looks like, the following image can help you recall it. You will see that textures of the terrain ground and trees have all been replaced by the texture attached via the sub-scene's **color buffer**. That is why such an extraordinary sight is produced as the final result of this example:

What just happened?

We just created a child camera under the main camera, as we have already done in the *Creating an HUD camera* example. However, this time it doesn't produce any result on the screen. The **render-to-textures** camera is traversed and executed in every frame, before the main camera (because of the PRE_RENDER setting). It renders the sub-scene to a texture object, which is then applied to all related state sets in the main **scene graph**. Use of the shared object mechanism and **FBO** make everything high performance.

Note that the setViewMatrixAsLookAt() method called in the customized **simulation loop** is not as safe as we wish, because of the multithread pipeline in the OSG backend. It is just a temporary implementation that demonstrates how to realize dynamic texturing. In the coming *Chapter 8*, *Animating Scene Objects*, we are going to introduce the node callbacks, and in *Chapter 9*, *Interacting with Outside Elements*, we will explain the event handlers, both of which can solve this in a thread-safe way.

Have a go hero – saving scene to an image file

Believe it or not, OSG can also attach an `osg::Image` object to the camera and save frame buffer data to the `data()` pointer of the image object. After that, we can save the image data to disk files by using the `osgDB::writeImageFile()` method, which corresponds to the `osgDB::readImageFile()` method:

```
osg::ref_ptr<osg::Image> image = new osg::Image;
image->allocateImage( width, height, 1, GL_RGBA, GL_UNSIGNED_BYTE );
camera->attach( osg::Camera::COLOR_BUFFER, image.get() );
...
// After running for a while
osgDB::writeImageFile( *image, "saved_image.bmp" );
```

Here, the `width` and `height` parameters are also set to the `camera` by using the `setViewport()` method. Now, could you save the scene image to a bitmap file at the time of exiting the application?

Summary

This chapter is mainly about the observation and transformation of the 3D world with the help of the `osg::Camera` class. In this chapter, we also introduced how to use the `osgViewer::Viewer` and `osgViewer::CompositeViewer`, which encapsulate the cameras, manipulators, and stereo supports in order to make them work together.

In this chapter, we specially covered:

- How to set the view point, the view, and the projection matrix of a camera node, and how to define the rendering order of cameras, by using `osg::Camera`
- Realization of the single viewer and composite viewer by using `osgViewer::Viewer` and `osgViewer::compositeViewer`
- The management of global display settings as well as the population of stereo visualization by using `osg::DisplaySettings`
- Different ways of implementing the **rendering-to-textures** technique by using **frame buffer**, **pixel buffer**, and FBO

8

Animating Scene Objects

OSG provides comprehensive toolkits for the realization of real-time animation, including transformation animation, key-frame animation, skeletal animation, and almost all other animations such as you may find in this chapter, which first explains basic concepts of animating scene objects, and then delivers implementation details for the most commonly-used types of scene animations, which can be applied in a variety of occasions.

In this chapter, we will tell you:

- The concept of callbacks and making use of them
- Realizing ease motions in different situations
- How to create simple path animations
- How to construct complex key-frame and animation channel systems
- How to generate character animations by using a preset skeleton system
- How to implement rendering state and texture animations

Taking references to functions

In the last chapter, we tried to animate the sub-scene graph for dynamically rendering to textures. A non-recommended method is to update the view matrix of the **render-to-textures** camera in the post-frame events, in which the major issue is in a multithread context. The "post-frame" events may overlap with separated cull or draw threads, thus causing data access conflicts.

To avoid the situation of data access conflicts, we may consider employing a reference of these animating functionalities for the **update traversal** and let OSG decide the execution timeline and when to call these functionalities according to the reference. The reference passed to an executable code fragment is called a callback.

A callback triggered in the update traversal is called an **update callback**. There is also an **event callback** and a **cull callback** for executing in event and cull traversals, respectively. Instead of just using the address of functions as their references, OSG provides its own implementation of the execution operation, which is called functor. To customize the execution code, we have to override the callback a functor's key operator or method, and attach it to a suitable scene object, for instance, a node or a drawable.

List of callbacks

There are several kinds of callbacks in the OSG scene graph and backend. Among them, the osg::NodeCallback class is an important implementer of update, event, and cull callbacks. It can be only attached to nodes. For drawables, we have osg::Drawable::UpdateCallback, osg::Drawable::EventCallback and osg::Drawable::CullCallback to achieve the same goal.

The osg::NodeCallback class has a virtual operator() method for users to override by customizing their own execution code. To make it work, we have to attach the callback object to a specific node in the **scene graph** with the setUpdateCallback() or addUpdateCallback() method. The operator() method will then be automatically called during the **update traversal** in every frame.

The following table provides a brief introduction to the main callbacks defined in OSG, each of which has a *virtual method* to be overridden by user subclasses, and an *attached to* property to indicate that it is attached to a certain class with corresponding methods.

Name	Callback functor	Virtual method	Attached to
Update callback	osg::NodeCallback	operator()	osg::Node:: setUpdateCallback()
Event callback	osg::NodeCallback	operator()	osg::Node:: setEventCallback()
Cull callback	osg::NodeCallback	operator()	osg::Node:: setCullCallback()
Drawable update callback	osg::Drawable:: UpdateCallback	update()	osg::Drawable:: setUpdateCallback()

Name	Callback functor	Virtual method	Attached to
Drawable event callback	`osg::Drawable::EventCallback`	`event()`	`osg::Drawable::setEventCallback()`
Drawable cull callback	`osg::Drawable::CullCallback`	`cull()`	`osg::Drawable::setCullCallback()`
State attribute update callback	`osg::StateAttributeCallback`	`operator()`	`osg::StateAttribute::setUpdateCallback()`
State attribute event callback	`osg::StateAttributeCallback`	`operator()`	`osg::StateAttribute::setEventCallback()`
Uniform update callback	`osg::Uniform::Callback`	`operator()`	`osg::Uniform::setUpdateCallback`
Uniform event callback	`osg::Uniform::Callback`	`operator()`	`osg::Uniform::setEventCallback`
Camera callback before drawing the sub-graph	`osg::Camera::DrawCallback`	`operator()`	`osg::Camera::setPreDrawCallback()`
Camera callback after drawing the sub-graph	`osg::Camera::DrawCallback`	`operator()`	`osg::Camera::setPostDrawCallback()`

Time for action – switching nodes in the update traversal

Do you remember that we have designed an animated switch node in *Chapter 5, Managing Scene Graph*? It is derived from `osg::Switch`, but will automatically change the states of its first two children according to an internal counter, through overriding the `traverse()` virtual method.

Now we would like to redo the same task, but this time using the **update callback** mechanism. This requires customizing a new class derived from the `osg::NodeCallback` base class, and overriding the `operator()` to perform the execution in the callback implementaton.

1. Include the necessary headers:

```
#include <osg/Switch>
#include <osgDB/ReadFile>
#include <osgViewer/Viewer>
```

2. Declare the `SwitchingCallback` class. It is an `osg::NodeCallback` based class, which can soon be used as update, event, or cull callbacks of scene nodes. The only important virtual method to implement is `operator()`. This is automatically called during the update, event, or cull traversal of the **scene graph**. Besides, we also initialize the member variable `_count`, as an internal counter:

```
class SwitchingCallback : public osg::NodeCallback
{
public:
    SwitchingCallback() : _count(0) {}
    virtual void operator()( osg::Node* node,
                             osg::NodeVisitor* nv );

protected:
    unsigned int _count;
};
```

3. The `operator()` has two input parameters: the node associated with the callback, and the node visitor calling the function during traversals. To animate the state switching of the two child nodes, we have to convert the node pointer to the type `osg::Switch`. A `static_cast<>` is used here because we are sure that the associated node is a switch node. Also, note that the `traverse()` method should be executed in a certain location, to ensure that the update traversal visitor can continue traversing the **scene graph**.

```
void SwitchingCallback::operator()( osg::Node* node,
                                    osg::NodeVisitor* nv )
{
    osg::Switch* switchNode = static_cast<osg::Switch*>( node );
    if ( !((++_count)%60) && switchNode )
    {
        switchNode->setValue( 0, !switchNode->getValue(0) );
        switchNode->setValue( 1, !switchNode->getValue(1) );
    }
    traverse( node, nv );
}
```

4. The next step was already introduced in *Chapter 5, Managing Scene Graph*. Load two models that show two different states of a Cessna, and put them under the `switch` node, which will be used in the customized **update callback** `SwitchingCallback`:

```
osg::ref_ptr<osg::Node> model1 = osgDB::readNodeFile(
    "cessna.osg" );
osg::ref_ptr<osg::Node> model2= osgDB::readNodeFile("cessnafire.
osg");

osg::ref_ptr<osg::Switch> root = new osg::Switch;
root->addChild( model1.get(), false );
root->addChild( model2.get(), true );
```

5. Don't forget to attach the **update callback** object to the node. And if you are tired of executing this callback in every frame, just retransfer a NULL argument to the `setUpdateCallback()` method. The callback object will be deleted if its **referenced count** is down to 0:

```
root->setUpdateCallback( new SwitchingCallback );
```

6. Now start the viewer:

```
osgViewer::Viewer viewer;
viewer.setSceneData( root.get() );
return viewer.run();
```

7. The rendering result is completely similar to the *Animating the switch node* example in *Chapter 5, Managing Scene Graph*. The Cessna will be intact and afire alternately, acting in cycles. Comparing with overriding a new node type, the solution is that using a callback is less intrusive to the **scene graph**, and can be easily removed or replaced by other callbacks at runtime.

What just happened?

So far we have dealt with the mysterious `traverse()` method for two purposes: customizing nodes by overriding the `traverse()` method for own-execution code; and calling the `traverse()` method of the `osg::NodeVisitor` class in order to continue the traversal while implementing node visitors. Although these two occurrences have different parameters, they actually represent the same processing pipeline.

Firstly, the `traverse()` method of node visitors, which has a single `osg::Node` parameter, simply calls the node's `traverse()` virtual method and passes itself as an argument.

Secondly, the node's traversing method must call its super class's `traverse()` at the end of the implementation. It will then determine if there are child nodes to be traversed with the current visitor object (using the `accept()` method of child nodes).

Finally, the visitor in turn calls the `apply()` virtual method to receive various types of nodes as its argument, and realizes customized visiting behaviors thereafter. Since each `apply()` method must call the visitor's `traverse()` to end itself, the cycle comes back to the first step, until the whole scene graph is traversed. The entire diagram can be explained with following image:

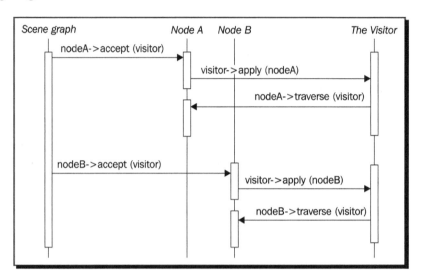

The callback's `operator()` method calls its `traverse()` in the third form, with a visitor and a node parameter. However, there is no need to worry about the complexity, as the only work it performs is to call the `traverse()` method of the visitor and continue the traversal. If you fail to call this in the callback's method, the traversal will simply be stopped and will return from current node at once.

Pop quiz – adding or setting callbacks

The `addUpdateCallback()` method can be used to attach callbacks to scene nodes besides `setUpdateCallback()`. It adds the new callback object to the end of the major one, and thus makes it possible to have more than one callback on a single node. Which one do you prefer? Can you point out when the nested callback is going to be executed during the run of the major one's `operator()` method?

Avoiding conflicting modifications

We have discussed OSG's multithread implementation and thread safety in a very simple and easy way. The theory of the processing architecture is really out of the scope of this book. But in order to show the importance of maintaining data variance of scene objects, we need to briefly talk about the threading model.

OSG can make the **draw traversal**, which transfers data to the OpenGL pipeline run in a separated thread. It must be synchronized with other draw traversals in every frame, but part of the draw traversal can usually overlap the **update traversal** coming from the next frame, which improves the rendering efficiency and reduces frame latency. That means that the `frame()` method of `osgViewer::Viewer` will return while the drawing work is still active. Data changes in update callbacks could then conflict with the unfinished rendering process and cause unexpected behaviors, and even crashes.

OSG supplies a solution in the `setDataVariance()` method, which belongs to the `osg::Object` class—the base class of all scene objects. This can be set to one of three enumerate values: UNSPECIFIED (by default), STATIC, and DYNAMIC. A DYNAMIC object in the **scene graph** must be processed at the beginning of the **draw traversal**. That is, the rendering backend should ensure all nodes and scene objects that are specified as DYNAMIC have finished being drawn before starting the next frame's update and cull traversals. However, STATIC objects, which are considered to be unchanged during updating and drawing, can thus be rendered later and won't hold back the frame rate.

By default, any newly-allocated objects are set to UNSPECIFIED, including nodes, drawables, state sets, and attributes. This allows OSG to predict the data variance. On the other hand, you can always reset the value and make it work from the next frame, for instance:

```
node->setDataVariance( osg::Object::DYNAMIC );
```

Time for action – drawing a geometry dynamically

It is common practice to modify geometries' vertices and primitive attributes dynamically. We can change the position, normal, color, and texture coordinate of each vertex, as well as related primitives per frame, in order to implement kinds of morph animations. During the modifications, it is important to keep an eye on the data variance, because the draw traversal might be running while updating vertices and primitives, which might cause conflicts and even crashes.

In this example, we will make use of the quad geometry that was created in *Chapter 4, Building Geometry Models*. We will simply alter its last vertex and make it rotate around the X axis, which results in a simple animation effect.

1. Include the necessary headers:
```
#include <osg/Geometry>
#include <osg/Geode>
#include <osgViewer/Viewer>
```

2. The creation of a quad is familiar to us. Specify the vertex, normal, and color array, and add a primitive set to indicate that all vertices are arranged and rendered with the type of GL_QUADS. Finally, return the newly-allocated geometry object:

```
osg::Geometry* createQuad()
{
    osg::ref_ptr<osg::Vec3Array> vertices = new osg::Vec3Array;
    vertices->push_back( osg::Vec3(0.0f, 0.0f, 0.0f) );
    vertices->push_back( osg::Vec3(1.0f, 0.0f, 0.0f) );
    vertices->push_back( osg::Vec3(1.0f, 0.0f, 1.0f) );
    vertices->push_back( osg::Vec3(0.0f, 0.0f, 1.0f) );

    osg::ref_ptr<osg::Vec3Array> normals = new osg::Vec3Array;
    normals->push_back( osg::Vec3(0.0f,-1.0f, 0.0f) );

    osg::ref_ptr<osg::Vec4Array> colors = new osg::Vec4Array;
    colors->push_back( osg::Vec4(1.0f, 0.0f, 0.0f, 1.0f) );
    colors->push_back( osg::Vec4(0.0f, 1.0f, 0.0f, 1.0f) );
    colors->push_back( osg::Vec4(0.0f, 0.0f, 1.0f, 1.0f) );
    colors->push_back( osg::Vec4(1.0f, 1.0f, 1.0f, 1.0f) );

    osg::ref_ptr<osg::Geometry> quad = new osg::Geometry;
    quad->setVertexArray( vertices.get() );
    quad->setNormalArray( normals.get() );
    quad->setNormalBinding( osg::Geometry::BIND_OVERALL );
    quad->setColorArray( colors.get() );
    quad->setColorBinding( osg::Geometry::BIND_PER_VERTEX );
    quad->addPrimitiveSet( new osg::DrawArrays(GL_QUADS, 0, 4) );
    return quad.release();
}
```

3. With the help of osg::Drawable::UpdateCallback, we can easily obtain the geometry pointer for altering each frame. The only method to be overridden is update(), which has a node visitor and a drawable pointer parameter. Its super class, osg::Drawable::UpdateCallback, is a little similar to the osg::NodeCallback class, except that a drawable's callback doesn't have to traverse to any "child" (a drawable has no child).

```
class DynamicQuadCallback : public osg::Drawable::UpdateCallback
{
public:
    virtual void update( osg::NodeVisitor*, osg::Drawable*
drawable );
};
```

4. In the implementation of the `update()` method, we read out the vertex array of the created quad geometry with two `static_cast<>` operators. The `dynamic_cast<>` keyword might be safer here if the `DynamicQuadCallback` class is not only applied to `osg::Geometry`, but is also applied to other customized drawables. After that, we quickly rotate the last vertex in the array around the origin (0, 0, 0), using the `osg::Quat` quaternion class. The last work before exiting the method is to recalculate the **display list** object and bounding box of the current geometry, which may need to be updated when any of the vertices are changed:

```
void DynamicQuadCallback::update( osg::NodeVisitor*,
                                  osg::Drawable* drawable )
{
    osg::Geometry* quad = static_cast<osg::Geometry*>( drawable );
    if ( !quad ) return;

    osg::Vec3Array* vertices = static_cast<osg::Vec3Array*>(
        quad->getVertexArray() );
    if ( !vertices ) return;

    osg::Quat quat(osg::PI*0.01, osg::X_AXIS);
    vertices->back() = quat * vertices->back();

    quad->dirtyDisplayList();
    quad->dirtyBound();
}
```

5. We define the geometry as `DYNAMIC`, so the drawing traversal of the OSG backend will automatically order the dynamic object to perform robust scene graph traversals. In addition, the drawable's modification callback is specified by the `setUpdateCallback()` method of the `osg::Drawable` class:

```
osg::Geometry* quad = createQuad();
quad->setDataVariance( osg::Object::DYNAMIC );
quad->setUpdateCallback( new DynamicQuadCallback );
```

6. Now, add the quad geometry to an `osg::Geode` node, and attach the root node to the viewer:

```
osg::ref_ptr<osg::Geode> root = new osg::Geode;
root->addDrawable( quad );

osgViewer::Viewer viewer;
viewer.setSceneData( root.get() );
return viewer.run();
```

7. The quad is animated this time. Its fourth vertex is dancing around the X axis, with the help of `osg::Quat` class. It is more dynamic than just showing a motionless image on the screen:

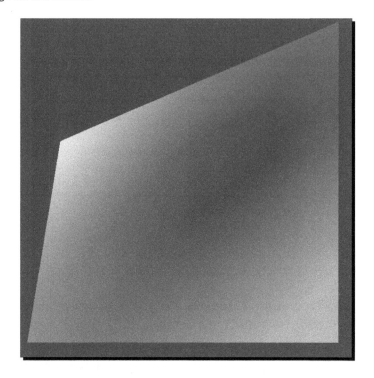

What just happened?

Try to remove the `setDataVariance()` line and see what happens. It is a little surprising that the example is still running perfectly, as if it is not affected by the threading model. That is because `UNSPECIFIED` objects can decide if they will be dynamically modified in callbacks or not, and reset the data variance to `DYNAMIC` automatically.

Try changing the enumeration `DYNAMIC` to `STATIC`, and you may occasionally find that the rendering result is flickering and there is an OpenGL error message "invalid operation" from the console. This is actually caused by thread conflicts.

Without calling the `dirtyDisplayList()` method, OSG will ignore all dynamic drawable changes and make use of the **display list** commands storing the previous vertex and primitive data. Also, without the `dirtyBound()` method, OSG will not know if the bounding box no longer fits the drawable size, and will make mistakes when doing view frustum culling work.

Have a go hero – dirtying geometry objects

We have to call the `dirtyDisplayList()` method to activate the update of drawable data for correct rendering. But an important prerequisite here is the drawable should support the **display list** mode, which is the default behavior of drawables and can be enabled or disabled with the `setUseDisplayList()` method.

OSG allows a better mechianism to be used while working in the **VBO** mode, which tends to be more efficient. Enable `setUseVertexBufferObjects()` and disable `setUseDisplayList()` to make it work. You will find the `dirtyDisplayList()` method is useless in this case. Try dirtying array data by issuing a `dirty()` command, such as:

```
osg::Vec3Array* vertices = …;
…     // Dynamically modify the vertex array data
vertices->dirty();
```

See if your modifications take effect, and identify the difference between these two strategies when dirtying the same geometry. Actually, **display list** is of no use here because it is regenerated in every frame. Therefore, we often prefer **VBO** for rendering changing geometry data.

Understanding ease motions

Assume that there is a train running from station A to station B within 15 minutes. We would like to simulate this scenario by altering the transformation matrix of the train in an **update callback**. The simplest way is to put the train at station A at time point 0, and at station B at time point 15 (minutes), and move it evenly in the transition phase. A heavily-employed method used here is the **linear interpolation**. This draws a straight line between two neighboring samples P0 and P1, and returns the appropriate point P along the line, which can be used to represent translation and scale operations of nodes. It is commonly expressed in the following form:

```
P = (1 - t) * P0 + t * P1
```

Here, t is a number between 0 and 1.

Unfortunately, the motion of a train is usually much more complex. It starts from station A, accelerates slowly, drives at an even speed, decelerates, and finally stops at station B. In that case, **linear interpolation** is always slightly unnatural.

So we have **ease motions**, or ease functions. These are mathematical functions that are used to interpolate values between two endpoints. An ease motion usually generates non-linear results, in order to produce more natural effects. The **osgAnimation** library defines a number of built-in ease motions. Each of them has at least two arguments: the start value (usually 0) and a duration (usually 1), and thus produces results in the range [start value, start value + duration]. They can be applied to the start (InMotion), to the end (OutMotion), or to both start and end of the animation (InOutMotion). We will list them in the following table:

Motion type	Ease-in class	Ease-out class	Ease-in/out class
Linear interpolation	LinearMotion	-	-
Quad function (y = t2)	InQuadMotion	OutQuadMotion	InOutQuadMotion
Cubic function (y = t3)	InCubicMotion	OutCubicMotion	InOutCubicMotion
Quart function (y = t4)	InQuartMotion	OutQuartMotion	InOutQuartMotion
Bounce effect function	InBounceMotion	OutBounceMotion	InOutBounceMotion
Elastic bounce function	InElasticMotion	OutElasticMotion	InOutElasticMotion
Sine function	InSineMotion	OutSineMotion	InOutSineMotion
Back function	InBackMotion	OutBackMotion	InOutBackMotion
Circle function	InCircMotion	OutCircMotion	InOutCircMotion
Exponent function	InExpoMotion	OutExpoMotion	InOutExpoMotion

To create a linear interpolation motion object, we just type:

```
// Start value is 0.0, and duration time is 1.0.
osg::ref_ptr<osgAnimation::LinearMotion> motion =
    new osgAnimation::LinearMotion(0.0f, 1.0f);
```

The examples/osganimationeasemotion file in the OSG source code can help you to discover these ease motions graphically. Try compiling and running it for details.

Animating the transformation nodes

Path animations are the most commonly-used animations in graphics applications. They can be used to describe a running car, a flight, a rotating ball, or the camera's motion. The path should always be set up first, including position, rotation, and scale values at different key time nodes. When the simulation loop is running, a transition state is calculated every frame, using the **linear interpolation** for position and scale vectors, and **spherical linear interpolation** for the rotation quaternion. The slerp() method of osg::Quat is used internally here.

OSG provides the osg::AnimationPath class to encapsulate a time varying transformation path. It has an insert() method that can be used to insert a control point at a specific time. A control point, declared by the osg::AnimationPath::ControlPoint class, accepts a position value, and optional rotation and scale values in order to construct the animation path. For example:

```
osg::ref_ptr<osg::AnimationPath> path = new osg::AnimationPath;
path->insert(t1, osg::AnimationPath::ControlPoint(pos1,rot1,scale1));
path->insert(t2, …);
```

Here, t1 and t2 are time nodes in seconds, and rot1 is an osg::Quat variable for representing the rotation of a object.

Besides that, we can set up the loop mode of the animation path with the setLoopMode() method. The default value is LOOP, that is, the animation will continuously run on the preset path over and over again. This parameter can be changed to NO_LOOPING (run once) or SWING (create a ping-pong path) for other purposes.

After that, we attach the osg::AnimationPath object to a built-in osg::AnimationPathCallback object, which is actually derived from osg::NodeCallback, and can help developers to control their animating scenes in an intuitive way.

Time for action – making use of the animation path

Now we are going to make our Cessna navigate a cruise. It will be moving in a circle with the centre at (0, 0, 0). The animation path is used for updating the position and orientation of the model continuously, using linear interpolation between key-frames. The only work is to add control points, including position, optional rotation, and scale key value, to the animation timeline.

1. Include the necessary headers:

```
#include <osg/AnimationPath>
#include <osg/MatrixTransform>
#include <osgDB/ReadFile>
#include <osgViewer/Viewer>
```

2. Create the animation path. This is in fact a circle with a specific *radius* on the XOY plane. The *time* parameter is used to indicate the total time required to finish a lap. The `osg::AnimationPath` object is set to loop the animation infinitely. It contains 32 control points to form a circle path, which is determined by the local variable `numSamples`:

```
osg::AnimationPath* createAnimationPath( float radius, float time
)
{
    osg::ref_ptr<osg::AnimationPath> path = new
osg::AnimationPath;
    path->setLoopMode( osg::AnimationPath::LOOP );

    unsigned int numSamples = 32;
    float delta_yaw = 2.0f * osg::PI / ((float)numSamples - 1.0f);
    float delta_time = time / (float)numSamples;
    for ( unsigned int i=0; i<numSamples; ++i )
    {
        float yaw = delta_yaw * (float)i;
        osg::Vec3 pos( sinf(yaw)*radius, cosf(yaw)*radius, 0.0f );
        osg::Quat rot( -yaw, osg::Z_AXIS );
        path->insert( delta_time * (float)i,
                    osg::AnimationPath::ControlPoint(pos, rot)
);
    }
    return path.release();
}
```

3. Load the Cessna model. You will have noticed that there is a significant difference between this and previous file names. The string `"0,0,90.rot"` seems redundant and ambiguous here. It is a kind of pseudo-loader, which is written as part of filename but actually does a 90 degrees rotation around the Z axis to the model `cessna.osg`. We are going to discuss this in detail in *Chapter 10, Creating Components and Extending Functionality*:

```
osg::ref_ptr<osg::Node> model =
    osgDB::readNodeFile( "cessna.osg.0,0,90.rot" );

osg::ref_ptr<osg::MatrixTransform> root = new
osg::MatrixTransform;
root->addChild( model.get() );
```

4. Add the animation path to the `osg::AnimationPathCallback` object, and attach the callback to a node. Note that the animation path can only affect `osg::MatrixTransform` and `osg::PositionAttitudeTransform` nodes, updating their transformation matrices or position and rotation attributes in the **update traversal**:

```
osg::ref_ptr<osg::AnimationPathCallback> apcb = new
osg::AnimationPathCallback;
apcb->setAnimationPath( createAnimationPath(50.0f, 6.0f) );

root->setUpdateCallback( apcb.get() );
```

5. Simply start the viewer now:

```
osgViewer::Viewer viewer;
viewer.setSceneData( root.get() );
return viewer.run();
```

6. The Cessna starts circling now. It may move beyond the scope of the screen, so we have to use the camera manipulator to change to a better viewing place than the initial one. Use the mouse buttons to adjust the view matrix and have an overview of the animation path that we have created:

What just happened?

The `osg::AnimationPath` class uses a `getMatrix()` method to compute and return a transitional transformation matrix according to the two control points just before and after a given time. It is then applied to the host `osg::MatrixTransform`, `osg::PositionAttitudeTransform`, or `osg::Camera` node in order to make it move along the path. This is done by the `osg::AnimationPathCallback` class, which is actually an **update callback** for a specific purpose.

If the `osg::AnimationPathCallback` object is attached to any kind of nodes other than transformation nodes previously described, it will become invalid. It is also not suggested to use the animation path callback as event or cull callbacks, as this may lead to unexpected results.

Have a go hero – more controls over the animation path

An animation must be able to be stopped, reset, and fast-forwarded, which makes it easy to be controlled by users. The `osg::AnimationPathCallback` class provides the `reset()`, `setPause()`, `setTimeMultiplier()`, and `setTimeOffset()` methods to implement these common operations. For example, to restart a preset animation path, callback `apcb` at any time:

```
apcb->setPause( false );
apcb->reset();
```

In order to set the time offset to 4.0s and move forward through the animation at a 2x speed, just use:

```
Apcb->setTimeOffset( 4.0f );
apcb->setTimeMultiplier( 2.0f );
```

Now, can you figure out how to create your own path animation player?

Changing rendering states

Rendering states can be animated, too. A number of effects can be generated by altering the properties of one or more rendering attributes, including fade-in and fade-out, density and variation of the atmosphere, fog, changing the direction of light beams, and so on. We can easily implement a state animation in the **update callback**. We may either retrieve the attribute object from the arguments of the overridden method, or just manage the object as a member variable of the user-defined callback. Remember to make use of **smart pointers**, to ensure that the member attribute won't be automatically destroyed if it is no longer referenced.

The ease motion classes can be used to improve the animation quality. We must allocate an ease motion object with the start value and duration parameters, and update it with a delta time as the time step size. For example:

```
osg::ref_ptr<osgAnimation::LinearMotion> motion =
    new osgAnimation::LinearMotion(0.0, 10.0);
...
motion->update( dt );
float value = motion->getValue();
```

This creates a linear motion object with the X axis (time) ranging from 0.0 to 10.0. The `getValue()` method uses specific formula on the current X value, and obtains a corresponding Y value.

You should add the **osgAnimation** library as a dependence if you would like the ease motion and more functionalities to be used in your projects.

Time for action – fading in

We already had experience of making a scene object translucent using `osg::BlendFunc` class and rendering orders. The fourth component of the color vector, called the alpha value, will do the trick for us. But what will happen if we have a continuously-changing alpha? The object will be completely transparent (invisible) when alpha is 0, and completely opaque when it is 1.0. The animating process from 0.0 to 1.0 will therefore cause the object to gradually appear to viewers, that is, the fade-in effect.

The **update callback** can be used in this task. It is no problem to create an `osg::NodeCallback` based class and set it to the node that will be fading in. But the state attribute callback, `osg::StateAttributeCallback`, is also available in this case.

The `osg::Material` class is used here to provide the alpha bit of each geometry vertex, instead of just setting a color array.

1. Include the necessary headers:

```
#include <osg/Geode>
#include <osg/Geometry>
#include <osg/BlendFunc>
#include <osg/Material>
#include <osgAnimation/EaseMotion>
#include <osgDB/ReadFile>
#include <osgViewer/Viewer>
```

2. To instantiate an `osg::StateAttributeCallback`, we have to override the `operator()` method and make use of its arguments: the state attribute itself and the visitor who is traversing it. An additional work item here is to declare an ease motion interpolator using a cubic function at the in and out position of the animation curve:

```
class AlphaFadingCallback : public osg::StateAttributeCallback
{
public:
    AlphaFadingCallback()
    { _motion = new osgAnimation::InOutCubicMotion(0.0f, 1.0f); }

    virtual void operator()(osg::StateAttribute*,
```

```
                                    osg::NodeVisitor*);

    protected:
        osg::ref_ptr<osgAnimation::InOutCubicMotion> _motion;
    };
```

3. In the `operator()`, we will obtain the material attribute of the scene object, which can be used for simulating transparent and translucent effects. There are two steps to follow: firstly, update the ease motion object with a customized delta time value; after that, retrieve the result of motion between 0 and 1, and apply it to the alpha component of the material's diffuse color:

```
void AlphaFadingCallback::operator()( osg::StateAttribute* sa,
                                      osg::NodeVisitor* nv )
{
    osg::Material* material = static_cast<osg::Material*>( sa );
    if ( material )
    {
        _motion->update( 0.005 );

        float alpha = _motion->getValue();
        material->setDiffuse( osg::Material::FRONT_AND_BACK,
                              osg::Vec4(0.0f, 1.0f, 1.0f, alpha)
);
    }
}
```

4. That is all we have done in `osg::StateAttribute`'s callback. Now, in the main function of the example, we would like to create a quad and apply the callback to its material. You may copy the code from *Chapter 4, Building Geometry Models* and *Chapter 6, Creating Realistic Rendering Effects* to create a geometry quad yourself. OSG supports a more convenient function named `osg::createTexturedQuad Geometry()`. It requires a corner point, a width vector, and a height vector, and returns a newly-created `osg::Geometry` object with preset vertex, normal, and texture coordinate data:

```
osg::ref_ptr<osg::Drawable> quad = osg::createTexturedQuadGeomet
ry(
    osg::Vec3(-0.5f, 0.0f, -0.5f),
    osg::Vec3(1.0f, 0.0f, 0.0f), osg::Vec3(0.0f, 0.0f, 1.0f)
);
osg::ref_ptr<osg::Geode> geode = new osg::Geode;
geode->addDrawable( quad.get() );
```

5. Configuring the material attribute is nothing special. With experience of using OpenGL `glMaterial()`, we can easily imagine how the `osg::Material` class sets ambient and diffuse colors with similar member methods. An important matter here is to attach the `AlphaFadingCallback` object to the material and make it work in every update traversal per frame:

```
osg::ref_ptr<osg::Material> material = new osg::Material;
material->setAmbient( osg::Material::FRONT_AND_BACK,
                      osg::Vec4(0.0f, 0.0f, 0.0f, 1.0f) );
material->setDiffuse( osg::Material::FRONT_AND_BACK,
                      osg::Vec4(0.0f, 1.0f, 1.0f, 0.5f) );
material->setUpdateCallback( new AlphaFadingCallback );
```

6. Add the material attribute and related mode to the state set of the `geode`. Meanwhile, we have to enable the OpenGL blend function to implement our fade-in effect, and ensure that transparent objects are rendered in an orderly manner:

```
geode->getOrCreateStateSet()->setAttributeAndModes(
  material.get() );
geode->getOrCreateStateSet()->setAttributeAndModes(
    new osg::BlendFunc(GL_SRC_ALPHA, GL_ONE_MINUS_SRC_ALPHA) );
geode->getOrCreateStateSet()->setRenderingHint(
    osg::StateSet::TRANSPARENT_BIN );
```

7. Add the quad to the root node. We will also add a glider model as the referenced model, half of which is covered by the quad and thus indicates whether the quad is fading in or not:

```
osg::ref_ptr<osg::Group> root = new osg::Group;
root->addChild( geode.get() );
root->addChild( osgDB::readNodeFile("glider.osg") );
```

8. OK, now start the viewer:

```
osgViewer::Viewer viewer;
viewer.setSceneData( root.get() );
return viewer.run();
```

9. The in-out cubic ease motion makes the changing of the alpha in a smooth way. You will find that it is more suitable for implementing realistic animations than simply linear interpolation motion. Now, can you figure out how to achieve a fade-out effect with the same structure? These two are often used in representing dynamic models and buildings in a huge city scene:

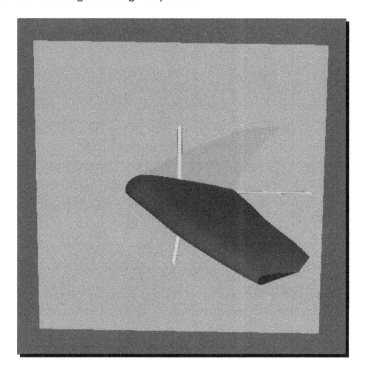

What just happened?

The `osgAnimation::InOutCubicMotion` class here generates values based on a cubic formula of time. The resultant curve is illustrated as follows:

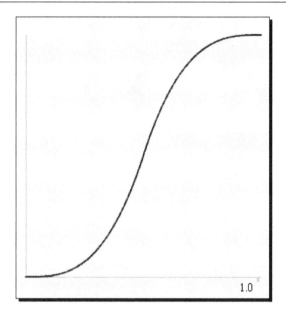

Assuming that the current time value is t (on the X axis), the motion object will return Y values according to the cubic formula. It is accelerating from zero velocity to halfway, and then decelerating to zero velocity. This allows the object to appear more natural than just using a simple constant speed. Try applying this and more ease motions to the alpha value of the material, as well as the path animation of osg::MatrixTransform nodes (alter its matrix in a customized node callback).

Pop quiz – choosing the alpha setter and the callback

What else can set the alpha value of vertices, besides the osg::Material class and the color array of osg::Geometry? And what callback types do you think can be used to control the fade-in effect, besides osg::StateAttributeCallback, for instance, node and drawable callbacks? Can you implement the fade-out effect by modifying the example above in the simplest way?

Have a go hero – animating in graphics shaders

It would be cool to use state animations in **graphics shaders**. In most cases, it is easier to control than the fixed pipeline, and gives you free imagination of various effects, such as the ocean wave, ripple, blaze, shadow, and complex particle effects.

The osg::Uniform class can define its own **update callback** with the setUpdateCallback() method and an osg::Uniform::Callback derived object. The virtual method operator() has two input arguments: the uniform pointer and the visitor who traverses it. Use the set() method to change uniform values (must be the same type as before) and see if it can work in **graphics shaders**.

Playing movies on textures

It is fantastic if we can watch movies or hold video conferences in the 3D world. We can place a big quad geometry as the movie screen and attach a dynamic 2D texture to its surface. The texture contains a series of images that make up the whole video. It is necessary that the image sequence can add new images on the fly, which may be transferred from files or mini cameras.

OSG uses the osg::ImageStream class to support an image stream, which manages sub-images in the data buffer. It can be derived to read data from video files or the Internet. In fact, OSG has already had a few built-in plugins that support the loading and playing of AVI, MPG, MOV, and other file formats. This will be described in details in *Chapter 10, Saving and Loading Files*.

Here, we are going to introduce another osg::ImageSequence class, which stores multiple image objects and renders them successively. It has the following public methods:

1. The addImage() method adds an osg::Image object to this sequence. There are also setImage() and getImage() methods for operating sub-images at specific indexes, and getNumImages() for counting the number of sub-images.

2. The addImageFile() and setImageFile() methods can also push image objects to the end of the sub-image list. But instead of specifying a pointer, they both accept a filename parameter, for reading the sub-image from the disk.

3. The setLength() method sets the total time of the image sequence in seconds. The time is divided equally between each sub-image during the animation.

4. The setTimeMultiplier() method sets the time multiplier. The default is 1.0, and a larger value indicates that the sequence should be fast-forwarded.

5. The play(), pause(), rewind(), and seek() methods give developers basic controls over the sequence. The seek() method accepts a time parameter, which should be less than the total time length.

Time for action – rendering a flashing spotlight

The key to rendering dynamic textures is to provide multiple images as the source, and draw them one after another. These images can be obtained from a video file, or created by developers and artists. In the following example, we will create a series of spotlights with varying radii, and output them to osg::Image objects, and then attach them to the texture attribute using the osg::ImageSequence class to produce a flashing effect on a specific model.

1. Include the necessary headers:

```cpp
#include <osg/ImageSequence>
#include <osg/Texture2D>
#include <osg/Geometry>
#include <osg/Geode>
#include <osgViewer/Viewer>
```

2. The spotlight can be defined as a follow spot projecting a bright beam of light onto a space. It usually produces a halo surrounding the central spot, and can be modified to use different color and power ranges. Here, the function createSpotLight() simply generates an osg::Image object with the center color, background color, and power arguments. The size parameter is used to define the final size of the image itself. Here, the data() method accepts the column and row indices, and returns a corresponding start address for assignment:

```cpp
osg::Image* createSpotLight( const osg::Vec4& centerColor,
                             const osg::Vec4& bgColor,
                             unsigned int size, float power )
{
    osg::ref_ptr<osg::Image> image = new osg::Image;
    image->allocateImage( size, size, 1, GL_RGBA,
                          GL_UNSIGNED_BYTE );

    float mid = (float(size)-1) * 0.5f;
    float div = 2.0f / float(size);
    for( unsigned int r=0; r<size; ++r )
    {
        unsigned char* ptr = image->data(0, r);
        for( unsigned int c=0; c<size; ++c )
        {
            float dx = (float(c) - mid)*div;
            float dy = (float(r) - mid)*div;
            float r = powf(1.0f - sqrtf(dx*dx+dy*dy), power);
            if ( r<0.0f ) r = 0.0f;
```

```
                              osg::Vec4 color = centerColor*r + bgColor*(1.0f - r);
                              *ptr++ = (unsigned char)((color[0]) * 255.0f);
                              *ptr++ = (unsigned char)((color[1]) * 255.0f);
                              *ptr++ = (unsigned char)((color[2]) * 255.0f);
                              *ptr++ = (unsigned char)((color[3]) * 255.0f);
                          }
                      }
                      return image.release();
                  }
```

3. With the convenient `createSpotLight()` function, we can quickly generate multiple images with different power values. We will then add all of them to the `osg::ImageSequence` object for unified management:

```
osg::Vec4 centerColor( 1.0f, 1.0f, 0.0f, 1.0f );
osg::Vec4 bgColor( 0.0f, 0.0f, 0.0f, 1.0f );

osg::ref_ptr<osg::ImageSequence> sequence = new
  osg::ImageSequence;
sequence->addImage( createSpotLight(centerColor, bgColor, 64,
  3.0f) );
sequence->addImage( createSpotLight(centerColor, bgColor, 64,
  3.5f) );
sequence->addImage( createSpotLight(centerColor, bgColor, 64,
  4.0f) );
sequence->addImage( createSpotLight(centerColor, bgColor, 64,
  3.5f) );
```

4. Because `osg::ImageSequence` is derived from the `osg::Image` class, it can be directly attached to a texture as the data source. This makes it possible to continuously display images on model surfaces:

```
osg::ref_ptr<osg::Texture2D> texture = new osg::Texture2D;
texture->setImage( imageSequence.get() );
```

5. Create a quad with the `osg::createTexturedQuadGeometry()` function, again. This is used to present the resultant image sequence. It can be even regarded as the screen for displaying movies in a visual cinema, if all images are captured from a video source.

```
osg::ref_ptr<osg::Geode> geode = new osg::Geode;
geode->addDrawable( osg::createTexturedQuadGeometry(
    osg::Vec3(), osg::Vec3(1.0,0.0,0.0), osg::Vec3(0.0,0.0,1.0))
  );
geode->getOrCreateStateSet()->setTextureAttributeAndModes(
    0, texture.get(), osg::StateAttribute::ON );
```

6. We have to configure the `osg::ImageSequence` object to determine the total length (in seconds), and start to play the sequence in an orderly manner. This can be done in an **update callback**, too.

```
imageSequence->setLength( 0.5 );
imageSequence->play();
```

7. Start the viewer:

```
osgViewer::Viewer viewer;
viewer.setSceneData( geode.get() );
return viewer.run();
```

8. You will see a spotlight flashing in the center of the quad. This is because we apply spotlight images with different radii to the sequence, and play them in a loop (by default). Now you can imagine some more realistic effects based on this basic implementation:

What just happened?

The osg::ImageSequence class updates the current rendering data from stored images in every frame. It uses a setImage() method to configure the dimensions, format, and pixel data, and will also dirty itself—this will remind all texture objects that keep the image to update the graphics memory and output new data to the rendering pipeline. This is not efficient as it causes already-high CPU-GPU bandwidth usage to increase if image switching is too frequent.

Another point of interest is the addFileName() and setFileName() methods. These use image files on the disk to form the image sequence, and all these files are loaded at once by default. This can be modified with a setMode() method. This accepts one of three values:

1. PRE_LOAD_ALL_IMAGES leads to the default behavior
2. PAGE_AND_RETAIN_IMAGES will load the image from file on the fly and retain it
3. PAGE_AND_DISCARD_USED_IMAGES removes any used images and reload them when the movie is reset

Thus, in order to force to load images with a pager mechanism, set the mode before starting the **simulation loop**:

```
imageSequence->setMode( osg::ImageSequence::PAGE_AND_RETAIN_IMAGES );
```

Creating complex key-frame animations

Now we can explore more about the osgAnimation library. Besides the ease motion implementations, osgAnimation supports a lot more generic animation features, including solid animations, morph animations, skeleton animations with rigged mesh, channel mixers with priorities, basic animation managers, and timeline schedulers. It defines a lot of concepts and template classes, which seems to be of high complexity, but can provide developers with great flexibility to build their own advanced animations.

With the foundation of using animation paths, we can quickly clarify some important concepts of osgAnimation, and get started with an example implementing the same result as the animation path example.

The basic element of animations is the key-frame. This defines the endpoints of any smooth transition. The osg::AnimationPath uses a ControlPoint class to create key-frames of position, rotation, and scale values.

A key-frame usually requires two parameters: the time point, and the value to be achieved. The `osgAnimation::TemplateKeyframe<>` class is used to define a generic key-frame in the `osgAnimation` library, and the `osgAnimation::TemplateKeyframeContai ner<>` class manages a list of key-frames with the same data type. It is derived from the `std::vector` class and can benefit from all vector methods, such as `push_back()`, `pop_back()`, and iterators. Thus, to add a position key-frame into a corresponding container object, we have:

```
osgAnimation::TemplateKeyframe<osg::Vec3> kf(0.0, osg::Vec3(…));
osgAnimation::TemplateKeyframeContainer<osg::Vec3>* container =
    new osgAnimation::TemplateKeyframeContainer<osg::Vec3>;
container->push_back( keyframe );
```

Here, `osg::Vec3` is the template argument of both the key-frame and the container. To simplify the code, we can simply replace the template class names with `osgAnimation::Vec3KeyFrame` and `osgAnimation::Vec3KeyFrameContainer` classes, that is:

```
osgAnimation::Vec3KeyframeContainer* container =
    new osgAnimation::Vec3KeyframeContainer;
container->push_back( osgAnimation::Vec3Keyframe(0.0, osg::Vec3(…)) );
```

The container object is actually derived from `osg::Referenced`, so it can be managed by **smart pointers**. A sampler is then used to interpolate elements in the key-frame container with a functor that defines the interpolation method.

The `osgAnimation::TemplateSampler<>` defines the low-level sampler template. It contains an internal interpolator object and an `osgAnimation::TemplateKeyframeC ontainer<>` with the same template argument. Samplers have aliases, too. For example, `osgAnimation::Vec3LinearSampler` defines a sampler including `osg::Vec3` data and a linear interpolator. Its public method `getOrCreateKeyframeContainer()` can return a valid 3D vector key-frame container object at any time.

The following table lists the types of samplers and the associated container and key-frame classes within the `osgAnimation` namespace:

Sampler class	Key-frame class	Value type
FloatStepSampler	FloatKeyframe	float
DoubleLinearSampler	DoubleKeyframe	double
Vec2LinearSampler	Vec2Keyframe	osg::Vec2
Vec3LinearSampler	Vec3Keyframe	osg::Vec3
Vec4LinearSampler	Vec4Keyframe	osg::Vec4
QuatSphericalLinearSampler	QuatKeyframe	osg::Quat
MatrixLinearSampler	MatrixKeyframe	osg::Matrixf

In order to add key-frames to a given sampler object, just type:

```
// Again, assume it is a 3D vector sampler
sampler->getOrCreateKeyframeContainer()->push_back(
    osgAnimation::Vec3Keyframe(0.0, osg::Vec3(…)) );   // Frame at 0s
sampler->getOrCreateKeyframeContainer()->push_back(
    osgAnimation::Vec3Keyframe(2.0, osg::Vec3(…)) );   // Frame at 2s
```

Channels and animation managers

Now it's time to handle samplers full of preset key-frames. The
osgAnimation::TemplateChannel<> class accepts a certain sampler class as the
argument and represents the association of the sampler and a "target". The channel's
name is set by the setName() method, and the target it is looking for is defined by the
setTargetName() method.

The target objects are often osgAnimation built-in **update callbacks**. They should be
attached to specific nodes with the setUpdateCallback() method. The osgAnimation:
:UpdateMatrixTransform is a typical one. It updates the host osg::MatrixTransform
node and changes the transformation matrix using the channel results per frame. We will
have a look at its usage in the following example.

A channel that contains a 3D vector's sampler can be replaced by the
osgAnimation::Vec3LinearChannel class, and the one with a spherical linear
quaternion sampler is called osgAnimation::QuatSphericalLinearChannel,
and so on.

After finishing designing all key-frames and animation channels, the last step in constructing
our animation scene is to declare a manager class for all channels. Before that, we define
the osgAnimation::Animation class for containing a series of animation channels, as
if they were in the same layer. Channels can be added into the animation object with the
addChannel() method.

The osgAnimation::BasicAnimationManager class is the final "butler" of all animation
objects. It manages osgAnimation::Animation objects via the registerAnimation(),
unregisterAnimation(), and getAnimationList() methods, and controls the playing
states of one or more animation objects via the playAnimation(), stopAnimation(),
and isPlaying() methods. It is an **update callback**, too, but should be set to the **root
node**, in order to give full control of animations all over the **scene graph**.

The entire process can be described with the following image:

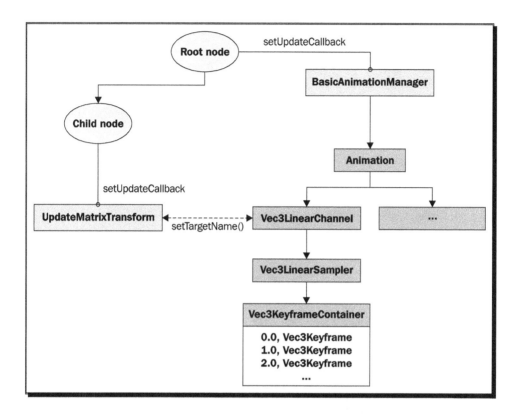

Time for action – managing animation channels

To achieve the same animation effect that the animation path example has already done, we have to create two channels, one with a *position animation* target and the other with a *rotation* one.

The createAnimationPath() function, which generates a circular path around the origin point, can be reused. But instead of just combining the position and rotation values into a control point structure, these two kinds of key frames should be added to separate containers that belong to different animation channels.

1. Include the necessary headers:

    ```cpp
    #include <osg/MatrixTransform>
    #include <osgAnimation/BasicAnimationManager>
    #include <osgAnimation/UpdateMatrixTransform>
    #include <osgAnimation/StackedTranslateElement>
    #include <osgAnimation/StackedQuaternionElement>
    #include <osgDB/ReadFile>
    #include <osgViewer/Viewer>
    ```

2. The algorithm of `createAnimationPath()` is still usable. The only difference is that the calculated values should be put into different types of key-frame objects (`Vec3KeyFrame` and `QuatKeyFrame`), and then added to input containers:

    ```cpp
    void createAnimationPath( float radius, float time,
        osgAnimation::Vec3KeyframeContainer* container1,
        osgAnimation::QuatKeyframeContainer* container2 )
    {
        unsigned int numSamples = 32;
        float delta_yaw = 2.0f * osg::PI/((float)numSamples - 1.0f);
        float delta_time = time / (float)numSamples;
        for ( unsigned int i=0; i<numSamples; ++i )
        {
            float yaw = delta_yaw * (float)i;
            osg::Vec3 pos( sinf(yaw)*radius, cosf(yaw)*radius, 0.0f );
            osg::Quat rot( -yaw, osg::Z_AXIS );
            container1->push_back(
                osgAnimation::Vec3Keyframe(delta_time * (float)i, pos)
        );
            container2->push_back(
                osgAnimation::QuatKeyframe(delta_time * (float)i, rot)
        );
        }
    }
    ```

3. In the main function, we are going to first declare a "position animation" channel and a "rotation animation" channel (the `QuatSphericalChannel` can realize the same effect as the `slerp()` method of `osg::Quat`). Their names should be unique, and the target name should be same as their updater. Otherwise, the channel will not be recognized correctly:

    ```cpp
    osg::ref_ptr<osgAnimation::Vec3LinearChannel> ch1 =
        new osgAnimation::Vec3LinearChannel;
    ch1->setName( "position" );
    ch1->setTargetName( "PathCallback" );
    ```

```
osg::ref_ptr<osgAnimation::QuatSphericalLinearChannel> ch2 =
    new osgAnimation::QuatSphericalLinearChannel;
ch2->setName( "quat" );
ch2->setTargetName( "PathCallback" );
```

4. The key-frame containers of the channels will receive proper animation data in the createAnimationPath() function, as described above:

```
createAnimationPath( 50.0f, 6.0f,
    ch1->getOrCreateSampler()->getOrCreateKeyframeContainer(),
    ch2->getOrCreateSampler()->getOrCreateKeyframeContainer() );
```

5. Now we are going to create an osg::Animation object to contain these two channels and define their general behaviors. The setPlayMode() method just equals to setLoopMode() of osg::AnimationPath:

```
osg::ref_ptr<osgAnimation::Animation> animation = new
osgAnimation::Animation;
animation->setPlayMode( osgAnimation::Animation::LOOP );
animation->addChannel( ch1.get() );
animation->addChannel( ch2.get() );
```

6. The animation is set, but is not attached to any scene elements. Because it will effect transformation nodes, we have to create a "transform updater" target here, to match all channels of the animation. Its stacked elements and the channels are put into a one-to-one relationship, by using the same name string:

```
osg::ref_ptr<osgAnimation::UpdateMatrixTransform> updater =
    new osgAnimation::UpdateMatrixTransform("PathCallback");
updater->getStackedTransforms().push_back(
    new osgAnimation::StackedTranslateElement("position") );
updater->getStackedTransforms().push_back(
    new osgAnimation::StackedQuaternionElement("quat") );
```

7. The Cessna is loaded with the help of a pseudo-loader, and placed under an osg::MatrixTransform parent. The transformation parent node, to which transformation animations can be applied, will accept the updater as an **update callback**. The data variance here ensures that the processing of animation is always safe:

```
osg::ref_ptr<osg::MatrixTransform> animRoot= new
osg::MatrixTransform;
animRoot->addChild( osgDB::readNodeFile("cessna.osg.0,0,90.rot")
);
animRoot->setDataVariance( osg::Object::DYNAMIC );
animRoot->setUpdateCallback( updater.get() );
```

8. As we have only one animation object to play, a basic manager is enough. The next step is to create an `osgAnimation::BasicAnimationManager` object and register the animation to it:

```
osg::ref_ptr<osgAnimation::BasicAnimationManager> manager =
    new osgAnimation::BasicAnimationManager;
manager->registerAnimation( animation.get() );
```

9. The manager is also an **update callback**, so attach it to the root node of the **scene graph**:

```
osg::ref_ptr<osg::Group> root = new osg::Group;
root->addChild( animRoot.get() );
root->setUpdateCallback( manager.get() );
```

10. Now, play the animation. Of course, you can also put this line in a customized callback:

```
manager->playAnimation( animation.get() );
```

11. Start the viewer:

```
osgViewer::Viewer viewer;
viewer.setSceneData( root.get() );
return viewer.run();
```

12. The result is completely the same as the animation path example. It is a little too complicated, with so many objects, to achieve such a simple animation. We introduce this example here only to illustrate the overall structure of `osgAnimation` elements, with the hope that it can inspire more brains and thoughts.

What just happened?

The `osgAnimation::UpdateMatrixTransform` object here is the target of both animation channels, because its name, `PathCallback`, set in the constructor, is also used by the `setTargetName()` method of channels.

But this is not enough. The updater should also know what action each channel will take, and link the channels to the correct action handlers. For example, an `osgAnimation::Vec3LinearChannel` object can be used to represent either a 3D position, or the Euler angles for implementing rotation. To judge the actual work it will be applied to, we have to push some stacked elements into the updater, each of which is associated with a predefined channel. This is done by adding to the list returned by `getStackedTransforms()` method, which is indirectly derived from `std::vector`.

Usable stacked elements include StackedTranslateElement (translation action), StackedScaleElement (scale action), StackedRotateAxisElement (Euler rotation action), StackedQuaternionElement (quaternion rotation action), and StackedMatrixElement (matrix assignment action). All of these are defined in the osgAnimation namespace, and are linked to channels of the same name.

Loading and rendering characters

The osgAnimation library has certain classes for implementing character animations. The osgAnimation::Bone and osgAnimation::Skeleton classes are used to construct a complete skeleton in the **scene graph**. The osgAnimation::UpdateBone class defines how to update bones from animation channels.

Unfortunately, it is not easy to build your own characters in OSG, especially when starting completely from scratch. A simpler way is to load a character model file and play it in your OSG applications. Collada DAE is a great royalty-free format that beginners can use to create and save animation characters. You may find more information about the open standards and tools at: https://collada.org.

Autodesk FBX is a good file format, too, but it can only be supported by commercial software.

OSG can read both formats directly via the osgDB::readNodeFile() function, assuming that you have the third party libraries and have compiled the corresponding OSG plugin. Please refer to *Chapter 10*, *Saving and Loading Files* for details of how to do this.

Time for action – creating and driving a character system

Now we are going to load and play animations for an existing OSG character: bignathan. This was created by the principal author of osgAnimation, and contains a few comic animations. The main work here is to obtain the animation manager from the **root node**, list all available animations, and play a certain animation within it.

1. Include the necessary headers:

```
#include <osgAnimation/BasicAnimationManager>
#include <osgDB/ReadFile>
#include <osgViewer/Viewer>
#include <iostream>
```

2. We would like to configure two arguments for the application. The argument `--animation` specifies a name string that will be played in the application, and `--listall` lists all available animations on the console:

```
osg::ArgumentParser arguments( &argc, argv );

bool listAll = false;
std::string animationName;
arguments.read( "--animation", animationName );
if ( arguments.read("--listall") ) listAll = true;
```

3. Make sure that `bignathan.osg` is loaded; otherwise, we can't continue with this example. It should be located in the sample data directory defined by the environment variable `OSG_FILE_PATH`. You may obtain it by running the installer, or by searching the OSG website:

```
osg::ref_ptr<osg::Node> model =
    osgDB::readNodeFile("bignathan.osg");
if ( !model ) return 1;
```

4. Try getting the animation manager from the **update callback** of the model root:

```
osgAnimation::BasicAnimationManager* manager =
    dynamic_cast<osgAnimation::BasicAnimationManager*>
    ( model->getUpdateCallback() );
if ( !manager ) return 1;
```

5. Now it's time to iterate over all animations recorded in the manager. If the `--listall` argument is read from the command line, each animation's name should also be printed on the screen. Play the animation that matches the input name following the `--animation` argument:

```
const osgAnimation::AnimationList& animations =
    manager->getAnimationList();
if ( listAll ) std::cout << "**** Animations ****" << std::endl;
for ( unsigned int i=0; i<animations.size(); ++i )
{
    const std::string& name = animations[i]->getName();
    if ( name==animationName )
        manager->playAnimation( animations[i].get() );
    if ( listAll ) std::cout << name << std::endl;
}
if ( listAll )
{
    std::cout << "********************" << std::endl;
    return 0;
}
```

6. Start the viewer, now:

```
osgViewer::Viewer viewer;
viewer.setSceneData( model.get() );
return viewer.run();
```

7. Start the prompt. The first step is to list all animations and see which one is more interesting. Type the following command and have a look at the output (assuming that the executable file is `MyProject.exe`):

 # MyProject.exe --listall

The output is as follows:

```
**** Animations ****
Idle_Head_Scratch.02
Idle_Nose_Scratch.02
Idle_Nose_Scratch.01
Idle_Head_Scratch.01
Idle_Main
MatIpo_ipo
*********************
```

8. Type the command with the `--animation` argument this time:

 # MyProject.exe --animation Idle_Head_Scratch_01

9. Now we are able to see the polygonal boy scratching his head all the time:

What just happened?

Maybe you are eager to learn how to create characters with animations, rather than loading them into OSG, and start rendering. But again, it is out of the scope of this book. There are a couple of 3D modeling software for you to use: Autodesk 3dsmax, Autodesk Maya, Blender, and so on. Try outputting your works to FBX format, or you may choose to convert it to OSG native formats by using some exporting tools, such as Cedric Pinson's Blender Exporter: `http://hg.plopbyte.net/osgexport/`. This is controlled by Mercurial, a popular source control management tool.

In addition to the character solution in `osgAnimation`, there exist more third-party projects that handle character animations. One of them is known as Cal3D project. This has an OSG wrapper project named `osgCal2`. It is suggested that you have a look at the following websites to see if they are more preferred in your applications:

* `http://cal3d.sourceforge.net/`
* `http://osgcal.sourceforge.net/`

Have a go hero – analyzing the structure of your character

Are you interesting in the structure of `bignathan`? As introduced before, it should be made up of `osgAnimation::Bone` and `osgAnimation::Skeleton` classes, which are actually nodes. Therefore, a node visitor can be used to analyze the scene graph and see how it is constructed and traversed.

Alter the node visitor example in *Chapter 5*, *Managing Scene Graph* and use it to view and operate all of the bone nodes in the character file. A suggestion is that you may read out the **update callback** attached with each `osgAnimation::Bone` node, and, if possible, build your own `biped` with `bignathan` used as a reference. They often have the same skeletons in design.

Summary

OSG supports all major types of animation that can be applied in 3D applications. The most common is transformation over time, which can be achieved by changing the spatial status or even rendering states of a 3D object, while the so called key-frame animation is designed to achieve smooth movement by interpolating between frames. Skeleton system is the key for character animation, in which a mesh is used to rig to a prebuilt skeleton.

In this chapter, we introduced the capabilities of OSG animation classes' and specifically covered:

- The reason for and methods to avoid conflicted modifications, especially when creating dynamic geometries
- Deriving from the callback base classes, including `osg::NodeCallback`, `osg::StateAttributeCallback`, and so on
- Interpolating transformation values in a path animation by using the `osg::AnimationPath` and `osg::AnimationPathCallback` classes
- Using ease motion classes such as `osgAnimation::LinearMotion` and `osgAnimation::InOutCubicMotion` to achieve nature motion effects
- Generating animated textures using the `osg::ImageSequence` class
- How to create complex generic key-frame animation by using the `osgAnimation` library, as well as the concept of animation channels and the way to control them
- Managing and animating rigged characters from existing files

9
Interacting with Outside Elements

*OSG provides a graphical user interface (GUI) abstraction library that centralizes the commonality of implementations of different windowing systems (MFC, Qt, GLUT, and so on). It handles GUI events, among which the most commonly seen is the user's real-time interaction with peripheral devices such as the mouse and keyboard. In addition, the **osgViewer** library encapsulates different windowing systems' graphics contexts for constructing rendering environments. These constitute the topic of this chapter: how OSG interacts with other elements—for instance, input devices and windowing systems.*

In this chapter, we will tell you:

- ◆ How to handle keyboard and mouse events with customized event handlers
- ◆ How to create and handle user-defined events
- ◆ How to understand the intersection test of scene objects
- ◆ How to configure traits of a window, and thus create the graphical context
- ◆ How to integrate the rendered scene into a windowing system

Various events

A **graphical user interface (GUI)** is a type of interface object that allows computer users to interact with programs in many ways, via so called GUI events. There are always different kinds of events that can be handled to respond to corresponding user operations, for instance, moving the mouse device, clicking a mouse button, pressing a key, resizing windows, and even waiting until a deadline has been reached.

In today's GUI framework, a widget element is always defined to receive these user actions and transfer them to an event handler object. The latter is written by high-level developers to implement specific functionalities. For example, to pop up a dialog when clicking the **Browse** button, or to save current content of a text editor to a file when pressing the *S* key.

Unfortunately, most frameworks, including MFC and .NET under Windows, GTK+ under Linux, Cocoa under Mac OS X, and some cross-platform systems like Qt and wxWidgets, are incompatible with each other. Therefore they are not so convenient for direct use in an OSG application. Instead, OSG provides a basic interface for anyone who wants to handle GUI events, called the `osgGA::GUIEventHandler`.

This event handler class should be attached to the scene viewer with the `addEventHandler()` method of the viewer, and removed with the `removeEventHandler()` method. It is a kind of callback that will automatically be called during the **event traversal**, which is introduced in the *Traversing the scene graph* section of *Chapter 5, Managing Scene Graph*.

When inheriting `osgGA::GUIEventHandler` to implement your own event handlers, the most important work is to override the `handle()` method. This has two arguments: the `osgGA::GUIEventAdapter` parameter that supplies the received events, and the `osgGA::GUIActionAdapter` parameter for feedback. The method can be written like this:

```
bool handle( const osgGA::GUIEventAdapter& ea,
             osgGA::GUIActionAdapter& aa )
{
    … // concrete operations
}
```

The `osgGA::GUIEventAdapter` class will be introduced in the next section. The `osgGA::GUIActionAdapter` allows the handler to ask the GUI to take some action in response to an incoming event. In most cases, this can actually be considered as the viewer object. That is because the `osgViewer::Viewer` class is also derived from `osgGA::GUIActionAdapter`. The `dynamic_cast<>` operator can be used here to perform the conversion in a safe way:

```
osgViewer::Viewer* viewer = dynamic_cast<osgViewer::Viewer*>(&aa);
```

Here, aa is the input parameter of the `handle()` method of `osgGA::GUIEventHandler`.

Handling mouse and keyboard inputs

The `osgGA::GUIEventAdapter` class manages all kinds of OSG supported events, including both setting and getting methods for them. The `getEventType()` method returns the current GUI event stored in an event adapter. Every time the overriding `handle()` method is called, we have to check this first to determine the event type and take appropriate countermeasures.

The following table shows the main event types in OSG, as well as the related methods used to get the necessary event arguments:

Event type value	Description	Related methods
PUSH/RELEASE/DOUBLECLICK	The push, release, and double-click events of the mouse	Get the current mouse position: `getX()`, `getY()`
		Get the related button: `getButton()`; return value can be one of:
		`LEFT_MOUSE_BUTTON`, `MIDDLE_MOUSE_BUTTON`, or `RIGHT_MOUSE_BUTTON`
SCROLL	The scrolling motion of the mouse	Get the motion value: `getScrollingMotion()`; return value can be one of:
		`SCROLL_UP`, `SCROLL_DOWN`, `SCROLL_LEFT`, or `SCROLL_RIGHT`
DRAG	The mouse drag event	Get the current mouse position: `getX()`, `getY()`
		Get the current mouse button state: `getButtonMask()`; return value is the same as `getButton()`
MOVE	The mouse move event	Get the current mouse position: `getX()`, `getY()`
KEYDOWN/KEYUP	The key up and down events of the keyboard	Get the related key value: `getKey()`; the return value can be any ASCII character for letter keys, or values in the `Key_Symbol` enumeration (for example `KEY_BackSpace` for the backspace key)
FRAME	An event that occurs every frame	None

Event type value	Description	Related methods
USER	A user-defined event for more extensions.	Get the user data pointer: `getUserData()`; the user data object must be derived from the `osg::Referenced` base class

There is another `getModKeyMask()` method that can be used to get the current modifier key when moving or clicking the mouse or pressing the keys on the keyboard. The return value is bitwise OR'ed with values including `MODKEY_CTRL`, `MODKEY_SHIFT`, `MODKEY_ALT`, and so on. So we can check to see if the `Ctrl` key is pushed with the following code segment:

```
if ( ea.getModKeyMask()&osgGA::GUIEventAdapter::MODKEY_CTRL )
{
    …   // Related operations
}
```

Be aware that the corresponding setting methods of all getting ones above, including `setEventType()`, `setX()`, `setY()`, and so on, are not suitable for use in the `handle()` implementation. They are often called by the low-level graphics window system of OSG to push new events to the event queue.

Time for action – driving the Cessna

We have learnt how to change the transformation matrix of a model with the `osg::MatrixTransform` nodes. With the help of the `osg::AnimationPath` class and the `osgAnimation` namespace, we can even create animation effects on these transformable objects. But this is not enough for an interactive scene. Our further requirement is to control scene graph nodes with user input devices. Imagine that we have a submarine, a tank, or a familiar Cessna in a modern warfare game. It will be really exciting if we can simulate driving it with the keyboard, mouse, or even joysticks.

1. Include the necessary headers:

    ```
    #include <osg/MatrixTransform>
    #include <osgDB/ReadFile>
    #include <osgGA/GUIEventHandler>
    #include <osgViewer/Viewer>
    ```

2. Our task is to take control of a Cessna model with some keys. To handle these user events, we have to declare a `ModelController` class, which is derived from the `osgGA::GUIEventHandler` base class, and override the `handle()` method to make sure that all user events are passed in as an `osgGA::GUIEventAdapter` object. The model pointer is also included in the handler class; otherwise there is no way to tell which model is going to be controlled:

```
class ModelController : public osgGA::GUIEventHandler
{
public:
    ModelController( osg::MatrixTransform* node )
: _model(node)
{}
    virtual bool handle( const osgGA::GUIEventAdapter& ea,
                         osgGA::GUIActionAdapter& aa );

protected:
    osg::ref_ptr<osg::MatrixTransform> _model;
};
```

3. In the implementation of the `handle()` method, we will modify the Euler angles of the member variable `_model`, which can be a transformation node representing a Cessna or other models. The character keys `w`, `s`, `a`, and `d` can easily describe the heading and pitch rotations of the aircraft via a common `KEYDOWN` event. Of course, function keys and navigation keys, including `KEY_Left`, `KEY_Right`, and so on, are also available for use here:

```
bool ModelController::handle( const osgGA::GUIEventAdapter& ea,
                              osgGA::GUIActionAdapter& aa )
{
    if ( !_model ) return false;
    osg::Matrix matrix = _model->getMatrix();

    switch ( ea.getEventType() )
    {
    case osgGA::GUIEventAdapter::KEYDOWN:
        switch ( ea.getKey() )
        {
        case 'a': case 'A':
            matrix *= osg::Matrix::rotate(-0.1f, osg::Z_AXIS);
            break;
        case 'd': case 'D':
            matrix *= osg::Matrix::rotate(0.1f, osg::Z_AXIS);
            break;
        case 'w': case 'W':
            matrix *= osg::Matrix::rotate(-0.1f, osg::X_AXIS);
            break;
        case 's': case 'S':
            matrix *= osg::Matrix::rotate(0.1f, osg::X_AXIS);
            break;
        default:
```

```
            break;
        }
        _model->setMatrix( matrix );
        break;
    default:
        break;
    }
    return false;
}
```

4. In the main function, we will first load the Cessna model and add it to an `osg::MatrixTransform` parent. The parent node will be used as the controlled object and transferred to a `ModelController` handler instance:

```
osg::ref_ptr<osg::Node> model = osgDB::readNodeFile( "cessna.osg"
);

osg::ref_ptr<osg::MatrixTransform> mt = new osg::MatrixTransform;
mt->addChild( model.get() );

osg::ref_ptr<osg::Group> root = new osg::Group;
root->addChild( mt.get() );
```

5. Initialize the model controller and pass the transformation node as an argument:

```
osg::ref_ptr<ModelController> ctrler =
    new ModelController( mt.get() );
```

6. We don't want the camera manipulator to work in this example, because it may also affect the **model-view matrix** of the viewer when using the keyboard and mouse, and confuse the result of handling GUI events. Therefore, in addition to adding the created event handler, we will prevent the **main camera** from receiving any user events with the `setAllowEventFocus()` method, and set a suitable **view matrix** by ourselves (because the manipulator can't contact the camera now):

```
osgViewer::Viewer viewer;
viewer.addEventHandler( ctrler.get() );
viewer.getCamera()->setViewMatrixAsLookAt(
    osg::Vec3(0.0f,-100.0f,0.0f), osg::Vec3(), osg::Z_AXIS );
viewer.getCamera()->setAllowEventFocus( false );
```

7. Now start the viewer:

```
viewer.setSceneData( root.get() );
return viewer.run();
```

8. We will find that the camera manipulator (its default behavior is trackball-like) losses control of the **main camera**, and none of the mouse buttons can navigate in the scene now. However, pressing the four character keys has an effect on the Cessna now. Be aware, that the keyboard event here only works on the model node, but not on the whole **scene graph**. You may add another stationary node to the **root node** and see if it can be changed at any time:

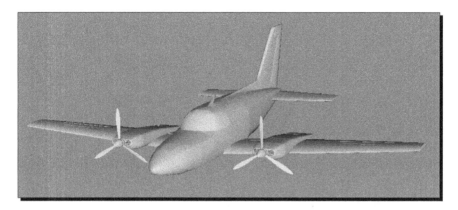

What just happened?

Event handlers can be used for many purposes. In a hander callback, we can move and rotate transformable nodes, record animation paths, add or remove children from a parent node, compute frame rates and free memory, and do anything we want. It is triggered in the **event traversal**, thus it is always safe for dynamic data modification.

An interesting question here is how to decide the return value of the handle() method. The required Boolean value here is used to indicate whether the event has already been handled or not. If true is returned, OSG believes that the user event is no longer needed by any subsequent handlers, including the camera manipulator. The event will be marked as "handled" and will be ignored by other handlers or event callbacks by default. In most cases in this book, we don't want this behavior. So false will always be returned without any doubts in this and subsequent examples.

Pop quiz – handling events within nodes

Similar to update callbacks, OSG also allows event callbacks to be set to nodes and drawables, using the `setEventCallback()` and `addEventCallback()` methods, both of which accept an `osg::NodeCallback` pointer as the unique parameter. To obtain the event variable in the overrode `operator()`, we can just convert the node visitor to an `osg::EventVisitor` pointer:

```
#include <osgGA/EventVisitor>
…
void operator()( osg::Node* node, osg::NodeVisitor* nv )
{
    std::list< osg::ref_ptr<osgGA::GUIEventAdapter> > events;

    osgGA::EventVisitor* ev = dynamic_cast<osgGA::EventVisitor*>(nv);
    if (ev) events = ev->getEvents();
    …  // Handle events with the node
}
```

Can you tell the major difference between using node callbacks and event handlers? Is it better to reproduce this example using a customized event callback on the transformation node?

Have a go hero – manipulating the cameras

Believe it or not, the `osgGA::CameraManipulator` class also has a virtual method named `handle()`. This is actually derived from the `osgGA::GUIEventHandler`, but is not suitable for adding to the viewer with the `addEventHandler()` method. It navigates the **main camera** by calling the `getInverseMatrix()` virtual method, which computes the inverse transformation matrix of the manipulator, that is, the **view matrix**, and set it to the **main camera** with the `setViewMatrix()` method during the **update traversal**. All OSG manipulators, including user customized ones, should override this method to make sure that they work properly.

The `osgGA::CameraManipulator` class also provides the `setByMatrix()` and `getMatrix()` virtual methods which can be overridden to specify or obtain the transformation matrix. Try rewriting all of these methods to produce your own camera manipulators. The standard manipulators, including `osgGA::TrackballManipulator`, among others, can be very good references for this activity.

Adding customized events

OSG uses an internal event queue to manage coming GUI events in a first in first out (FIFO) list. Events at the beginning will be handled first and then erased from the list. That is, the `handle()` method of each added event handler will be executed as many times as the size of the event queue. The event queue class, named `osgGA::EventQueue`, allows new events to be pushed in with the `addEvent()` method at any time. Its argument is an `osgGA::GUIEventAdapter` pointer, which uses setting methods like `setEventType()` and `setButton()` to define its behavior.

There are some additional methods of the `osgGA::EventQueue` class that can be used to quickly set and add new GUI events. One of them is the `userEvent()` method, which adapts user-defined events with a user data pointer as the argument. This user data can be used to represent any kind of customized event, for instance, the timer event described in the following section.

It is of no use to create a completely new event queue object. The viewer class has already defined one to operate on:

```
viewer.getEventQueue()->userEvent( data );
```

Here, the variable `data` is an object derived from `osg::Referenced`. After adding this new event, the event handler will receive a `USER` event and developers can then read from the `getUserData()` method of the handler and do anything they want.

Time for action – creating a user timer

A timer event is emitted whenever the internal counter reaches a specified interval. This is common in various GUI systems, and allows users to set a customized timer callback to receive the timing message and implement related operations.

Now we are able to realize the same work in OSG. As there are no standard timer events defined in the `osgGA::GUIEventAdapter` class, we have to make use of the `USER` event type, as well as an additional data pointer.

1. Include the necessary headers:

```
#include <osg/Switch>
#include <osgDB/ReadFile>
#include <osgGA/GUIEventHandler>
#include <osgViewer/Viewer>
#include <iostream>
```

2. A `TimerInfo` structure is first defined to manage the parameters (mainly the trigger time of the timer) of the timer event. We have to attach this `osg::Referenced` derived pointer to the `userEvent()` method, because it is the only element for distinguishing between different customized events:

```cpp
struct TimerInfo : public osg::Referenced
{
    TimerInfo( unsigned int c ) : _count(c) {}
    unsigned int _count;
};
```

3. The `TimerHandler` is used for both processing the timer object and handling timer events. We would like to switch between normal and afire states of a Cessna model every time we receive such an event. In *Chapter 5*, *Managing Scene Graph* and *Chapter 8*, *Animating Scene Object*, this is done by customizing the `osg::Node` class and the update callback. But this time we will try using the event handler with an input `osg::Switch` pointer as the argument:

```cpp
class TimerHandler : public osgGA::GUIEventHandler
{
public:
    TimerHandler( osg::Switch* sw ) : _switch(sw), _count(0) {}
    virtual bool handle( const osgGA::GUIEventAdapter& ea,
                         osgGA::GUIActionAdapter& aa );

protected:
    osg::ref_ptr<osg::Switch> _switch;
    unsigned int _count;
};
```

4. There are two kinds of events to handle in the overrode `handle()` method. The FRAME event is automatically emitted with every frame and can be used to manage and increase an internal counter, and send `userEvent()` to the event queue when time is ripe. In this example, we assume that the timer event is emitted every 100 counts. The other one is the USER event, which doesn't contain any information except a `TimerInfo` object as the "user data" to indicate the timer and its counts. Here, we will print the count number and switch between child nodes of the variable `_switch`:

```cpp
bool TimerHandler::handle( const osgGA::GUIEventAdapter& ea,
                           osgGA::GUIActionAdapter& aa )
{
    switch ( ea.getEventType() )
    {
    case osgGA::GUIEventAdapter::FRAME:
```

```
        if (_count % 100 == 0 )
        {
            osgViewer::Viewer* viewer =
                dynamic_cast<osgViewer::Viewer*>(&aa);
            if ( viewer )
            {
                viewer->getEventQueue()->userEvent(
                    new TimerInfo(_count) );
            }
        }
        _count++;
        break;
    case osgGA::GUIEventAdapter::USER:
        if ( _switch.valid() )
        {
            const TimerInfo* ti =
                dynamic_cast<const TimerInfo*>( ea.getUserData()
);
            std::cout << "Timer event at: " <<ti->_count<<
            std::endl;

            _switch->setValue( 0, !_switch->getValue(0) );
            _switch->setValue( 1, !_switch->getValue(1) );
        }
        break;
    default:
        break;
    }
    return false;
}
```

5. In the main function, we simply create the switch node, which contains a normal Cessna model and an afire one:

```
osg::ref_ptr<osg::Node> model1= osgDB::readNodeFile("cessna.osg");
osg::ref_ptr<osg::Node> model2= osgDB::readNodeFile("cessnafire.
osg");

osg::ref_ptr<osg::Switch> root = new osg::Switch;
root->addChild( model1.get(), false );
root->addChild( model2.get(), true );
```

6. Add the timer event sender and handler to the viewer, and start it:

```
osgViewer::Viewer viewer;
viewer.setSceneData( root.get() );
viewer.addEventHandler( new TimerHandler(root.get()) );
return viewer.run();
```

7. As we have seen for times, the Cessna is alternating between intact and afire. In addition, there are messages appearing on the console screen, which tell us when the timer is trigged:

```
Timer event at: 0
Timer event at: 100
Timer event at: 200
Timer event at: 300
Timer event at: 400
Timer event at: 500
Timer event at: 600
```

What just happened?

We made use of the FRAME event here to check and emit user events to the event queue. This leads to an architecture that is a little weird: the event sender and the receiver is the same TimeHandler class. This is similar to the postman and the addressee being the same person!

In fact, we can easily avoid this problem. The occasion to emit a user event is determined every frame. A new user event can be added to the event queue at any time in an update or cull traversal. That is, callbacks, customized nodes,and drawables can all be used as an event sender, rather than the event handler itself. This makes it possible to obtain and handle complex events like joysticks and data gloves. Declare a structure named JoyStickInfo or DataGloveInfo with the necessary information, set its attributes, emit user events with the instance of the structure in an **update callback**, and handle user events in the handler. That is all we need to make the user event mechanism work.

Pop quiz – global and node-related events

We have already demonstrated two kinds of event handlers in the last two examples: the `ModelController`, which controls a node's orientations, and the `TimerHandler`, which simulates timer events. So, continue our discussion and quiz: do you think an event callback is suitable for re-implementing the timer example? And what about implementing the picking example in the next section with callbacks (read it first and then come back to this question)?

Picking objects

The picking functionality allows users to move the mouse over a portion of a rendered scene and click a button. The result may be an action of opening or closing a door, or shooting on an intruding alien in the 3D world. There are three main steps required to perform these kinds of actions.

Firstly, we use an event handler to receive mouse events. For example, a mouse push event comes along with the X and Y positions of the cursor, which are of course the most important factors of the picking operation.

Secondly, we have to determine which part of the scene graph is under the mouse cursor. This can be done by using the intersection tools provided by the **osgUtil** library. The result is a set of intersections that includes the picked drawable, its parent node path, the intersecting point, and so on.

Finally, we are going to make use of the intersection result to achieve our goals of picking objects or making them fight.

Intersection

OSG has its own intersection strategy that makes use of the node visitor mechanism to reduce time consumption. It is always more efficient than OpenGL's selection feature. The `osgUtil::IntersectionVisitor` class is the implementer. It is derived from the `osg::NodeVisitor` class and can test nodes' bounding volumes against the input intersector and quickly skip sub-scene graphs that are not intersectable during the traversal.

The `osgUtil::IntersectionVisitor` object takes an `osgUtil::Intersector` derived object as the argument of its constructor. It can be configured for intersection tests with several intersectors, including line segments, planes, and polytopes. An intersector can work in four kinds of coordinate system, each of which has different input parameters and can convert them to world space with different transformation matrices. In the following table, we will take the line segment intersector class `osgUtil::LineSegmentIntersector`, to use as an example:

Coordinate system	Input parameters	Requirement
MODEL	Two osg::Vec3 vertices in the local space as the endpoints	No more requirements. The vertices in the world space will be automatically computed during the traversal.
VIEW	Two osg::Vec3 vertices in the view space as the endpoints	One or more osg::Camera nodes must exist in the **scene graph** to be traversed to provide a valid **view matrix**.
PROJECTION	Two double values are required as a point on the projection plane, ranging from (-1, -1) to (1, 1)	One or more osg::Camera nodes must exist to provide a valid **view matrix** and a **projection matrix**.
WINDOW	Two double values are required as a point on the screen	One or more osg::Camera nodes must exist to provide a valid **view matrix**, **projection matrix**, and **window matrix**.

Assume that we are going to make an intersection test in the handle() method of an event handler. The WINDOW coordinate system can then be used here to obtain a ray from the mouse position into the 3D scene. The following code segment shows how this works on a camera node camera:

```
osg::ref_ptr<osgUtil::LineSegmentIntersector> intersector =
    new osgUtil::LineSegmentIntersector(
        osgUtil::Intersector::WINDOW, ea.getX(), ea.getY()
    );
osgUtil::IntersectionVisitor iv( intersector.get() );
camera->accept( iv );
```

The containsIntersections() method of the intersector can be used to check if there is any intersecting result. The getIntersections() method of osgUtil::LineSegmentIntersector returns a set of Intersection variables, ascending from the nearest to the viewer, to the farthest. The intersection point can be found by calling the getLocalIntersectPoint() method or getWorldIntersectPoint() method of one of these result variables, for example:

```
osgUtil::LineSegmentIntersector::Intersection& result =
    *( intersector->getIntersections().begin());
osg::Vec3 point = result.getWorldIntersectPoint();  // in world space
```

The first line can also be rewritten as:

```
osgUtil::LineSegmentIntersector::Intersection& result =
    intersector->getIntersections().front();
```

Similarly, we can obtain the intersected `drawable` object, its parent node path `nodePath`, and even the `indexList` which lists all vertices and indices of triangles intersected with the line segment, from the result's member variables, for future use.

Time for action – clicking and selecting geometries

Our task this time is to implement a very common task in 3D software—clicking to select an object in the world and showing a selection box around the object. The bounding box of the selected geometry should be good for representing a selection box, and the `osg::ShapeDrawable` class can quickly generate a simple box for display purposes. The `osg::PolygonMode` attribute will then make the rendering pipeline only draw the wireframes of the box, which helps to show the selection box as brackets. These are all we need to produce practical picking object functionalities.

1. Include the necessary headers:

```
#include <osg/MatrixTransform>
#include <osg/ShapeDrawable>
#include <osg/PolygonMode>
#include <osgDB/ReadFile>
#include <osgUtil/LineSegmentIntersector>
#include <osgViewer/Viewer>
```

2. The `PickHandler` will do everything required for our task, including an intersection test of the mouse cursor and the **scene graph**, creating and returning the selection box node (the `_selectionBox` variable in this example), and transforming the box around the selected object when pressing the mouse button:

```
class PickHandler : public osgGA::GUIEventHandler
{
public:
    osg::Node* getOrCreateSelectionBox();
    virtual bool handle( const osgGA::GUIEventAdapter& ea,
                         osgGA::GUIActionAdapter& aa );

protected:
    osg::ref_ptr<osg::MatrixTransform> _selectionBox;
};
```

3. In the following method, we will allocate and return a valid selection box node to the main function. There are several points to note here: firstly, the `osg::Box` object will not be changed at runtime, but a parent transformation node will be used and modified instead, for the reason of simplifying operations; secondly, the `GL_LIGHTING` mode and the `osg::PolygonMode` attribute should be used to make the selection box more natural; finally, there is also a confusing `setNodeMask()` call, which will be explained later:

```
osg::Node* PickHandler::getOrCreateSelectionBox()
{
    if ( !_selectionBox )
    {
        osg::ref_ptr<osg::Geode> geode = new osg::Geode;
        geode->addDrawable(
            new osg::ShapeDrawable(new osg::Box(osg::Vec3(),
                                   1.0f)) );

        _selectionBox = new osg::MatrixTransform;
        _selectionBox->setNodeMask( 0x1 );
        _selectionBox->addChild( geode.get() );

        osg::StateSet* ss = _selectionBox->getOrCreateStateSet();
        ss->setMode( GL_LIGHTING, osg::StateAttribute::OFF );
        ss->setAttributeAndModes(new osg::PolygonMode(
            osg::PolygonMode::FRONT_AND_
BACK,osg::PolygonMode::LINE));
    }
    return _selectionBox.get();
}
```

4. We are going to strictly limit the occasion of picking scene objects to make sure camera manipulation operations can work. It will only be called when the user is holding the `Ctrl` key and releasing the left mouse button. After that, we obtain the viewer by converting the `osgGA::GUIActionAdapter` object, and create an intersection visitor to find a node that can possibly be picked by the mouse cursor (be aware of the `setTraversalMask()` method here, which will be introduced along with the `setNodeMask()` method). Then the resulting drawable object and its parent node path can be used to describe the world position and scale of the bounding selection box:

```
bool PickHandler::handle( const osgGA::GUIEventAdapter& ea,
                          osgGA::GUIActionAdapter& aa )
{
    if ( ea.getEventType()!=osgGA::GUIEventAdapter::RELEASE ||
```

```
            ea.getButton()!=osgGA::GUIEventAdapter::LEFT_MOUSE_BUTTON
    ||
            !(ea.getModKeyMask()&osgGA::GUIEventAdapter::MODKEY_CTRL)
    )
        return false;

    osgViewer::Viewer* viewer =
      dynamic_cast<osgViewer::Viewer*>(&aa);
    if ( viewer )
    {
        osg::ref_ptr<osgUtil::LineSegmentIntersector>
            intersector =
            new osgUtil::LineSegmentIntersector(
                osgUtil::Intersector::WINDOW, ea.getX(), ea.getY()
            );
        osgUtil::IntersectionVisitor iv( intersector.get() );
        iv.setTraversalMask( ~0x1 );
        viewer->getCamera()->accept( iv );

        if ( intersector->containsIntersections() )
        {
            osgUtil::LineSegmentIntersector::Intersection&
                result =
                *(intersector->getIntersections().begin());

            osg::BoundingBox bb = result.drawable->getBound();
            osg::Vec3 worldCenter = bb.center() *
                osg::computeLocalToWorld(result.nodePath);
            _selectionBox->setMatrix(
                osg::Matrix::scale(bb.xMax()-bb.xMin(),
                                   bb.yMax()-bb.yMin(),
                                   bb.zMax()-bb.zMin()) *
                osg::Matrix::translate(worldCenter) );
        }
    }
    return false;
}
```

5. The remaining work is not hard to understand. We will first construct the **scene graph** by adding two models to the root node:

```
osg::ref_ptr<osg::Node> model1 = osgDB::readNodeFile( "cessna.osg"
);
osg::ref_ptr<osg::Node> model2 = osgDB::readNodeFile( "cow.osg" );
```

```
osg::ref_ptr<osg::Group> root = new osg::Group;
root->addChild( model1.get() );
root->addChild( model2.get() );
```

6. We create the picking handler, and add the value of `getOrCreateSelectionBox()` to the root node, too. This will make the selection box visible in the **scene graph**:

```
osg::ref_ptr<PickHandler> picker = new PickHandler;
root->addChild( picker->getOrCreateSelectionBox() );
```

7. OK, start the viewer with the `PickHandler` object as a customized event handler:

```
osgViewer::Viewer viewer;
viewer.setSceneData( root.get() );
viewer.addEventHandler( picker.get() );
return viewer.run();
```

8. Hold the *Ctrl* key and press on the cow. You will see a white selection box appear. Try moving your mouse and clicking on the Cessna, without releasing the *Ctrl* key. The selection box now migrates to the Cessna model, enclosing all of its vertices. All other operations will not be affected if the *Ctrl* key is not held down:

What just happened?

The `setNodeMask()` method of `osg::Node` class is introduced for some special purposes. It performs a bitwise logical AND operation with a certain scene controller to indicate that the node is available for use to the controller or not. For example, to make a node and its sub-scene graph untouchable to the intersection visitor, we can adjust the two operators, one of which is defined by `setNodeMask()` and the other is defined by the `setTraversalMask()` method of the `osg::NodeVisitor` class, to make the result of the logical AND zero. That is why we have these two lines in the previous example:

```
_selectionBox->setNodeMask( 0x1 );
...
iv.setTraversalMask( ~0x1 );
```

That makes the selection box itself not pickable by the visitor, as shown in the following diagram:

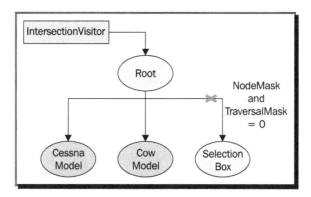

Have a go hero – selecting geometries in a rectangular region

osgUtil::LineSegmentIntersector is used for computing the intersection between a line segment and the **scene graph**. It accepts both model and window coordinate systems, thus the mouse position on the screen can be converted to a line segment from the near plane to the far plane, leading to desired results.

But what will happen if we left click and drag a rectangular region around all scene objects to be selected? There are four points to be recorded to form a rectangle, and actually eight points in the model coordinates, which constitutes a polyhedron. The osgUtil::PolytopeIntersector is recommended for this purpose. This accepts the coordinate frame and four screen points as input arguments, and returns a list of intersections as the result. Try making use of this class to select multiple geometries, and list all of them.

Windows, graphics contexts, and cameras

In *Chapter 7, Viewing the World* we have already seen that the osg::Camera class manages the OpenGL **graphics context** associated with it, which is done via a simple setGraphicsContext() method. The **graphics context** actually encapsulates information on the way in which scene objects are drawn and rendering states are applied. It can be a graphics window providing a related windowing API or some other buffer objects, for example, the OpenGL pixel buffer, which stores pixel data without transferring it to the frame buffer.

OSG uses the `osg::GraphicsContext` class to represent the abstract graphics context, and the `osgViewer::GraphicsWindow` class to represent the abstract graphics window. The latter also has a `getEventQueue()` method for managing GUI events. Its platform-specific subclasses will continuously add new events to this event queue.

Because of the agnostic type of the windowing API (Windows, X11, Mac OS X, and so on), a graphics context must be created as a platform-specific one. The `createGraphicsContext()` method of the `osg::GraphicsContext` class will automatically make the decision for us. Its only argument, an `osg::GraphicsContext::Traits` pointer, will provide the specification of what type of graphics window or buffer is required.

The Traits class

The `osg::GraphicsContext::Traits` class can set up properties of a specific **graphics context**. This is different from the `osg::DisplaySettings` class, which manages the characteristics of all newly-created cameras' graphics contexts. Instead of a number of setting and getting property methods, the traits class uses public class member variables to indicate a property. This will take effect once the `createGraphicsContext()` is called. The main components of the traits are listed in the following table:

Member attribute	Data type	Default value	Description
x	int	0	The initial horizontal position of the graphics context
y	int	0	The initial vertical position of the graphics context
width	int	0	The width of the graphics context (always affect the window rectangle)
height	int	0	The height of the graphics context (always affect the window rectangle)
windowName	std::string	""	The name of the generated graphics window
windowDecoration	bool	false	The decoration (title bar) of the generated graphics window
red	unsigned int	8	Number of bits of red in the OpenGL color buffer
green	unsigned int	8	Number of bits of green in the OpenGL color buffer
blue	unsigned int	8	Number of bits of blue in OpenGL color buffer

Member attribute	Data type	Default value	Description
`alpha`	`unsigned int`	0	Number of bits in the OpenGL alpha buffer
`depth`	`unsigned int`	24	Number of bits in the OpenGL depth buffer
`stencil`	`unsigned int`	0	Number of bits in the OpenGL stencil buffer
`doubleBuffer`	`bool`	false	Use double or single buffering
`samples`	`unsigned int`	0	Number of multisampling buffer samples
`quadBufferStereo`	`bool`	false	Use NVIDIA's quad-buffering stereo mode or not
`inheritedWindowData`	`osg::ref_ptr<osg::Referenced>`	NULL	The associated window handle, which will be described later

To initialize a new traits pointer and set one or more of its member variables, just type:

```
osg::ref_ptr<osg::GraphicsContext::Traits> traits =
    new osg::GraphicsContext::Traits;
traits->x = 50;
...
```

Time for action – configuring the traits of a rendering window

We will create a fixed-size window to contain the rendering result of an OSG scene. The brief steps are: configure the traits of the rendering window, create a **graphics context** according to the traits, attach the **graphics context** to a camera, and finally set the camera as the **main camera** of the viewer.

1. Include the necessary headers:

```
#include <osg/GraphicsContext>
#include <osgDB/ReadFile>
#include <osgViewer/Viewer>
```

2. Create a traits structure and set its attributes. The samples value here is set to enable the global multisampling functionality of the current window, but leave others to their defaults (no multisampling). This is different from the `setNumMultiSamples()` method of the `osg::DisplaySettings` class:

```
osg::ref_ptr<osg::GraphicsContext::Traits> traits =
    new osg::GraphicsContext::Traits;
traits->x = 50;
traits->y = 50;
traits->width = 800;
traits->height = 600;
traits->windowDecoration = true;
traits->doubleBuffer = true;
traits->samples = 4;
```

3. Create the **graphics context** with the `createGraphicsContext()` function. Note here, never create new graphic's contexts with the `new` operator, otherwise OSG can't decide the low-level windowing platform for it:

```
osg::ref_ptr<osg::GraphicsContext> gc =
    osg::GraphicsContext::createGraphicsContext( traits.get() );
```

4. The graphics context is then attached to a newly-created camera node. It will be used as the **main camera** of the whole scene, so we have to specify the clear mask and color to make it work like ordinary OSG cameras. It is also very important to preset the **projection matrix** here. But we don't need to alter this **projection matrix** all the time, as it will be recomputed and updated by the rendering backend at an appropriate time:

```
osg::ref_ptr<osg::Camera> camera = new osg::Camera;
camera->setGraphicsContext( gc );
camera->setViewport(
    new osg::Viewport(0, 0, traits->width, traits->height) );
camera->setClearMask( GL_DEPTH_BUFFER_BIT | GL_COLOR_BUFFER_BIT );
camera->setClearColor( osg::Vec4f(0.2f, 0.2f, 0.4f, 1.0f) );
camera->setProjectionMatrixAsPerspective(
    30.0f, (double)traits->width/(double)traits->height,
    1.0,1000.0 );
```

5. Load a model as the **scene graph**:

```
osg::ref_ptr<osg::Node> root = osgDB::readNodeFile(
  "cessna.osg" );
```

6. Set the camera to the viewer and start it as usual:

```
osgViewer::Viewer viewer;
viewer.setCamera( camera.get() );
viewer.setSceneData( root.get() );
return viewer.run();
```

7. Now we have the Cessna model shown in a rendering window. We can still navigate in the window, run previous examples, and test the code. To make it rendered in full-screen mode again, set the `width` and `height` attributes to the size of the screen, and set `windowDecoration` to false.

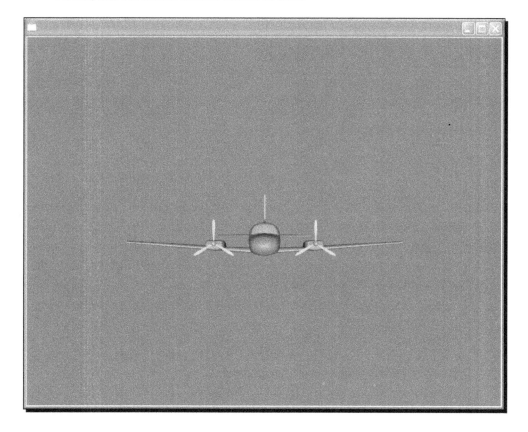

What just happened?

We have already made use of the setUpViewInWindow() method in *Chapter 7, Viewing the World*. It constructs a window instead of full-screen mode to display rendering results. Believe it or not, the content of the setUpViewInWindow() method is nearly the same as the example here. It configures the traits, creates a specific graphics context, attaches it to a new camera, and finally sets the camera as the **main camera** of the viewer. Other methods, like setUpViewFor3DSphericalDisplay(), do the similar work at the beginning of implementations to generate rendering containers. But after that, they always produce multiple camera objects with special projection matrices to realize rich effects. The **rendering-to-textures** technique is also useful in these cases.

Integrating OSG into a window

Interface developers may work under various GUI systems, and have to integrate the OSG **scene graph** into their UI widgets. According to the different working strategies of GUIs, it is technically hard to have a universal method of embedding OSG viewers. However, there do exist some tricks we can use to make the integration easier:

- Attach the window handle to the inheritedWindowData of the osg::GraphicsContext::Traits class. The window handle's type can be Win32's HWND, X11's Window, and Cocoa's WindowRef. After that, OSG will manage the OpenGL rendering context and drawing calls on the inherited window and thus render the whole scene to the window surface.

- The frame() method of the osgViewer::Viewer class should be executed continuously. For this purpose, we can either use a separate thread, or a GUI timer event handler with a short enough interval.

- For widgets that support OpenGL drawing calls directly (Qt's QGLWidget, GLUT, FLTK, and so on), use the osgViewer::GraphicsWindowEmbedded class to create a graphic's context without worrying about the rendering context and related buffer attributes. The frame() method of the OSG viewer must be executed in a continuous-updating method of the widget class.

- Never modify the **scene graph** (dynamic changing node and state attributes, adding or removing child nodes, and so on) in a GUI's callbacks or event handlers. Use OSG native ones instead to prevent thread conflicts. Another inefficient solution is to force the viewer to use the single-threaded mode, which will be introduced in *Chapter 12, Improving Rendering Efficiency*.

Time for action – attaching OSG with a window handle in Win32

A window handle (HWND) in Win32 applications allows the system resources to know what kind of window objects it referring to. The HWND variable may encapsulate a dialog, a push button, an MDI or SDI window, and so on. In that case, attaching this handle to the OSG traits and then to the graphics context will make it possible to integrate OSG and Win32 GUI controls, and thus display 3D scenes in all kinds of user interface objects.

1. Include the necessary headers:

    ```
    #include <windows.h>
    #include <process.h>
    #include <osgDB/ReadFile>
    #include <osgGA/TrackballManipulator>
    #include <osgViewer/api/win32/GraphicsWindowWin32>
    #include <osgViewer/Viewer>
    ```

2. Two global variables are declared here; these will be explained later:

    ```
    osg::ref_ptr<osgViewer::Viewer> g_viewer;
    bool g_finished;
    ```

3. We would like to create a classic pop-up window with the CreateWindow() function from the Win32 API. It must use a WNDCLASS structure to define the styles and customized procedure of the window. In most cases, the procedure is a pointer to a static function, which handles windowing messages that are passed to this window:

    ```
    static TCHAR szAppName[] = TEXT("gui");

    WNDCLASS wndclass;
    wndclass.style = CS_HREDRAW | CS_VREDRAW;
    wndclass.lpfnWndProc = WndProc;
    wndclass.cbClsExtra = 0;
    wndclass.cbWndExtra = 0;
    wndclass.hInstance = 0;
    wndclass.hIcon = LoadIcon(NULL, IDI_APPLICATION);
    wndclass.hCursor = LoadCursor(NULL, IDC_ARROW);
    wndclass.hbrBackground = (HBRUSH)GetStockObject(WHITE_BRUSH);
    wndclass.lpszMenuName = NULL;
    wndclass.lpszClassName = szAppName;
    if ( !RegisterClass(&wndclass) )
        return 0;
    ```

4. Create an 800x600 window at the position (100, 100). It returns the window handle if it succeeds, which is required by the OSG rendering window traits for integrating work. We can either put the initialization code of the graphics context here, or put it in the WM_CREATE case:

```
HWND hwnd = CreateWindow( szAppName, // window class name
                          TEXT("OSG and Win32 Window"),
                          // caption
                          WS_OVERLAPPEDWINDOW, // window style
                          100, // initial x position
                          100, // initial y position
                          800, // initial x size
                          600, // initial y size
                          NULL, // parent window handle
                          NULL, // window menu handle
                          0, // program instance handle
                          NULL ); // creation parameters
ShowWindow( hwnd, SW_SHOW );
UpdateWindow( hwnd );
```

5. Create a message loop to retrieve messages from the internal queue and dispatch them to the appropriate window procedure:

```
MSG msg;
while ( GetMessage(&msg, NULL, 0, 0) )
{
    TranslateMessage( &msg );
    DispatchMessage( &msg );
}
return 0;
```

6. Now, in the implementation of the procedure WndProc(), we will try initializing an OSG viewer and embedding it into the created window. This is going to be done in the WM_CREATE statement. Firstly, a WindowData structure is created to include the HWND handle. Then it is applied to the traits and the graphic's context is created platform-specific. The camera and the viewer objects are then initialized one after another. The setKeyEventSetsDone() here is used to disable quitting OSG applications with the *Esc* key. Finally, we start a new rendering thread for advancing the frames in the viewer. That is why we declare two global variables at the beginning:

```
case WM_CREATE:
{
    osg::ref_ptr<osg::Referenced> windata =
        new osgViewer::GraphicsWindowWin32::WindowData( hwnd );

    osg::ref_ptr<osg::GraphicsContext::Traits> traits =
```

```
        new osg::GraphicsContext::Traits;
    traits->x = 0;
    traits->y = 0;
    traits->width = 800;
    traits->height = 600;
    traits->windowDecoration = false;
    traits->doubleBuffer = true;
    traits->inheritedWindowData = windata;

    osg::ref_ptr<osg::GraphicsContext> gc =
        osg::GraphicsContext::createGraphicsContext( traits.get()
);

    osg::ref_ptr<osg::Camera> camera = new osg::Camera;
    camera->setGraphicsContext( gc );
    camera->setViewport(
        new osg::Viewport(0, 0, traits->width, traits->height) );
    camera->setClearMask( GL_DEPTH_BUFFER_BIT |
                          GL_COLOR_BUFFER_BIT );
    camera->setClearColor( osg::Vec4f(0.2f, 0.2f, 0.4f, 1.0f) );
    camera->setProjectionMatrixAsPerspective(
      30.0f,(double)traits->width/(double)traits
                        ->height,1.0,1000.0 );

    g_viewer = new osgViewer::Viewer;
    g_viewer->setCamera( camera.get() );
    g_viewer->setSceneData( osgDB::readNodeFile("cessna.osg") );
    g_viewer->setKeyEventSetsDone( 0 );
    g_viewer->setCameraManipulator(
      new osgGA::TrackballManipulator );

    g_finished = false;
    _beginthread( render, 0, NULL );
    return 0;
}
```

7. In the case of WM_DESTROY, we have to force exiting the OSG rendering thread before releasing the window handle. The setDone() method tells OSG to stop all work and wait for the application to quit. A Sleep() method is good for handling multiple threads here, because it yields the current time slice to the rendering thread until it is finished:

```
case WM_DESTROY:
    g_viewer->setDone( true );
    while ( !g_finished ) Sleep(10);
    PostQuitMessage( 0 );
    return 0;
```

8. The routine that begins execution of the extra rendering thread will only do one thing, that is, it will continue rendering new frames until the viewer is told to stop:

```
void render( void* )
{
    while ( !g_viewer->done() )
        g_viewer->frame();
    g_finished = true;
}
```

9. Now start the application. You will see the Cessna model appearing in a new window. The run() method of osgViewer::Viewer is not used directly, but a separate rendering thread is used to draw OSG **scene graph** to the graphics context of the window. Of course, the WM_TIMER message is also available for advancing frames continuously, if the time interval is short enough for simulating an active 3D world:

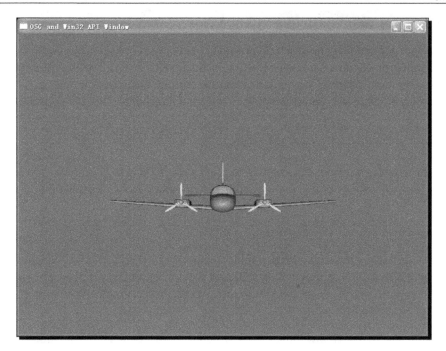

What just happened?

Almost all kinds of operating systems supply functionalities for specifying the rendering contexts of OpenGL-based applications. Under the Windows systems, WGL (Windows GL) functions are used to bring related Windows API support into OpenGL, such as `wglCreateContext()` and `wglMakeCurrent()`. Developers should first create and set up the handle to a GDI-like rendering context, and execute OpenGL calls only when the current context is enabled. All of the above are encapsulated in the internal `osgViewer::GraphicsWindowWin32` class. Similarly, there are also `GraphicsWindowX11`, `GraphicsWindowCarbon`, and `GraphicsWindowCocoa` classes for different operating systems, which liberates OSG programmers from maintaining the portability of their applications, especially in cross-platform GUI systems like Qt.

In other platform-dependant GUI systems like MFC, the most important step to follow is to obtain and attach the window handle (HWND) to the traits of the graphic's contexts. This can be always acquired from `CWND` objects with the `GetSafeHwnd()` method. It is also smart to use a separate thread for rendering frames, if the GUI system permits this.

Have a go hero – embedding into GUI systems

There is a special graphics context in OSG, named `osgViewer::GraphicsWindowEmbedded`. It assumes that the window containing the graphic's context can support OpenGL without any other operations (like making rendering context current, and so on). In this case, we can allocate a new embedded graphics window directly and attach it to the camera, as follows:

```
gw = new osgViewer::GraphicsWindowEmbedded(x,y,width,height);
camera-> setGraphicsContext( gw );
```

Then we have to draw frames at a certain frequency when the GUI is running, and send keyboard and mouse events to the event queue of the graphics context all the time, for example:

```
gw->getEventQueue()->keyPress( 'W' );
```

A good GUI for testing the embedded graphic's contexts is the GLUT library, which supports OpenGL calls directly. Try implementing OSG and GLUT integration with the `osgViewer::GraphicsWindowEmbedded` class. The `osgviewerGLUT` example in the `examples` subdirectory can also help a lot.

For your information, OSG now implements integration with GUI systems including Qt, MFC, wxWidgets, GTK, SDL, GLUT, FLTK, FOX, and Cocoa. You can find all of the implementations in the `examples` folder of the OSG source code.

Summary

This chapter taught us how users can interact with the 3D scene using OSG's GUI event adapters and handlers. Events of different windowing systems under different platforms are translated into a compatible interface named `osgGA::GUIEventAdapter`.

We also introduced a common solution for integrating OSG scene graph with a 2D windowing system. The key element here is to create the graphic's context with the appropriate window traits, including the size, display settings, and window handle arguments.

In this chapter, we specifically covered:

- Handling ordinary user events with the `osgGA::GUIEventHandler` class, which uses an `osgGA::GUIEventAdapter` to pass in events, and an `osgGA::GUIActionAdapter` to receive further requests (actually, a viewer object in most cases).
- The customization and emitting of user-defined GUI events using `osgGA::EventQueue`.

- Intersection tests of scene objects with the `osgUtil::IntersectionVisitor` visitor, and operators like `osgUtil::LineSegmentIntersector`.

- How to set up the traits of the to-be-rendered window using `osg::GraphicsContext::Traits`.

- Embedding the graphic context for rendering scenes into a windowing system, for example, a Win32 API window handler. More examples can be found in the `examples` folder of the source code.

10
Saving and Loading Files

One of the more important concepts in programming is the ability to store information after the program has terminated. This has many advantages, such as a small executable size, easy to implement modularity, and the ability of the program remember different user information.

*The **osgDB** library provides support for reading and writing the **scene graph** nodes, images and other objects. It also implements a plugin framework and file I/O utility classes. It allows various file formats, including the OSG native formats that wrap up the entire **scene graph** elements into text or binary files, to be dynamically loaded, on demand.*

In this chapter, we will discuss:

- The file I/O mechanism implemented in OSG
- A complete list of presently-supported file formats, including models, images, fonts, and so on
- The concept and usage of OSG's pseudo-loaders
- How to customize OSG plugin interface and provide support for user-defined formats
- How to create class wrappers for supporting serialized I/O of the OSG native formats

Understanding file I/O plugins

We have already learnt a little about the plugin mechanism of reading and writing data files, in *Chapter 2, Compilation and Installation of OpenSceneGraph*. With the help of specific format-managing plugins, OSG can load various models, images, fonts, and even video data from external files. A plugin here is a separate functionality component that customizes the supported file formats of an OSG-based application. It is recognized as a shared library file implementing the necessary reading or writing interface (or both). Different plugins are always required by user applications to load and construct large and complex scene graphs without too much programming work.

All file I/O plugins conform to the same naming convention; otherwise they are not recognizable and can't be used to read files. Take the native .osg file format as an example: under the Windows system, the plugin library file is osgdb_osg.dll. Under Linux, it is named osgdb_osg.so. Both have the prefix osgdb_ and the following name usually represents the file extension.

However, a plugin may support multiple extensions. For instance, the JPEG image format uses .jpeg and .jpg as the most common file extensions. There are no essential differences between them, so a unified osgdb_jpeg plugin should be enough to input and output files with either of these extensions. Fortunately, the **osgDB** library can support such kinds of plugins with an internal extension-to-handler map, which will be introduced later.

After the file I/O plugins are prepared and placed at locations at which they can be referenced, we can read OSG scene nodes or images with the **osgDB** namespace functions below:

```
osg::Node* node = osgDB::readNodeFile( "cow.osg" );
osg::Image* image = osgDB::readImageFile( "Images/lz.rgb" );
```

As we just discussed, OSG will automatically look for plugin library files named osgdb_osg and osgdb_rgb and read these two files from the hard disk. The required data files should exist in specified relative or absolute paths, or in the OSG search path defined by the environment variable OSG_FILE_PATH.

Discovery of specified extension

The basic principles of searching and locating a plugin for the handling of a specified file type can be described in two steps:

Firstly, OSG manages a commonly-used plugin list in the osgDB::Registry class. This class is designed as a singleton and can be only instantiated and obtained with the instance() method. The protected plugin list of the **osgDB** registry can help quickly find and call the corresponding reading or writing entries of the required format, based on the **chain-of-responsibility** design pattern. This means that each plugin object, called a reader-writer in OSG, will try to process the extension of the input file, and pass it off to the next plugin in the list if the extension is unrecognizable to that plugin.

In case all prestored reader-writers fail to handle the file extension, OSG will use the extension as a keyword to find and load a plugin from an external shared module, that is, the osgdb_<ext> library file. Here, <ext> represents the extension string, but the extension-to-handler map is also used here to decide the relationship between the extension and the special plugin library name. For example, we can define the relation of the extension string and plugin name with the addFileExtensionAlias() method:

```
// Add alias extensions for specified plugin
osgDB::Registry::instance()->addFileExtensionAlias( "jpeg", "jpeg" );
osgDB::Registry::instance()->addFileExtensionAlias( "jpg", "jpeg" );

// Now OSG can read .jpg files with the osgdb_jpeg plugin
osg::Image* image = osgDB::readImageFile( "picture.jpg" );
```

Calling these two lines before any other reading or writing operations will automatically link both *.jpeg and *.jpg files to the osgdb_jpeg library file, which is dynamically loaded when such types of files are required for use.

Note that we don't have to add such aliases for the JPEG support, because it is already embedded when the registry object is being initialized. Other OSG predefined plugins that support multiple file formats will be listed in the table in the following section.

Supported file formats

Here, we would like to list all of the supported plugins in OSG 3.0. Some of these require third-party dependencies, which are shown in the *Notes* column. The *Interface* property identifies whether a plugin supports the reading (R) or writing (W) interface. The ellipsis in the **Extensions** column signals whether the plugin supports additional file formats. More details can also be found in the `src/osgPlugins` directory of the source code.

Plugin name	Extensions	Interface	Requirements
osgdb_3dc (3DC Point cloud)	*.3dc, *.asc	R/W	-
osgdb_3ds (Autodesk 3DS)	*.3ds	R/W	-
osgdb_ac (AC3D)	*.ac	R/W	-
osgdb_bmp (Windows Bitmap)	*.bmp	R/W	-
osgdb_bsp (Valve BSP)	*.bsp	R	-
osgdb_bvh (Biovision Motion)	*.bvh	R	-
osgdb_curl (Web data with URL)	*.curl (pseudo-loader)	R	Needs **libcurl** (http://curl.haxx.se)
osgdb_dae (COLLADA DOM)	*.dae	R/W	Needs **COLLADA** (http://collada.org)
osgdb_dds (DirectDraw Surface)	*.dds	R/W	-
osgdb_dicom (NEMA DICOM)	*.dicom, *.dcm, ...	R	Needs **DCMTK** (http://dicom.offis.de/dcmtk) or **ITK** (http://www.itk.org)
osgdb_directshow (DirectShow)	*.avi, *.wmv, ...	R	Needs **DirectX SDK** (http://msdn.microsoft.com/en-us/directx)
osgdb_dot (DOT graph)	*.dot	W	Needs **Graphviz** (http://www.graphviz.org/)
osgdb_dw (Designer Workbench)	*.dw	R	-

Plugin name	Extensions	Interface	Requirements
osgdb_dxf (Autodesk DXF)	*.dxf	R/W	-
osgdb_exr (ILM OpenEXR)	*.exr	R	Needs **OpenEXR** (http://www.openexr.com)
osgdb_fbx (Autodesk FBX)	*.fbx	R/W	Needs **Autodesk FBX SDK** (http://www.autodesk.com/fbx)
osgdb_ffmpeg (FFmpeg)	*.ffmpeg (pseudo-loader)	R	Needs **FFmpeg** (http://www.ffmpeg.org)
osgdb_freetype (FreeType)	*.ttf, *.ttc, ...	R	Needs **FreeType** (http://www.freetype.org)
osgdb_gdal (GDAL)	*.gdal (pseudo-loader)	R	Needs **GDAL** (http://www.gdal.org)
osgdb_geo (Carbon Graphics)	*.gem, *.geo	R	-
osgdb_gecko (Mozilla Gecko)	*.gecko	R	Needs **XULRunner** (https://developer.mozilla.org/en/XULRunner)
osgdb_gif (Graphics Interchange format)	*.gif	R	Needs **libungif** (http://sourceforge.net/projects/libungif)
osgdb_hdr (Radiance HDR)	*.hdr	R/W	-
osgdb_imageio (Mac OS X ImageIO)	*.bmp, *.jpg, ...	R/W	Available only under Mac OS X
osgdb_iv (Inventor)	*.iv, *.wrl	R/W	Needs **OpenInventor** (http://oss.sgi.com/projects/inventor) or Coin3D (www.coin3d.org)
osgdb_ive (OSG binary format, deprecated)	*.ive	R/W	-
osgdb_jp2 (JPEG 2000)	*.jp2, *.jpc	R/W	Needs **JasPer** (http://www.ece.uvic.ca/~mdadams/jasper)

Plugin name	Extensions	Interface	Requirements
osgdb_jpeg (JPEG)	*.jpeg, *.jpg	R/W	Needs **libjpeg** (http://www.ijg.org)
osgdb_lwo (Lightwave 3D Object)	*.lwo	R	-
osgdb_lws (Lightwave 3D Scene)	*.lws	R	-
osgdb_md2 (Quake2 models)	*.md2	R	-
osgdb_mdl (Valve MDL)	*.mdl	R	-
osgdb_obj (Wavefront OBJ)	*.obj	R/W	-
osgdb_ogr (OGR)	*.ogr (pseudo-loader)	R	Needs **OGR** (http://www.gdal.org/ogr)
osgdb_openflight (OpenFlight)	*.flt	R/W	-
osgdb_osg (OSG extendable format)	*.osg, *.osgt, *.osgb, *.osgx	R/W	-
osgdb_p3d (Present3D)	*.p3d	R	-
osgdb_pdf (Acrobat PDF)	*.pdf	R	Needs **libpoppler** (http://poppler.freedesktop.org)
osgdb_pfb (Performer)	*.pfb, *.pfs, ...	R	Needs **OpenPerformer** (http://oss.sgi.com/projects/performer)
osgdb_pic (PC-Paint)	*.pic	R	-
osgdb_ply (Stanford Triangle Format)	*.ply	R	-
osgdb_png (Portable Network Graphics)	*.png	R/W	Needs **libpng** (http://www.libpng.org/pub/png)

Plugin name	Extensions	Interface	Requirements
osgdb_pnm (Netpbm)	*.pnm	R/W	-
osgdb_pov (POV-Ray)	*.pov	W	-
osgdb_qfont (Qt font engine)	*.qfont (pseudo-loader)	R	Needs **Qt** (http://qt.nokia.com)
osgdb_QTKit (QTKit media)	*.mov, *.mpg, ...	R	Available only under Mac OS X, needs the **QTKit/CoreVideo** framework
osgdb_quicktime (Apple Quicktime)	*.mov, *.avi, ...	R	Needs **Quicktime SDK** (http://developer.apple.com/quicktime/download)
osgdb_rgb (SGI Images)	*.rgb, *.rgba, ...	R/W	-
osgdb_rot (Rotation)	*.rot (pseudo-loader)	R	Needs Euler angles as parameters
osgdb_scale (Scale)	*.scale (pseudo-loader)	R	Needs scale values along axes as parameters
osgdb_shp (ESRI Shapefile)	*.shp	R	-
osgdb_stl (Stereolithography)	*.stl, *.sta	R/W	-
osgdb_svg (Scalar Vector Graphics)	*.svg	R	Needs **librsvg** (http://librsvg.sourceforge.net)
osgdb_tga (Truevision Targa)	*.tga	R/W	-
osgdb_tiff (Tagged Image File)	*.tiff; *.tif	R/W	Needs **libtiff** (http://www.libtiff.org)
osgdb_trans (Translation)	*.trans (pseudo-loader)	R	Needs translation values along axes as parameters
osgdb_txf (Textured Font)	*.txf	R	-
osgdb_txp (TerraPage)	*.txp	R	-

Plugin name	Extensions	Interface	Requirements
osgdb_vnc (VNC Client)	*.vnc	R	Needs **libVNCClient** (http://libvncserver. sourceforge.net)
osgdb_vrml (VRML)	*.wrl	R	Needs **OpenVRML** (http:// openvrml.org)
osgdb_vtf (Valve Texture)	*.vtf	R/W	-
osgdb_x (Microsoft DirectX)	*.x	R	-
osgdb_xine (Xine)	*.xine (pseudo-loader)	R	Needs **Xine** (http://www. xine-project.org)

Details about configuring third-party dependencies that have been listed for certain plugins can be found in the *Configuring third-party dependencies* section of this chapter. Besides, there is another important project called **Zlib** (http://www.zlib.net), which is used as an optional part of the **osgDB** library and the osgdb_ive plugin to enable the compression of OSG native file formats, and is also required by some third-party projects referred into the *Notes* property.

The pseudo-loader

In the previous table, some extensions are marked as **pseudo-loader**. This means they are not actually file extensions, but just add a suffix to the end of the real filename to indicate that the file should be read by the specified plugin. For example:

```
osgviewer worldmap.shp.ogr
```

The real file on the disk is worldmap.shp, which may store the entire world map in ESRI's shapefile format. The suffix .ogr forces osgdb_ogr to read the .shp file and construct the **scene graph**; otherwise osgdb_shp will be automatically found and used by default.

Another good example is the osgdb_ffmpeg plugin. The **FFmpeg** library supports over 100 different codecs. To read any of these, we can simply add a suffix .ffmpeg behind the filename and leave the work to **FFmpeg** itself.

In addition, we have already seen some other pseudo-loaders in the following form:

```
node = osgDB::readNodeFile( "cessna.osg.0,0,90.rot" );
```

The string 0,0,90 between the real filename and the suffix is the parameter. Some pseudo-loaders need specific parameters to make them work properly.

Time for action – reading files from the Internet

To understand the use of a **pseudo-loader**, we will try to read a model from the Internet. The osgviewer utility is enough to perform this example, but you can always make use of the osgDB::readNodeFile() function to achieve the same result in your OSG-based applications.

1. The model file already exists at the following URL: http://www. openscenegraph.org/data/earth_bayarea/earth.ive.

2. Before trying to read files from the Internet or intranet, we'd better have a check of the OSG plugin directory to see if there is an osgdb_curl plugin. It should exist if you are installing OSG from the installer described in *Chapter 2, Compilation and Installation of OpenSceneGraph*. But for developers who build OSG from the source code, it may be ignored during the CMake configuration. In this latter case, please refer to the next section and obtain this important plugin first.

3. Start the osgviewer utility with the following argument:

   ```
   # osgviewer http://www.openscenegraph.org/data/earth_bayarea/
   earth.ive.curl
   ```

4. The .curl suffix tells OSG to load the specified file using the osgdb_curl plugin. The redundancy will be automatically removed by the reader-writer interface.

5. Now you will see an earth model on the screen. Rotate and scale the view matrix using your camera manipulator and try to find your home on the earth:

What just happened?

Although the whole earth model is rough for navigation, you can still find that some parts of it can become more detailed if you zoom in. The model is actually constructed from a tree of osg::PagedLOD nodes, each of which is stored in a separate file on the remote site, and manages a piece of terrain geometry of different level. This technique, called the quad-tree, is described in detail in the last chapter of this book.

The osgdb_curl plugin helps a lot when parsing and loading files from specified URLs. It depends upon a third-party library named **libcurl**, which provides an easy-to-use client-side URL transferring interface. The **pseudo-loader** mechanism here can quickly decide whether the required filename should be directly sent to osgdb_curl; otherwise OSG will check if the filename contains a remote address first, and make the final decision.

Pop quiz – getting rid of pseudo-loaders

Somebody may rename a pseudo-loader, for instance, the osgdb_ffmpeg library which can read .avi, .mpg, and many other media formats, to other plugin names like osgdb_avi. After that, the .ffmpeg suffix will become invalid, and only .avi files can be read directly using the osgDB::readNodeFile() function. Now, can you figure out the reason why the pseudo-loader lost its ability, and how to make the *new* osgdb_avi plugin still available for .mpg and other formats that were originally supported?

Configuring third-party dependencies

Have you ever built OSG from source code with your native compiler and the CMake system introduced in *Chapter 2, Compilation and Installation of OpenSceneGraph*? Then you may find that there are lots of mis-compiled components in the self-made OSG libraries, when compared with the installer provided in the same chapter. For example:

```
# osgviewer --image picture.jpg
```

The image picture.jpg may not be displayed even though it exists in the proper search path. If you encounter this situation, look into the plugin directory, and you may find that the osgdb_jpg or osgdb_jpeg library is missed. That is simply because we din't configure the options for an important third-party library, libjpeg, which is required by the JPEG reader-writer.

OSG doesn't load most file formats by itself, but delegates the loading of the data to third-party dependencies. Especially when handling various kinds of model, image, and miscellaneous files, a huge number of excellently-written open source projects can be used by different plugins as third-party dependencies. This effective methodology can share the ideas of developers all over the world during the design and implementation phases of the OSG engine, and support a continuous, stable, and team-style design.

Time for action – adding libcurl support for OSG

In this section, we will build the `osgdb_curl` support for compiling and linking OSG binaries from the source code. Without the necessary third-party library **libcurl**, the `osgdb_curl` plugin will be ignored in the entire solution and thus will not be generated. In *Chapter 2, Compilation and Installation of OpenSceneGraph*, we did not introduce the steps to add **libcurl** to the CMake configuration options. But with the CMake cache files and intermediate files kept in the build directory, we can quickly restart the configuration and rebuild our OSG libraries and development files. The Visual Studio solution file will be automatically updated to include the new `osgdb_curl` project.

1. Download the **libcurl** prebuilt package from the following website: `http://curl.haxx.se/download.html`. Visual Studio users should choose a download link in the section **Win32 – MSVC** and uncompress the ZIP file into an independent folder.

2. The folder includes the most important development files for use: the header files in the `include` sub-directory, the static-link file `libcurl.lib`, and the dynamic library `libcurl.dll`. Their locations will be specified to the CMake system:

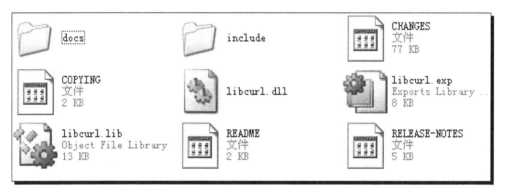

3. Now it's time for us to restart the CMake GUI environment. Instead of loading the `CMakeLists.txt` file in the source directory, we can drag the `CMakeCache.txt` from the **out-of-source** build directory and into the main window (you didn't remove the whole build directory, did you?) to quickly apply the previous settings. Change to **Grouped View** and expand the group `CURL`.

4. Set the `CURL_INCLUDE_DIR` to the `include` directory in the uncompressed folder. It will be used as the additional dependency directories of the generated Visual Studio project. `CURL_LIBRARY` and `CURL_LIBRARY_DEBUG` can both be set to the `libcurl.lib` file, which is automatically added to the dependency library list of the same project. Our prebuilt **libcurl** has a dynamic library file named `libcurl.dll`, so the option `CURL_IS_STATIC` should be cancelled:

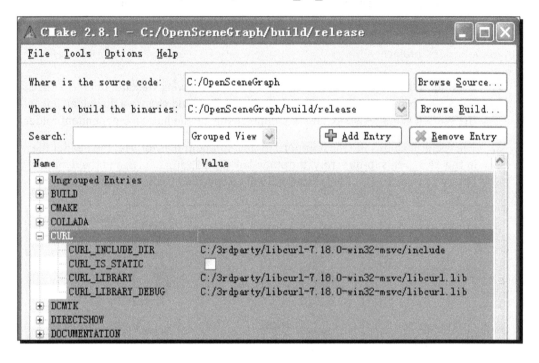

5. That is all! Click on **Configure** and then **Generate**, open the updated `OpenSceneGraph.sln`, and see if there are any changes. You will soon find that a new *Plugins curl* project has appeared among the plugin projects.

6. Repeat the steps of compiling and linking the OSG libraries and plugins. Then build the `ALL_BUILD` project and then `INSTALL`. The `osgdb_curl` library will be created during the entire process.

7. It is possible to view models and images from the Internet, now. Let's go back to the last example and browse the earth model with our generated `osgdb_curl` plugin.

What just happened?

Have a look at the CMake options used while configuring the CURL group; you will find a number of option groups that indicate different third-party dependencies, like JPEG, GIFLIB, TIFF, and ZLIB. Some groups will only appear when the necessary precursor groups are set up, for instance, the PNG group. Most of them require a <PROJ>_INCLUDE_DIR option to set the include directory, and the <PROJ>_LIBRARY and <PROJ>_LIBRARY_DEBUG options to locate the static-link libraries (both release and debug). Here, the name <PROJ> will vary according to the group name in CMake.

Under Windows, these options are then applied to the Visual Studio project properties for correctly compiling and linking it. Under a UNIX system, these can affect the Makefile.

To start from the **cmake** command-line and configure these third-party dependencies, you can add each option with a -D prefix as follows:

```
# cmake -DCMAKE_BUILD_TYPE=Release
-DCURL_INCLUDE_DIR=/usr/local/include
-DCURL_LIBRARY=/usr/local/lib/libcurl.so …
```

You may worry about obtaining so many third-party projects for building different kinds of OSG plugins. It is really heavy but interesting work to compile each of them from the source code and learn how to live in the open source world. But for developers who are eager to taste the most common OSG file I/O plugins (often including osgdb_jpeg, osgdb_gif, osgdb_tiff, and osgdb_png, for which the **zlib** library is required as the prerequisite), the following website may provide some useful prebuilt libraries and development files: http://gnuwin32.sourceforge.net/packages.html.

The following link may also help if you are familiar with SVN tools and the SourceForge website (http://sourceforge.net/): http://osgtoy.svn.sourceforge.net/viewvc/osgtoy/3rdParty/.

In addition, OSG also provides a CMake option ACTUAL_3RDPARTY_DIR to avoid manually setting too many include, dir, and library options. Developers may first create an empty directory called 3rdparty, as well as three subdirectories named include, lib, and bin. Then we have to put all of the headers of third-party dependencies into include, all static-link libraries (*.lib) into lib, and all dynamic libraries (*.dll) into the bin subfolder. After that, open **Ungrouped entries**, set ACTUAL_3RDPARTY_DIR to the newly-created 3rdparty directory, click on **Configure**, and see if OSG could automatically find some of the most common dependencies' include paths and libraries (including **FreeType, gdal, glut, libcurl, libjpeg, libpng, libtiff, libungif**, and **zlib**).

Have a go hero – adding FreeType support for OSG

FreeType is used by the **osgText** library to enable the loading and rendering of fonts for 2D and 3D texts. It is highly recommended that this is built for the `osgdb_freetype` plugin. Otherwise the **osgText** functionalities will not work properly with multi-languages and **True Type** fonts.

OSG requires a **FreeType** version higher than 2.35. The source code can be downloaded from: `http://savannah.nongnu.org/download/freetype/`.

The prebuilts can be found at `http://gnuwin32.sourceforge.net/packages/freetype.htm`.

The `FreeType` group in the CMake GUI window is a little different from the others. It needs two extra options: `FREETYPE_INCLUDE_DIR_freetype2` and `FREETYPE_INCLUDE_DIR_ft2build`. The first one points to the parent path of the `freetype` subdirectory, and the second points to the location of `ft2build.h`. All of these should be configured correctly to make sure that `osgdb_freetype` can be created without errors. We will introduce its usage when creating scene texts in the next chapter.

Writing your own plugins

Extending the virtual reader-writer interface, OSG allows developers to add additional customized file formats as plugins. The virtual interface is defined by the `osgDB::ReaderWriter` class. It has several important virtual methods to be used or re-implemented to achieve reading and writing functionalities.

Virtual method	Description
`supportsExtension()`	This has two string arguments: the extension name and the description. It is always called in the constructor of the reader-writer subclasses to indicate supported file extensions.
`acceptsExtension()`	This returns `true` if a specified extension argument is supported by the reader-writer.
`fileExists()`	This is used to determine if a file exists. It returns `true` if the input filename and options indicate that a local or remote file is accessible.
`readNode()`	This accepts a filename and an `osgDB::Option` object as parameters. Developers have to override it in order to read a file from the disk with user options. The options are parsed and used by specific plugin implementations.

Virtual method	Description
writeNode()	This has an extra osg::Node pointer besides the filename and options arguments. It can be re-implemented to write the **scene graph** to a file on the disk on the contrary.
readImage()	This reads image data from disk files. It is not necessary to override this method unless you are developing image file reader plugins.
writeImage()	This writes image data to disk. It is not necessary to override this method unless you are developing image file writer plugins.

The implementation of the readNode() method can be described as follows:

```
osgDB::ReaderWriter::ReadResult readNode(
                        const std::string& file,
                        const osgDB::Options* options) const
{
    // Check if the file extension is recognizable and file exists
    bool recognizableExtension = …;
    bool fileExists = …;
    if (!recognizableExtension) return ReadResult::FILE_NOT_HANDLED;
    if (!fileExists) return ReadResult::FILE_NOT_FOUND;
    …
    // Construct the scene graph according to format specification
    osg::Node* root = …;
    …
    // In case there are fatal errors during the process,
    // return an invalid message; otherwise return the root node
    bool errorInParsing = …;
    if (!errorInParsing) return ReadResult::ERROR_IN_READING_FILE;
    return root;
}
```

It is a little surprising that an osgDB::ReaderWriter::ReadResult object is returned by the readNode() method, and not an expected node pointer. This read result object can be used as a container of a node, an image, a status enumeration (like FILE_NOT_FOUND), some other special object, or even an error message string. It has multiple implicit constructors to achieve such a purpose. That is why we return the **root node** directly at the end of the above example code.

Another useful class here is osgDB::Options. This can set or get a general option string with the setOptionString() and getOptionString() methods, which are passed into different plugins to control their operations. Passing the string as an argument of the constructor is also OK.

Developers may design their plugin features and behaviors according to different option strings. Note that the option object is set and passed in the `readNodeFile()` function, so the plugin interface may always receive a `NULL` pointer, which means that there is no input options. This is actually the default setting of `readNodeFile()`:

```
osg::Node* node1 = osgDB::readNodeFile("cow.osg");  // Option is NULL!
osg::Node* node2 = osgDB::readNodeFile("cow.osg",
                                    new osgDB::Options(string));
```

Handling the data stream

The `osgDB::ReaderWriter` base class involves a set of stream data handling methods, which can also be overridden by user-defined plugins. The only difference is that the input filename argument is replaced by a `std::istream&` or `std::ostream&` variable. Making use of the file stream is always preferred rather than directly operating on physical files. To perform stream operations when reading a file, we may design the reader-writer interface like this:

```
osgDB::ReaderWriter::ReadResult readNode(
                         const std::string& file,
                         const osgDB::Options* options) const
{
    …
    osgDB::ifstream stream( file.c_str(), std::ios::binary );
    if ( !stream ) return ReadResult::ERROR_IN_READING_FILE;
    return readNode(stream, options);
}

osgDB::ReaderWriter::ReadResult readNode(
                         std::istream& stream,
                         const osgDB::Options* options) const
{
    // Construct the scene graph according to format specification
    osg::Node* root = …;
    return root;
}
```

We can then use `osgDB::readNodeFile()` to load and parse the file as usual, but it actually creates and handles stream data in the reader-writer implementation. The problem here is how to directly perform operations on some existing streams, for instance, a string stream in a data buffer or transferred over the socket? As we have seen already, OSG doesn't define a direct user interface, like the famous `osgDB::readNodeFile()` and `osgDB::readImageFile()`, for analyzing streams.

A solution is to retrieve a specific reader-writer and use it to parse the current stream in the buffer, using the `getReaderWriterForExtension()` method of `osgDB::Registry`. The obtained reader-writer must have implemented the stream operating interface, and the developer himself must ensure that the stream data format corresponds to the parser's specification definition. This means that a 3Ds reader-writer must only be used to read a 3Ds format stream; otherwise a not-so-well-written plugin may even cause a system crash when trying to explain unpredictable data.

Example code for reading stream data with the `osgdb_osg` plugin is as follows:

```
osgDB::ReaderWriter* rw =
    osgDB::Registry::instance()->getReaderWriterForExtension("osg");
if (rw)
{
    osgDB::ReaderWriter::ReadResult rr = reader->readNode(stream);
    if ( rr.success() )
        node = rr.takeNode();
}
```

The `node` variable can be used as the loaded **scene graph** later. The `success()` and `takeNode()` methods read status information and the stored `osg::Node` pointer from the read result.

Time for action – designing and parsing a new file format

We will design a new file format and create the I/O plugin for it in this example. Its format specification should be simple enough so that we won't take much time in explaining the usage and parsing it to a **scene graph**.

The new format will only focus on quickly creating triangle strips—that is, a series of connected triangles with N+2 shared vertices, where N is the number of triangles to be drawn. The file is in text format, and has one extension, `.tri`, which means *triangle file format*. The total number of vertices will always be written at the first line of every `.tri` file. The following lines provide the vertices data fields. Each vertex is stored as three float values in a row. An example of the content of the new format is as follows:

```
8
0 0 0
1 0 0
0 0 1
1 0 1
0 0 2
1 0 2
0 0 3
1 0 3
```

Save these values to an `example.tri` file, which will be used later. Now it's time to start implementing our reader-writer interface.

1. Include the necessary headers:

```
#include <osg/Geometry>
#include <osg/Geode>
#include <osgDB/FileNameUtils>
#include <osgDB/FileUtils>
#include <osgDB/Registry>
#include <osgUtil/SmoothingVisitor>
```

2. We would like to implement the reading methods of the new format. So two `readNode()` methods should be overridden here, one for reading data from files and the other for reading from streams:

```
class ReaderWriterTRI : public osgDB::ReaderWriter
{
public:
    ReaderWriterTRI();

    virtual ReadResult readNode(
        const std::string&, const osgDB::ReaderWriter::Options*)
const;
    virtual ReadResult readNode(
        std::istream&, const osgDB::ReaderWriter::Options*) const;
};
```

3. In the constructor, we have to announce that the extension `.tri` is supported by this plugin. Support for extensions can be added here with the same `supportExtension()` method:

```
ReaderWriterTRI::ReaderWriterTRI()
{ supportsExtension( "tri", "Triangle strip points" ); }
```

4. Now we are going to implement the `readNode()` method for reading files from the disk. It will check if the input extension and filename are available, and try to redirect the content of the file into the `std::fstream` object for further operations:

```
ReaderWriterTRI::ReadResult ReaderWriterTRI::readNode(
        const std::string&, const osgDB::ReaderWriter::Options*)
const
{
    std::string ext = osgDB::getLowerCaseFileExtension( file );
    if ( !acceptsExtension(ext) ) return
        ReadResult::FILE_NOT_HANDLED;
```

```
    std::string fileName = osgDB::findDataFile( file, options );
    if ( fileName.empty() ) return ReadResult::FILE_NOT_FOUND;

    std::ifstream stream( fileName.c_str(), std::ios::in );
    if( !stream ) return ReadResult::ERROR_IN_READING_FILE;
    return readNode( stream, options );
}
```

5. This is the core implementation of the new file format. All that we need to do is to read the total number and every vertex from the data stream, and push them into the osg::Vec3Array variable. A new osg::Geometry object is then created to include the vertex array and related primitive object. Finally, we generate the normals of the geometry and return a new osg::Geode containing it as the reading result:

```
ReaderWriterTRI::ReadResult ReaderWriterTRI::readNode(
    std::istream&, const osgDB::ReaderWriter::Options*) const
{
    unsigned int index = 0, numPoints = 0;
    stream >> numPoints;

    osg::ref_ptr<osg::Vec3Array> va = new osg::Vec3Array;
    while ( index<numPoints && !stream.eof() &&
            !(stream.rdstate()&std::istream::failbit) )
    {
        osg::Vec3 point;
        stream >> point.x() >> point.y() >> point.z();
        va->push_back( point );
        index++;
    }

    osg::ref_ptr<osg::Geometry> geom = new osg::Geometry;
    geom->setVertexArray( va.get() );
    geom->addPrimitiveSet(
        new osg::DrawArrays(GL_TRIANGLE_STRIP, 0, numPoints) );

    osgUtil::SmoothingVisitor smoother;
    smoother.smooth( *geom );

    osg::ref_ptr<osg::Geode> geode = new osg::Geode;
    geode->addDrawable( geom.get() );
    return geode.release();
}
```

6. Register the reader-writer class with the following macro. This must be done for every OSG plugin at the end of the source file. The first parameter indicates the plugin library name (without the `osgdb_` prefix), and the second one provides the class name:

```
REGISTER_OSGPLUGIN( tri, ReaderWriterTRI )
```

7. Note that the output target name should be `osgdb_tri` this time, and must be a shared library file instead of an executable. So the CMake script for generating our project should use the macro `add_library()` to replace `add_executable()`, such as:

```
add_library( osgdb_tri SHARED readerwriter.cpp )
```

8. Now, start a console and run `osgviewer` with the `example.tri` as the input filename:

```
# osgviewer example.tri
```

9. The result clearly shows whether the vertices are read out correctly and form the geometry as triangular strips:

What just happened?

A few utility functions are used here to judge the validity of the input filename in the `readNode()` method. The `osgDB::getLowerCaseFileExtension()` obtains the file extension, which is checked by `acceptsExtension()` of the `osgDB::ReaderWriter` base class. The `osgDB::findDataFile()` function then looks for the file in possible paths (current and system paths). It will return the full path of the first valid file found, or an empty string if nothing is found.

Another important point to mention is the macro `REGISTER_OSGPLUGIN`. This actually defines a global variable that registers the user-defined reader-writer to the `osgDB::Registry` instance in the constructor. When the dynamic library is first loaded, the global variable is automatically allocated, and the reader-writer can be found in order to handle the input file or stream then.

Have a go hero – finishing the writing interface of the plugin

We have already demonstrated the reading operation of the `.tri` format, by implementing the two virtual `readNode()` methods. Now it's your turn to re-implement the `writeNode()` methods and finish the reader-writer interface. Of course, a plugin can work with only the reading functionality or the writing functionality, but why not make things perfect if we have the chance?

 A customized node visitor may be used to find all `osg::Geode` nodes and geometries of a `scene graph`. You can improve the format specification to support saving and loading multiple triangle strips from `.tri` files, if necessary.

Serializing OSG native scenes

The OSG native formats, implemented by the `osgdb_ive` and `osgdb_osg` plugins, are used for encapsulating OSG native classes and converting them to representations that can be written to a data stream. This makes it possible to save the **scene graph** to a disk file and read it back without missing any information.

For example, the Cessna model is stored in a file named `cessna.osg`. It is actually made up of an `osg::Group` root node, an `osg::Geode` child node, and an `osg::Geometry` object with specific materials and some other rendering attributes. In a text file, it may be defined by the following lines:

```
osg::Group {
    Name "cessna.osg"
    DataVariance STATIC
```

```
        UpdateCallback FALSE
        ...
        Children 1 {
            osg::Geode {
                ...
                Drawables 1 {
                    osg::Geometry {
                        ...
                    }
                }
            }
        }
    }
```

Every scene object (node, drawable, and so on) is defined by a class name and begin and end brackets. The object's properties, including properties of its parent classes, are written into a sequence of bits for storing in files and buffers. For example, the `Name` and `DataVariance` fields are defined in the `osg::Object` base class, `UpdateCallback` is defined in `osg::Node`, and `Children` is the only native property of `osg::Group`. They are all saved for the Cessna's root node to record all of the information required for a complete model.

These properties can be soon reread to create a semantically-identical clone of the original Cessna **scene graph**, according to the same sequence of bits. The process of serializing (writing to a series of data) and deserializing (resurrecting the series of data) the **scene graph** is called **I/O serialization**. Each property that can be saved into and reread from a sequence is called a **serializable** object, or a **serializer** for short.

Creating serializers

The OSG native formats, including `.osg`, `.osgb`, `.osgt`, and `.osgx`, are extensible for saving to and loading from files and data streams. With the exception of the deprecated `.ive` format, they all need special helper classes called wrappers, which wrap up primitive values that offer the utility methods and properties of the API's classes. When new methods and classes are introduced into the OSG core libraries, there should be corresponding wrappers for them in order to make sure that any new features can be immediately supported in the native format files. The theory of serializing is extremely useful in this situation, enabling simple and common input/output interfaces to be utilized.

The `.osg` format has been widely used in the OSG community for many years. Almost all of the models referred to in this book are written in this format. It supports only ASCII formats and uses a slightly complex interface for implementing wrappers.

But there is another "second generation" format in development, which is well serialized, easy-to-extend, and even *cross-format*. ASCII format (`.osgt`), binary format (`.osgb`), and XML style format (`.osgx`) files are all supported with one set of core class wrappers, in each of which a series of serializers are used to bind reading and writing members. In the following example, we will discuss how to write wrappers for user-defined classes in your own applications or dynamic libraries. The to-be-wrapped class must be derived from `osg::Object`, and must have a namespace for the wrapper manager in **osgDB** to use.

All OSG predefined wrappers are stored in the `src/osgWrappers` directory of the source code. They are always a good reference for user-customized designing and programming.

Time for action – creating serializers for user-defined classes

To create serializers for a class and make it accessible from OSG native formats, there are some preconditions: firstly, the class must be derived from `osg::Object`, either directly or indirectly; secondly, the class must be declared in a namespace, and uses `META_Object` to define the correct namespace and class names; finally and most importantly, the class must have at least a getter and a setter method for each member property, which makes it serializable, that is, it can be stored to OSG native scene files and deserialized to a cloned scene object at any time.

1. Include the necessary headers:

```
#include <osg/Node>
#include <osgDB/ObjectWrapper>
#include <osgDB/Registry>
#include <osgDB/ReadFile>
#include <osgDB/WriteFile>
#include <iostream>
```

2. We define the `testNS::ExampleNode` class to be serialized. It is easy to understand and will do nothing except record an unsigned integer number, `_exampleID`. You will easily find that the setter and getter methods are defined in strict naming conventions (the same string after the `set` or `get` prefix, the same input and return value type, and a constant keyword to the getter method):

```
namespace testNS {

class ExampleNode : public osg::Node
{
public:
    ExampleNode() : osg::Node(), _exampleID(0) {}

    ExampleNode(const ExampleNode& copy,
```

```
                           const osg::CopyOp& copyop=osg::CopyOp::SHALLOW_
COPY)
    : osg::Node(copy, copyop), _exampleID(copy._exampleID) {}

    META_Node(testNS, ExampleNode)

    void setExampleID( unsigned int id ) { _exampleID = id; }
    unsigned int getExampleID() const { return _exampleID; }
protected:
    unsigned int _exampleID;
};

}
```

3. The `REGISTER_OBJECT_WRAPPER` macro is used to define a wrapper class. It has four arguments: the unique wrapper name, the prototype, the class name, and the inheritance relations in the form of a string. The only serializer object to be added is the `_exampleID` property. Its shared name (shared by the setter and getter) is `ExampleID`, and the default value is 0:

```
REGISTER_OBJECT_WRAPPER( ExampleNode_Wrapper,
                         new testNS::ExampleNode,
                         testNS::ExampleNode,
                         "osg::Object osg::Node
                         testNS::ExampleNode" )
{
    ADD_UINT_SERIALIZER( ExampleID, 0 );
}
```

4. Now we enter the main entry. We hope this tiny application can demonstrate both the writing and reading operations. When the `-w` argument is specified, a newly-allocated node is saved to a `.osgt` file (OSG native ASCII format); otherwise the saved file will be loaded and the `_exampleID` will be printed on the screen:

```
osg::ArgumentParser arguments( &argc, argv );

unsigned int writingValue = 0;
arguments.read( "-w", writingValue );
```

5. Write the `ExampleNode` node to the `examplenode.osgt` file, if there is a valid value that can be set with the `setExampleID()` method:

```
if ( writingValue!=0 )
{
    osg::ref_ptr<testNS::ExampleNode> node = new
testNS::ExampleNode;
    node->setExampleID( writingValue );
    osgDB::writeNodeFile( *node, "examplenode.osgt" );
}
```

6. Read back the node from the same file and print the written value with
`getExampleID()`:

```
else
{
    testNS::ExampleNode* node = dynamic_
cast<testNS::ExampleNode*>(
        osgDB::readNodeFile("examplenode.osgt") );
    if ( node!=NULL )
    {
        std::cout << "Example ID: " << node->getExampleID()
                << std::endl;
    }
}
```

7. We will first set a `_exampleID` value and write the **scene graph** to the
`.osgt` file, assuming the executable name is `MyProject.exe`:

 # MyProject.exe -w 20

8. A file named `examplenode.osgt` will be created in current path. Now
let's read it back to the memory and print the stored `_exampleID`:

 # MyProject.exe

9. It simply shows the value we just inputted. It is certainly obtained when loading
the file on the disk and reconstructing the clone of the previous **scene graph**:

```
Example ID: 20
```

What just happened?

Open the `examplenode.osgt` file with any text editors. It may contain the following lines:

```
testNS::ExampleNode {
  UniqueID 1
  ExampleID 20
}
```

The namespace and class names are leading a block of properties, including the `ExampleID`
field which saves our input value. OSG will gain the namespace and class names and look for
appropriate wrapper object that is already registered in the system memory. The wrapper, if
found, will create the `ExampleNode` instance from the prototype, and then traverse every
superclass in the inheritance relations string to read out all of the properties (properties with
default values will not be saved to or read from ASCII files).

The REGISTER_OBJECT_WRAPPER macro will define the prototype and inheritance relations for a specified class. Similar to REGISTER_OSGPLUGIN, it is actually a global variable, which registers the wrapper to the OSG registry object. When a dynamic library containing these wrappers is loaded, or the global variable is allocated in the executable segment of the application, all of the wrappers will be immediately ready-to-use for the native .osgt, .osgb, and .osgx formats.

Pop quiz – understanding the inheritance relations

As we have implemented it, the ExampleNode class is derived from osg::Node. According to the inheritance relations, it must record all changed properties in its super classes and itself. But what will happen if we remove the string osg::Node from the inheritance relations string? Will the wrapper fail or lose its effectiveness? Or it will just miss some information and still work in most cases? Do you have any good ideas or test code to verify your answer?

Have a go hero – adding more serializers

Obviously, the ADD_UINT_SERIALIZER() macro is used to call class methods to set or get an unsigned integer property. In fact, there are some more predefined serializers, including ADD_BOOL_SERIALIZER(), ADD_FLOAT_SERIALIZER(), ADD_VEC3_SERIALIZER(), and so on. To define enumeration properties, the BEGIN_ENUM_SERIALIZER(), ADD_ENUM_VALUE(), and END_ENUM_SERIALIZER() macros should be used to form a complete **serializer**. There is also an ADD_USER_SERIALIZER() macro that is used to design user-defined serializers. Any source files in the src/osgWrappers/serializers should be useful to learn about them, and the following link can also be used as a quick reference document: http://www.openscenegraph.org/projects/osg/wiki/Support/KnowledgeBase/SerializationSupport.

Now, let's try adding some more properties to the ExampleNode class, as well as the corresponding setter and getter methods. Could you implement different serializers for additional properties and make the class always serializable to OSG native formats?

Summary

In this chapter, we mainly discussed about the file I/O mechanism, including the use of plugins and the **chain-of-responsibility** design pattern in OSG. The `osgDB::Registry` is the singleton class storing all of the reader-writers and wrappers which are linked in at runtime for reading native and non-native file formats. By the end of this chapter, we were able to understand how OSG plugins work, and how to implement a new plugin reading and writing interface with user-defined subclasses of the `osgDB::ReaderWriter` base class.

In this chapter, we have learnt:

◆ How to load files of a specified extension, and searching for a specific plugin in the table provided

◆ How to understand the pseudo-loaders, and how to load files from the Internet, using the `osgdb_curl` plugin

◆ Re-configuring the CMake build system to set third-party dependency options for OSG plugins, which will enable related file formats to be readable or writable

◆ A basic way to construct the native compiling tool-chain of OSG and third-party dependencies

◆ How to implement customized reader-writer interfaces from the `osgDB::ReaderWriter` base class

◆ How to design serializable classes for OSG native formats

11
Developing Visual Components

*In the past 10 chapters, we have introduced the history and installation of OSG, and the concepts and tutorials of geometries, **scene graph** nodes, rendering states, cameras, animations, interactions and the file I/O mechanism. However, there are still many aspects of a complete 3D rendering API, including text display, particles, shadows, special effects, volume rendering, and a lot more modules that are collectively called **NodeKits**. It is impossible to explain all of them in this or any book, but it is worth showing you how to make use of some typical visual components and get the ball rolling by providing a list of practical NodeKits at the end of this chapter.*

In this chapter, we will learn:

♦ How to create geometries as billboards in the scene

♦ How to display 2D and 3D texts in the scene

♦ How to design a particle system and animate it

♦ How to cast shadows onto scene objects

♦ The theory and implementation of special effects

Creating billboards in a scene

In the 3D world, a billboard is a 2D image that is always facing a designated direction. Applications can use billboard techniques to create many kinds of special effects, such as explosions, flares, sky, clouds, and trees. In fact, any object can be treated as a billboard with itself cached as the texture, while looking from a distance. Thus, the implementation of billboards becomes one of the most popular techniques, widely used in computer games and real-time visual simulation programs.

The osg::BillBoard class is used to represent a list of billboard objects in a 3D scene. It is derived from osg::Geode, and can orient all of its children (osg::Drawable objects) to face the viewer's viewpoint. It has an important method, setMode(), that is used to determine the rotation behavior, which must set one of the following enumerations as the argument:

Enumeration	Usage
POINT_ROT_EYE	Set if all of the drawables are to be rotated about the viewer's position with the object coordinate Z axis constrained to the window coordinate Y axis
POINT_ROT_WORLD	Set if all of the drawables are to be rotated about the viewer directly from their original orientation to the current eye direction in the world space.
AXIAL_ROT	Set if all of the drawables are to be rotated about an axis specified by setAxis().

Every drawable in the osg::BillBoard node should have a pivot point position, which is specified via the overloaded addDrawable() method, for example:

```
billboard->addDrawable( child, osg::Vec3(1.0f, 0.0f, 0.0f) );
```

All drawables also need a unified initial front face orientation, which is used for computing rotation values. The initial orientation is set by the setNormal() method. And each newly-added drawable must ensure that its front face orientation is in the same direction as this normal value; otherwise the billboard results may be incorrect.

Time for action – creating banners facing you

The prerequisite for implementing billboards in OSG is to create one or more quad geometries first. These quads are then managed by the osg::BillBoard class. This forces all child drawables to automatically rotate around a specified axis, or face the viewer. These can be done by presetting a unified normal value and rotating each billboard according to the normal and current rotation axis or viewing vector.

We will create two banks of OSG banners, arranged in a V, to demonstrate the use of billboards in OSG. No matter where the viewer is and how he manipulates the scene camera, the front faces of banners are facing the viewer all the time. This feature can then be used to represent textured trees and particles in user applications.

1. Include the necessary headers:

```
#include <osg/Billboard>
#include <osg/Texture2D>
#include <osgDB/ReadFile>
#include <osgViewer/Viewer>
```

2. Create the quad geometry directly from the osg::createTexturedQuadGe ometry() function. Every generated quad is of the same size and origin point, and uses the same image file. Note that the osg256.png file can be found in the data directory of your OSG installation path, but it requires the osgdb_png plugin for reading image data. Please refer to *Chapter 10, Saving and Loading Files* if you have any problems in configuring and compiling this plugin.

```
osg::Geometry* createQuad()
{
    osg::ref_ptr<osg::Texture2D> texture = new osg::Texture2D;
    osg::ref_ptr<osg::Image> image =
        osgDB::readImageFile( "Images/osg256.png" );
    texture->setImage( image.get() );

    osg::ref_ptr<osg::Geometry> quad=
        osg::createTexturedQuadGeometry(
                                osg::Vec3(-0.5f, 0.0f,-0.5f),
                                osg::Vec3(1.0f,0.0f,0.0f),
                                osg::Vec3(0.0f,0.0f,1.0f) );
    osg::StateSet* ss = quad->getOrCreateStateSet()
    ss->setTextureAttributeAndModes( 0, texture.get() );
    return quad.release();
}
```

3. In the main entry, we first create the billboard node and set the mode to POINT_ROT_EYE. That is, the drawable will rotate to face the viewer and keep its Z axis upright in the rendering window. The default normal setting of the osg::BillBoard class is the negative Y axis, so rotating it to the viewing vector will show the quads on the XOZ plane in the best appearance:

```
osg::ref_ptr<osg::Billboard> geode = new osg::Billboard;
geode->setMode( osg::Billboard::POINT_ROT_EYE );
```

4. Now let's create the banner quads and arrange them in a V formation:

```
osg::Geometry* quad = createQuad();
for ( unsigned int i=0; i<10; ++i )
{
    float id = (float)i;
    geode->addDrawable( quad, osg::Vec3(-2.5f+0.2f*id, id, 0.0f)
);
    geode->addDrawable( quad, osg::Vec3( 2.5f-0.2f*id, id, 0.0f)
);
}
```

5. All quad textures' backgrounds are automatically cleared because of the alpha test, which is performed internally in the `osgdb_png` plugin. That means we have to set correct rendering order of all the drawables to ensure that the entire process is working properly:

```
osg::StateSet* ss = geode->getOrCreateStateSet();
ss->setRenderingHint( osg::StateSet::TRANSPARENT_BIN );
```

6. It's time for us to start the viewer, as there are no important steps left to create and render billboards:

```
osgViewer::Viewer viewer;
viewer.setSceneData( geode.get() );
return viewer.run();
```

7. Try navigating in the scene graph:

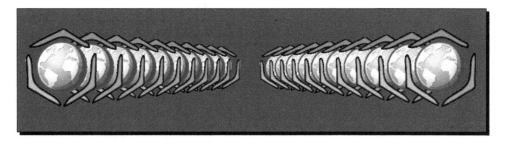

8. You will find that the billboard's children are always rotating to face the viewer, but the images' Y directions are never changed (point to the window's Y coordinate all along). Replace the mode `POINT_ROT_EYE` to `POINT_ROT_WORLD` and see if there is any difference:

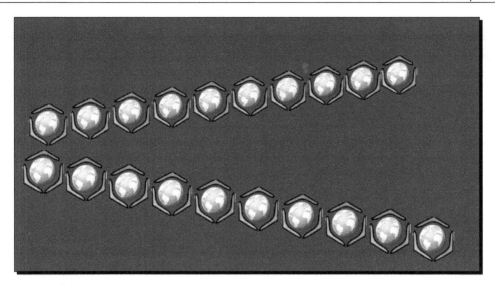

What just happened?

The basic usage of billboards in OSG **scene graph** is shown in this example. But it is still possible to be further improved. All the banner geometries here are created with the createQuad() function, which means that the same quad and the same texture are reallocated at least 20 times! The object sharing mechanism is certainly an optimization here. Unfortunately, it is not clever enough to add the same drawable object to osg::Billboard with different positions, which could cause the node to work improperly. What we could do is to create multiple quad geometries that share the same texture object. This will highly reduce the video card's texture memory occupancy and the rendering load.

Another possible issue is that somebody may require loaded nodes to be rendered as billboards, not only as drawables. A node can consist of different kinds of child nodes, and is much richer than a basic shape or geometry mesh. OSG also provides the osg::AutoTransform class, which automatically rotates an object's children to be aligned with screen coordinates.

Have a go hero – planting massive trees on the ground

Billboards are widely used for simulating massive trees and plants. One or more tree pictures with transparent backgrounds are applied to quads of different sizes, and then added to the billboard node. These trees will automatically face the viewer, or to be more real, rotate about an axis as if its branches and leaves are always at the front. Now let's try to create some simple billboard trees. We only need to prepare an image nice enough (for instance, `Images/tree0.rgba` in the `data` folder of the OpenSceneGraph prebuilts introduced in *Chapter 2, Compilation and Installation of OpenSceneGraph*), and follow the steps given for the previous example to create your own trees and plants.

Creating texts

Text is one of the most important components in all kinds of virtual reality programs. It is used everywhere—for displaying stats on the screen, labeling 3D objects, logging, and debugging. Texts always have at least one font to specify the typeface and qualities, as well as other parameters, including size, alignment, layout (left-to-right or right-to-left), and resolution, to determine its display behaviors. OpenGL doesn't directly support the loading of fonts and displaying texts in 3D space, but OSG provides full support for rendering high quality texts and configuring different text attributes, which makes it much easier to develop related applications.

The **osgText** library actually implements all font and text functionalities. It requires the `osgdb_freetype` plugin to work properly. This plugin can load and parse `TrueType` fonts with the help of **FreeType**, a famous third-party dependency. After that, it returns an `osgText::Font` instance, which is made up of a complete set of texture glyphs. The entire process can be described with the `osgText::readFontFile()` function.

The `osgText::TextBase` class is the pure base class of all OSG text types. It is derived from `osg::Drawable`, but doesn't support display lists by default. Its subclass, `osgText::Text`, is used to manage flat characters in the world coordinates. Important methods includes `setFont()`, `setPosition()`, `setCharacterSize()`, and `setText()`, each of which is easy to understand and use, as shown in the following example.

Time for action – writing descriptions for the Cessna

This time we are going to display a Cessna in the 3D space and provide descriptive texts in front of the rendered scene. A **heads-up display** (HUD) camera can be used here, which is rendered after the **main camera**, and only clears the **depth buffer** for directly updating texts to the **frame buffer**. The HUD camera will then render its child nodes in a way that is always visible.

1. Include the necessary headers:

```
#include <osg/Camera>
#include <osgDB/ReadFile>
#include <osgText/Font>
#include <osgText/Text>
#include <osgViewer/Viewer>
```

2. The `osgText::readFontFile()` function is used for reading a suitable font file, for instance, an undistorted `TrueType` font. The OSG data paths (specified with `OSG_FILE_PATH`) and the windows system path will be searched to see if the specified file exists:

```
osg::ref_ptr<osgText::Font> g_font =
    osgText::readFontFile("fonts/arial.ttf");
```

3. Create a standard HUD camera and set a 2D orthographic projection matrix for the purpose of drawing 3D texts in two dimensions. The camera should not receive any user events, and should never be affected by any parent transformations. These are guaranteed by the `setAllowEventFocus()` and `setReferenceFrame()` methods:

```
osg::Camera* createHUDCamera( double left, double right,
                              double bottom, double top )
{
    osg::ref_ptr<osg::Camera> camera = new osg::Camera;
    camera->setReferenceFrame( osg::Transform::ABSOLUTE_RF );
    camera->setClearMask( GL_DEPTH_BUFFER_BIT );
    camera->setRenderOrder( osg::Camera::POST_RENDER );
    camera->setAllowEventFocus( false );
    camera->setProjectionMatrix(
        osg::Matrix::ortho2D(left, right, bottom, top) );
    return camera.release();
}
```

4. The text is created by a separate global function, too. It defines a font object describing every character's glyph, as well as the size and position parameters in the world space, and the content of the text. In the HUD text implementation, texts should always align with the XOY plane:

```
osgText::Text* createText( const osg::Vec3& pos,
                           const std::string& content,
                           float size )
{
    osg::ref_ptr<osgText::Text> text = new osgText::Text;
    text->setFont( g_font.get() );
    text->setCharacterSize( size );
    text->setAxisAlignment( osgText::TextBase::XY_PLANE );
    text->setPosition( pos );
    text->setText( content );
    return text.release();
}
```

5. In the main entry, we create a new osg::Geode node and add multiple text objects to it. These introduce the leading features of a Cessna. Of course, you can add your own explanations about this type of monoplane by using additional osgText::Text drawables:

```
osg::ref_ptr<osg::Geode> textGeode = new osg::Geode;
textGeode->addDrawable( createText(
    osg::Vec3(150.0f, 500.0f, 0.0f),
    "The Cessna monoplane",
    20.0f)
);
textGeode->addDrawable( createText(
    osg::Vec3(150.0f, 450.0f, 0.0f),
    "Six-seat, low-wing and twin-engined",
    15.0f)
);
```

6. The node including all texts should be added to the HUD camera. To ensure that the texts won't be affected by OpenGL normals and lights (they are textured geometries, after all), we have to disable lighting for the camera node:

```
osg::Camera* camera = createHUDCamera(0, 1024, 0, 768);
camera->addChild( textGeode.get() );
camera->getOrCreateStateSet()->setMode(
    GL_LIGHTING, osg::StateAttribute::OFF );
```

7. The last step is to add the Cessna model and the camera to the scene graph, and start the viewer as usual:

```
osg::ref_ptr<osg::Group> root = new osg::Group;
root->addChild( osgDB::readNodeFile("cessna.osg") );
root->addChild( camera );

osgViewer::Viewer viewer;
viewer.setSceneData( root.get() );
return viewer.run();
```

8. In the rendering window, you will see two lines of text over the Cessna model. No matter how you translate, rotate, or scale on the **view matrix**, the HUD texts will never be covered. Thus, users can always read the most important information directly, without looking away from their usual perspectives:

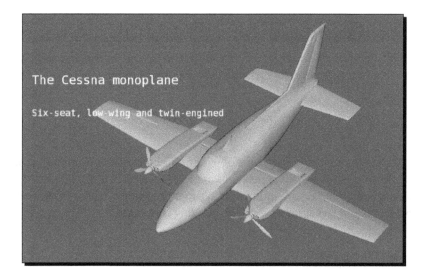

What just happened?

To build the example code with CMake or other native compilers, you should add the **osgText** library as dependence, and include the **osgParticle**, **osgShadow**, and **osgFX** libraries.

Here we specify the font from the `arial.ttf` file. This is a default font in most Windows and UNIX systems, and can also be found in OSG data paths. As you can see, this kind of font offers developers highly-precise displayed characters, regardless of font size settings. This is because the outlines of `TrueType` fonts are made of mathematical line segments and Bezier curves, which means they are not vector fonts. Bitmap (raster) fonts don't have such features and may sometimes look ugly when resized. Disable `setFont()` here, to force `osgText` to use a default 12x12 bitmap font. Can you figure out the difference between these two fonts?

We define our text objects with the following code:

```
text->setAxisAlignment( osgText::TextBase::XY_PLANE );
text->setPosition( pos );
```

There are two questions for you to think about:

1. Firstly, why must the flat text be placed in the XOY plane? What will happen if we don't do that? Should we use an HUD camera or not?

2. Secondly, what is the reference frame of these text positions? That is, when setting a text object's position, how can we locate it in the rendering window? Is it related with the orthographic **projection matrix**? Could you move the two lines of our example to the right-bottom corner?

The setText() method of osgText::Text accepts std::string variables directly. Meanwhile, it also accepts wide characters as the input argument. For example:

```
wchar_t* wstr = …;
text->setText( wstr );
```

This makes it possible to support multi-languages, for instance, Chinese and Japanese characters. Now, try obtaining a sequence of wide characters either by defining them directly or converting from multi-byte characters, and apply them to the osgText::Text object, to see if the language that you are interested in can be rendered. Please note that the font should also be changed to support the corresponding language.

Creating 3D texts

Believe it or not, OSG also provides support for 3D texts in the **scene graph**. Each character will be extruded with a depth parameter and finally rendered with OpenGL's **vertex array** mechanism. The implementer class, osgText::Text3D, is also derived form osgText::Textbase and thus has nearly the same methods as osgText::Text. It requires an osgText::Font3D instance as the font parameter, which can be obtained by the osgText::readFont3DFile() function.

Time for action – creating texts in the world space

A simple 3D text object will be created in this example. Like the 2D text class
osgText::Text, the osgText::Text3D class also inherits a list of methods to set basic
text parameters, including position, size, alignment, font object, and the content. 3D texts
are most likely to be used as a special effect of games and applications.

1. Include the necessary headers:

```
#include <osg/MatrixTransform>
#include <osgDB/ReadFile>
#include <osgText/Font3D>
#include <osgText/Text3D>
#include <osgViewer/Viewer>
```

2. Read an appropriate font file with the osgText::readFont3DFile() function,
which is similar to osgText::readFontFile(). Using the osgdb_freetype
plugin, TrueType fonts can be parsed into finely-detailed 3D character glyphs:

```
osg::ref_ptr<osgText::Font3D> g_font3D =
    osgText::readFont3DFile("fonts/arial.ttf");
```

3. So we are going to imitate the createText() function in the last example.
The only difference is that we have to set an extra depth parameter for the text
character to make it stand out in the 3D world. The setAxisAlignment() method
here indicates that the text object is placed on the XOZ plane, with its front faces
facing the negative Y axis:

```
osgText::Text3D* createText3D( const osg::Vec3& pos,
                               const std::string& content,
                               float size, float depth )
{
    osg::ref_ptr<osgText::Text3D> text = new osgText::Text3D;
    text->setFont( g_font3D.get() );
    text->setCharacterSize( size );
    text->setCharacterDepth( depth );
    text->setAxisAlignment( osgText::TextBase::XZ_PLANE );
    text->setPosition( pos );
    text->setText( content );
    return text.release();
}
```

4. Create a 3D text object with short words. Note that because 3D texts are actually made up of vertices and geometry primitives, abuse of them may cause high resource consumption:

```
osg::ref_ptr<osg::Geode> textGeode = new osg::Geode;
textGeode->addDrawable(
    createText3D(osg::Vec3(), "The Cessna", 20.0f, 10.0f) );
```

5. This time we add an `osg::MatrixTransform` as the parent of `textGeode`. It will apply an additional transformation matrix to the **model-view matrix** when rendering all text drawables, and thus change their displayed positions and attitudes in the world coordinates:

```
osg::ref_ptr<osg::MatrixTransform> textNode= new
osg::MatrixTransform;
textNode->setMatrix( osg::Matrix::translate(0.0f, 0.0f, 10.0f) );
textNode->addChild( textGeode.get() );
```

6. Add our Cessna to the scene graph again, and start the viewer:

```
osg::ref_ptr<osg::Group> root = new osg::Group;
root->addChild( osgDB::readNodeFile("cessna.osg") );
root->addChild( textNode.get() );

osgViewer::Viewer viewer;
viewer.setSceneData( root.get() );
return viewer.run();
```

7. You will see some big letters above the model, but in fact the initial position of the 3D text object should be at (0, 0, 0), which is also the origin of the Cessna. The `osg::MatrixTransform` node here prevents the model and the text from overlapping each other, by translating `textGeode` to a new position (0, 0, 10):

What just happened?

Both 2D and 3D texts can be transformed by their parent nodes. This is always helpful when we have to compose a paragraph or move a model followed by a text label. Similar to OSG's transformation nodes, the setPosition() method of osgText::TextBase only sets the location under the **relative reference frame** of the text object's parent. The same thing happens to the setRotation() method, which determines the rotation of the text, and setAxisAlignment(), which aligns the text with a specified plane.

The only exception is the SCREEN alignment mode:

```
text->setAxisAlignment( osgText::TextBase::SCREEN );
```

This mimics the billboard technique of scene objects, and makes the text (either osg::Text or osg::Text3D) always face the viewer. In 3D Geographic Information Systems (3DGIS), placing landmarks on earth or cities as billboards is a very common operation, and can be implemented with the SCREEN mode. In this case, rotation and parent transformations are not available and should not be used, as they may cause confusion and potential problems.

Creating particle animations

Particles are used in various 3D applications for special effects such as smoke, dust, explosions, fluid, fire, and rain. It is much more difficult to build and manage a complete particle system rather than construct other simple scene objects. In fact, OSG provides a large number of classes in the **osgParticle** library to enable customization of complex particle systems, most of which may be extended and overridden using inheritance, if user-defined algorithms are needed.

The particle class, osgParticle::Particle, represents the atomic particle unit. It is often used as a design template before the simulation loop starts, and copied and regenerated by the particle system in run-time to render massive particles.

The particle system class, osgParticle::ParticleSystem, manages the creation, updating, rendering, and destruction of all particles. It is derived from osg::Drawable, so it can accept different rendering attributes and modes, just like normal drawables. It should be added to an osg::Geode nod, as the last class.

The emitter abstract class (osgParticle::Emitter) defines the number and basic properties of newly-generated particles every frame. Its descendant class, osgParticle::ModularEmitter, works like a standard emitter, which provides the mechanism for controlling particles to be created. It always holds three kinds of sub-controllers:

- The placer (osgParticle::Placer) sets the initial position of every particle
- The shooter (osgParticle::Shooter) sets the initial velocities of particles
- The counter (osgParticle::Counter) determines how many particles should be created

The program's abstract class (osgParticle::Program) manipulates the position, velocity, and other properties of each individual particle during its lifetime. Its descendant class, osgParticle::ModularProgram, is composed of a list of osgParticle::Operator subclasses to perform operations on existing particles.

Both the emitter and program classes are indirectly derived from osg::Node, which means that they can be treated as nodes in the **scene graph**. During the update and cull traversals, they will be automatically traversed, and sub-controllers and operators will be executed. The particle system will then make use of their results to re-compute and draw its managed particles. The re-computing process can be done with the osgParticle::ParticleSys temUpdater, which is actually a node, too. The updater should be placed after the emitter and the program in the scene graph, in order to ensure that updates are carried out in the correct order. For example:

```
root->addChild( emitter );
root->addChild( program );
root->addChild( updater );  // Added last
```

The following diagram shows the hierarchy of the above **osgParticle** classes:

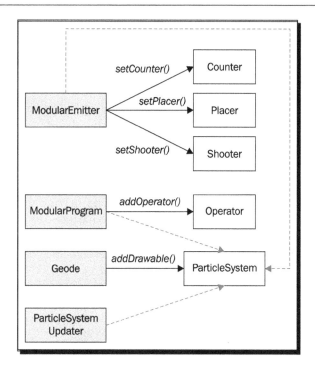

Time for action – building a fountain in the scene

We will demonstrate how to implement a basic particle fountain. The simulation of a fountain can be described as follows: firstly, the water emitted from a point rises with a certain initial speed; then the speed decreases due to gravity of the earth, until reaching the highest point; after that, the water drops fall down onto the ground or into the pool. To achieve this, an `osgParticle::ParticleSystem` node, along with an emitter and a program processor, should be created and added to the scene graph.

1. Include the necessary headers:

```
#include <osg/MatrixTransform>
#include <osg/Point>
#include <osg/PointSprite>
#include <osg/Texture2D>
#include <osg/BlendFunc>
#include <osgDB/ReadFile>
#include <osgGA/StateSetManipulator>
#include <osgParticle/ParticleSystem>
#include <osgParticle/ParticleSystemUpdater>
#include <osgParticle/ModularEmitter>
#include <osgParticle/ModularProgram>
#include <osgParticle/AccelOperator>
```

```
#include <osgViewer/ViewerEventHandlers>
#include <osgViewer/Viewer>
```

2. The entire process of creating a particle system can be implemented in a separate user function:

```
osgParticle::ParticleSystem* createParticleSystem(
    osg::Group* parent )
{
    ...
}
```

3. Now we are inside the function. Every particle system has a template particle that determines the behaviors of all newly-generated particles. Here, we set the shape of each particle in this system to POINT. With the help of OpenGL's **point sprite** extension, these points can be rendered as textured billboards, which is enough in most cases:

```
osg::ref_ptr<osgParticle::ParticleSystem> ps =
    new osgParticle::ParticleSystem;
ps->getDefaultParticleTemplate().setShape(
    osgParticle::Particle::POINT );
```

4. Set the rendering attributes and modes of the particle system. These will automatically affect every rendered particle. Here, we attach a texture image to particles, and define a blending function in order to make the background of the image transparent:

```
osg::ref_ptr<osg::BlendFunc> blendFunc = new osg::BlendFunc;
blendFunc->setFunction( GL_SRC_ALPHA, GL_ONE_MINUS_SRC_ALPHA );

osg::ref_ptr<osg::Texture2D> texture = new osg::Texture2D;
texture->setImage( osgDB::readImageFile("Images/smoke.rgb") );
```

5. Another two important attributes are osg::Point and osg::PointSprite. The first will set the point size (diameter of a rasterized point), and the latter will enable point sprites, which can effectively replace a four-point quad with a single vertex, without requiring to specify the texture coordinates and rotate the front face to the viewer. Besides, we had better turn off the lighting of particles, and we set a suitable rendering order to enable it to be drawn correctly in the whole **scene graph**:

```
osg::StateSet* ss = ps->getOrCreateStateSet();
ss->setAttributeAndModes( blendFunc.get() );
ss->setTextureAttributeAndModes( 0, texture.get() );

ss->setAttribute( new osg::Point(20.0f) );
```

```
ss->setTextureAttributeAndModes( 0, new osg::PointSprite );
```

```
ss->setMode( GL_LIGHTING, osg::StateAttribute::OFF);
ss->setRenderingHint( osg::StateSet::TRANSPARENT_BIN );
```

6. The `osgParticle::RandomRateCounter` class generates a random number of particles every frame. It is derived from `osgParticle::Counter` and has a `setRateRange()` method that is used to specify the minimum and maximum number of elements:

```
osg::ref_ptr<osgParticle::RandomRateCounter> rrc =
    new osgParticle::RandomRateCounter;
rrc->setRateRange( 500, 800 );
```

7. Add the random rate counter to the standard emitter. Also, we have to attach the particle system to it as the operation destination. By default, the modular emitter already includes a point-shape placer at (0, 0, 0), and a radial shooter that chooses a direction and an initial speed randomly for each particle, so we don't need to specify new ones here:

```
osg::ref_ptr<osgParticle::ModularEmitter> emitter =
    new osgParticle::ModularEmitter;
emitter->setParticleSystem( ps.get() );
emitter->setCounter( rrc.get() );
```

8. The `osgParticle::AccelOperator` class applies a constant acceleration to all particles, on the fly. To simulate gravity, we can either use `setAcceleration()` to specify the acceleration vector of gravity, or call the `setToGravity()` method directly:

```
osg::ref_ptr<osgParticle::AccelOperator> accel =
    new osgParticle::AccelOperator;
accel->setToGravity();
```

9. Add the only operator to the standard program node, and attach the particle system, too:

```
osg::ref_ptr<osgParticle::ModularProgram> program =
    new osgParticle::ModularProgram;
program->setParticleSystem( ps.get() );
program->addOperator( accel.get() );
```

10. The particle system, which is actually a drawable object, should be added to a **leaf node** of the **scene graph**. After that, we add all particle-related nodes to the `parent` node. Here is an interesting issue of world and local coordinates, which will be discussed later:

```
osg::ref_ptr<osg::Geode> geode = new osg::Geode;
geode->addDrawable( ps.get() );

parent->addChild( emitter.get() );
parent->addChild( program.get() );
parent->addChild( geode.get() );
return ps.get();
```

11. Now let's return to the main entry. Firstly, we create a new transformation node for locating the particle system:

```
osg::ref_ptr<osg::MatrixTransform> mt = new osg::MatrixTransform;
mt->setMatrix( osg::Matrix::translate(1.0f, 0.0f, 0.0f) );
```

12. Create all particle system components and, add them to the input transformation node. The particle system should also be registered to a particle system updater, using the `addParticleSystem()` method.

```
osgParticle::ParticleSystem* ps = createParticleSystem( mt.get()
);

osg::ref_ptr<osgParticle::ParticleSystemUpdater> updater =
    new osgParticle::ParticleSystemUpdater;
updater->addParticleSystem( ps );
```

13. Add all of the nodes above to the scene's **root node**, including a small axes model (that can be found in the sample data folder, see *Chapter 2, Compilation and Installation of OpenSceneGraph* for details) as a reference. After that, start the viewer and just take a seat:

```
osg::ref_ptr<osg::Group> root = new osg::Group;
root->addChild( updater.get() );
root->addChild( mt.get() );
root->addChild( osgDB::readNodeFile("axes.osg") );
osgViewer::Viewer viewer;
viewer.setSceneData( root.get() );
return viewer.run();
```

14. Our particle fountain is finally finished! Zoom in and you will find that all particles start from a point on the positive X axis, at x = 1. Now, with just a few simple fixed-function attributes, particles are rendered as well-textured points, and each particle element appears much like a water drop because of the blending operation:

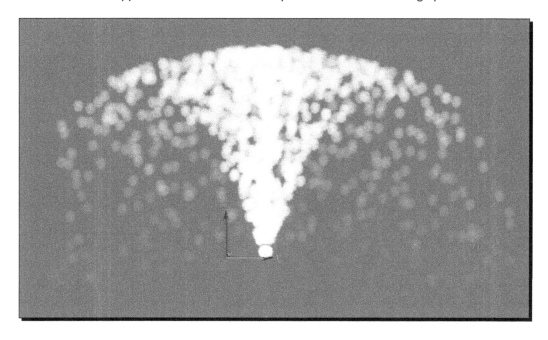

What just happened?

In the above image, we can find out that the whole particle system is translated to (1, 0, 0) in the world. That's because we add the emitter, the program, and the particle system's parent to a transformation node. But, in fact, the result will be different if we put one of the three elements under the transformation node and the other two under the root node. Adding only the `osg::Geode` node to an `osg::Transform` will make the entire particle system move with it; but adding only the emitter will change the transform behavior of new-born particles but will leave any existing ones in the world coordinate. Similarly, only adding the program node will make the parent transformation node only affect the operators.

A good example is to design flight jets. While spiraling in the sky, the flight plume's location and direction will vary at any time. Using an `osg::MatrixTransform` as the parent of the particle emitter will be helpful in representing such a particle-based scenario. The particle system and the updater should not be placed under the same transformation node; otherwise all old particles in the air will move and rotate with it, too, which is certainly unreasonable in reality.

Have a go hero – designing a rotary sprinkler

Have you ever seen a rotary sprinkler? It consists of at least one rounded head that can automatically rotate 360 degrees and spray water around the sprinkler's diameter. To create such a machine with a simple cylinder model and the particle system, you have to design a modular emitter with the shooter shooting particles to a specified horizontal direction, and a modular program with the gravity acceleration operator.

As a hint, the default radial shooter (`osgParticle::RadialShooter`) uses two angles, `theta` and `phi`, within specified ranges, in order to determine a random direction of particles, for example:

```
osg::ref_ptr<osgParticle::RadialShooter> shooter =
    new osgParticle::RadialShooter;
// Theta is the angle between the velocity vector and Z axis
shooter->setThetaRange( osg::PI_2 - 0.1f, osg::PI_2 + 0.1f );
// Phi is the angle between X axis and the velocity vector projected
// onto the XOY plane
shooter->setPhiRange( -0.1f, 0.1f );
// Set the initial speed range
shooter->setInitialSpeedRange( 5.0f, 8.0f );
```

To rotate the initial direction of emitting particles, you can either use an update callback that changes the theta and phi ranges, or consider adding a transformation node as the emitter's parent.

Creating shadows on the ground

Shadow is also an important component of 3D applications. When constructing massive 3D scenes like digital cities, modelers may first design and compute lights on buildings, models, and the ground in modeling software like 3dsmax, Maya, and Blender, and then bake the shadows to these models' textures. Then, real-time applications will read the model files with textures, and the shadows are then rendered statically in the rendering window.

Real-time shadows are also possible, but not for unlimited use. The **osgShadow** library provides a range of shadow techniques on a **scene graph** that needs to have shadows cast upon it. The core class, named `osgShadow::ShadowedScene`, should be used as the root node of these shadowy sub-graphs. It accepts an `osgShadow::ShadowTechnique` instance as the technique used to implement shadowing. Deriving the technique class will extend the **scene graph** to support more algorithms and solutions, which will enrich the shadow functionalities.

Time for action – receiving and casting shadows

Our goal is to show you the construction of a scene by casting shadows on models. It always includes a specific shadow scene root, an inbuilt or custom **shadow technique**, and child nodes with a distinguishable receiving or casting mask. A normal scene can't be shadowed without adding a shadow scene as the parent, and on the contrary, a shadowed scene graph can either remove the osgShadow::ShadowedScene **root node** or remove the **shadow technique** object (by simply setting a null one) applied to the node to exclude all **shadow** computations and effects. In this example, we just create and manage the **scene graph** under the shadow scene root, and make use of the predefined shadow mapping technique to render both real objects and shadows correctly.

1. Include the necessary headers:

```
#include <osg/AnimationPath>
#include <osg/MatrixTransform>
#include <osgDB/ReadFile>
#include <osgShadow/ShadowedScene>
#include <osgShadow/ShadowMap>
#include <osgViewer/Viewer>
```

2. The code for creating the animation path is copied from *Chapter 8, Animating Scene Objects*. It uses a few sample control points to generate a circle, which can then be applied to an osg::AnimationPathCallback to implement a time-varying transformation pathway:

```
osg::AnimationPath* createAnimationPath( float radius, float time
)
{
    osg::ref_ptr<osg::AnimationPath> path =
        new osg::AnimationPath;
    path->setLoopMode( osg::AnimationPath::LOOP );

    unsigned int numSamples = 32;
    float delta_yaw = 2.0f * osg::PI/((float)numSamples - 1.0f);
    float delta_time = time / (float)numSamples;
    for ( unsigned int i=0; i<numSamples; ++i )
    {
        float yaw = delta_yaw * (float)i;
        osg::Vec3 pos( sinf(yaw)*radius, cosf(yaw)*radius, 0.0f );
        osg::Quat rot( -yaw, osg::Z_AXIS );
        path->insert( delta_time * (float)i,
                    osg::AnimationPath::ControlPoint(pos, rot)
);
    );
```

```
    }
    return path.release();
}
```

3. Set masks of shadow receivers and casters. The AND operation of these two masks must yield 0:

```
unsigned int rcvShadowMask = 0x1;
unsigned int castShadowMask = 0x2;
```

4. Create the ground model. This only receives shadows from other scene objects, so performing an AND operation on its node mask and the receiver mask should return a non-zero value, and the bitwise AND between the node mask and the caster mask should always return 0. Therefore, we can determine the node mask according to such principles:

```
osg::ref_ptr<osg::MatrixTransform> groundNode =
    new osg::MatrixTransform;
groundNode->addChild( osgDB::readNodeFile("lz.osg") );
groundNode->setMatrix( osg::Matrix::translate(0.0f, 0.0f,-200.0f)
);
groundNode->setNodeMask( rcvShadowMask );
```

5. Set the Cessna model, which also accepts an update callback to perform path animation. In our example, it only casts a shadow on the ground and other scene objects:

```
osg::ref_ptr<osg::MatrixTransform> cessnaNode =
    new osg::MatrixTransform;
cessnaNode->addChild( osgDB::readNodeFile("cessna.osg.0,0,90.rot")
);
cessnaNode->setNodeMask( castShadowMask );

osg::ref_ptr<osg::AnimationPathCallback> apcb =
    new osg::AnimationPathCallback;
apcb->setAnimationPath( createAnimationPath(50.0f, 6.0f) );
cessnaNode->setUpdateCallback( apcb.get() );
```

6. Add a dump truck model onto the ground using an approximate translation matrix. It receives a shadow from the Cessna circling overhead, and casts a shadow onto the ground. This means that we have to set an appropriate node mask to retrieve a non-zero value while performing a bitwise AND with the union of both the receiver and caster masks:

```
osg::ref_ptr<osg::MatrixTransform> truckNode =
    new osg::MatrixTransform;
truckNode->addChild( osgDB::readNodeFile("dumptruck.osg") );
```

```
truckNode->setMatrix( osg::Matrix::translate(0.0f, 0.0f,-100.0f)
);
truckNode->setNodeMask( rcvShadowMask|castShadowMask );
```

7. Set a light source for producing shadows. We specify the parallel light's direction with the `setPosition()` method to generate declining shadows here:

```
osg::ref_ptr<osg::LightSource> source = new osg::LightSource;
    source->getLight()->setPosition( osg::Vec4(4.0, 4.0, 10.0,
0.0) );
    source->getLight()->setAmbient( osg::Vec4(0.2, 0.2, 0.2, 1.0)
);
    source->getLight()->setDiffuse( osg::Vec4(0.8, 0.8, 0.8, 1.0)
);
```

8. We must set a shadow technique here. There are already several OpenGL-based shadow techniques implemented by organizations and individuals, including **shadow mapping** using projective texture mapping, shadow volumes realized by **stencil buffer**, and other implementations. We choose the famous and effective **shadow mapping** (`osgShadow::ShadowMap`) technique, and set its necessary parameters including the light source, shadow texture's size, and unit:

```
osg::ref_ptr<osgShadow::ShadowMap> sm = new osgShadow::ShadowMap;
sm->setLight( source.get() );
sm->setTextureSize( osg::Vec2s(1024, 1024) );
sm->setTextureUnit( 1 );
```

9. Set the shadow scene's root node, and apply the technique instance, as well as shadow masks to it:

```
osg::ref_ptr<osgShadow::ShadowedScene> root =
    new osgShadow::ShadowedScene;
root->setShadowTechnique( sm.get() );
root->setReceivesShadowTraversalMask( rcvShadowMask );
root->setCastsShadowTraversalMask( castShadowMask );
```

10. Add all models and the light source to the root and start the viewer:

```
root->addChild( groundNode.get() );
root->addChild( cessnaNode.get() );
root->addChild( truckNode.get() );
root->addChild( source.get() );

osgViewer::Viewer viewer;
viewer.setSceneData( root.get() );
return viewer.run();
```

11. With a simple light source, and the most frequently-used and stable shadow mapping technique, we can now render the ground, Cessna, and dump truck in a shadowed scene. You may change the texture resolution with `setTextureSize()` method, or switch to other shadow techniques to see if there are any changes or improvements:

What just happened?

The `setNodeMask()` was introduced in *Chapter 9, Interacting with Outside Elements*. There, it was used for indicating the intersection visitor to pass a specified sub-scene graph. But this time, we make use of this method to distinguish between the receiver and casters of shadows. Here, it performs a bitwise logical AND operation on the shadow scene node's masks, instead of the previous node visitor's traversal mask.

The `setNodeMask()` can even be used to cull the node from the to-be-rendered scene, that is, to remove certain sub-graphs from the rendering pipeline. In the **cull traversal** of the OSG backend, each node's mask value will be computed with the camera node's cull mask, which is set by `setCullMask()` method of the `osg::Camera` class. Therefore, nodes and their sub-graphs will not be drawn if the node mask is 0, because the AND operation always returns 0 in the culling process.

Note that the current OSG shadow map implementation only handles cast shadow masks of nodes. It will adapt the shadow map to fit the bounds of all objects set to cast shadows, but you have to handle objects that do not need to receive shadows yourselves, for example, don't add them to the shadow scene node. In practice, almost all objects will be set to receive shadows, and only the ground should be set to not cast shadows.

Have a go hero – testing other shadow techniques

There are more shadow techniques besides **shadow mapping**, including the simplest implementation using only textures and fixed-functions, volume algorithm using the **stencil buffer** (not fully completed at present), soft-edged shadows, parallel-split shadows, light space perspective shadows, and so on.

You may find a brief introduction to them at: `http://www.openscenegraph.org/ projects/osg/wiki/Support/ProgrammingGuide/osgShadow`.

The knowledge of how to create advanced graphical effects (shadows is only one field) is profound. If you have an interest in learning more, you can read some advanced books, such as *Real-time rendering* by *Akenine-Möller, Haines, and Hoffman*, and *Computer Graphics: Principles and Practice* by *Foley, Van Dam* et al.

Now, choose one of the best performers among these shadow techniques. Another option is to design your own shadow techniques, if your application development requirements cannot be met by existing shadow techniques and there is a tangible benefit to developing at your own risk.

Implementing special effects

The **osgFX** library provides a special effects framework. It is a little analogous to the **osgShadow NodeKits**, which has a shadow scene as the parent of all shadowy sub-graphs. The `osgFX::Effect` class, which is derived from `osg::Group`, implements special effects on its child nodes, but never affects its siblings and parent nodes.

The `osgFX::Effect` is a pure base class that doesn't realize actual effects at all. Its derivatives include anisotropic lighting, highlights, cartoons, bump mapping, and outline and scribe effect implementations, and it can be extended at any time for different purposes.

Time for action – drawing the outline of models

Outlining an object is a practical technique for representing special effects in gaming, multimedia, and industry applications. One implementation in OpenGL is to write a constant value into the **stencil buffer** and then render the object with thick wireframe lines. After the two-pass rendering process, an outline around the object will be populated, the thickness of which is just one half of the wireframe's. Fortunately, this has already been implemented in the **osgFX** library, in the `osgFX::Outline` class—a derived class of `osgFX::Effect`.

1. Include the necessary headers:

   ```
   #include <osg/Group>
   #include <osgDB/ReadFile>
   #include <osgFX/Outline>
   #include <osgViewer/Viewer>
   ```

2. Load a Cessna model for outlining:

   ```
   osg::ref_ptr<osg::Node> model = osgDB::readNodeFile( "cessna.osg"
   );
   ```

3. Create a new outline effect node. Set the width and color parameters, and add the model node as the child:

   ```
   osg::ref_ptr<osgFX::Outline> outline = new osgFX::Outline;
   outline->setWidth( 8 );
   outline->setColor( osg::Vec4(1.0f, 0.0f, 0.0f, 1.0f) );
   outline->addChild( model.get() );
   ```

4. As discussed before, outlining requires the **stencil buffer** in order to accurately render the results. So we have to set valid stencil bits for the rendering windows in the `osg::DisplaySettings` instance. The stencil bits is setting 0 by default, which means that the **stencil buffer** will not be available.

   ```
   osg::DisplaySettings::instance()->setMinimumNumStencilBits( 1 );
   ```

5. Before starting the viewer, don't forget to reset the clear mask, in order to also clear stencil bits every frame. The outline effect node is used as the **root node** here. It can also be added to a more complex **scene graph** for rendering.

   ```
   osgViewer::Viewer viewer;
   viewer.getCamera()->setClearMask(
       GL_COLOR_BUFFER_BIT|GL_DEPTH_BUFFER_BIT|GL_STENCIL_BUFFER_BIT
   );
   ```

```
viewer.setSceneData( outline.get() );
return viewer.run();
```

6. That's it! This is really a simple example when compared to other examples in this chapter. However, it may not be easy to realize a similar one by using traditional nodes and attached state sets. The **osgFX** library uses the concept of multi-pass rendering here to realize such kinds of special effects:

What just happened?

OSG's effect classes are actually collections of state attributes and modes. They allow multiple state sets to be managed for a single host node. When traversing the **scene graph**, the node is traversed as many times as the number of predefined state sets. As a result, the model will be drawn multiple times (so-called multiple passes) in the rendering pipeline, each of which applies different attributes and modes, and is then combined with previous passes.

For outlining implementation, there are two passes defined internally: firstly, the model is drawn with the stencil buffer set to 1 if passable; secondly, the model is drawn again in wireframe mode, with a thick enough line width and another stencil test process. Pixels will only be drawn to the **frame buffer** if the **stencil buffer** is not set the last time, and thus the result has a colored outline. For better understanding of how this works, you are encouraged to take a look into the implementation of the osgFX::Outline class in the src/osgFX folder of the OSG source code.

Playing with more NodeKits

There are a lot more **NodeKits**, either in the OSG source code or contributed by third parties. Each one provides a specific functionality to be used in the **scene graph**. Most of them also extend OSG native formats (`.osg`, `.osgb`, and so on) to support reading or writing extended node and object types.

Here is a table of some of the existing **NodeKits** (and practical applications) that may enrich the visual components in OSG-based applications. Play with them freely, or attend one of these communities to share your ideas and codes. Note that not all of these **NodeKits** are available for direct use, but they are always believed to be worthy, and will be sure to draw the attention of more contributors:

Name	Description	Website
`osgART`	Augmented reality (AR) support	`http://www.osgart.org/`
`osgAudio`	Sound toolkits in OSG	`http://code.google.com/p/osgaudio/`
`osgBullet`	Physics engine support using the **Bullet** library	`http://code.google.com/p/osgbullet/`
`osgcal`	Character animation support using the **Cal3D** library	`http://osgcal.sourceforge.net/`
`osgCairo`	**Cairo** interface support	`http://code.google.com/p/osgcairo/`
`osgCompute (osgCUDA)`	Parallel streaming processor support	`http://www.cg.informatik.uni-siegen.de/svt/osgcompute/`
`osgEarth`	Scalable terrain rendering toolkit	`http://osgearth.org/`
`osgIntrospection`	An introspection or reflection framework	`http://www.openscenegraph.org/svn/osg/osgIntrospection/` (only available in SVN at present)
`osgManipulator`	3D interactive manipulators	In the core OSG source code
`osgMaxExp`	3dsmax's OSG scene exporter	`http://sourceforge.net/projects/osgmaxexp/`
`osgModeling`	Parametric modeling and polygon techniques support	`http://code.google.com/p/osgmodeling/`
`osgNV`	Cg and NVIDIA extensions support	`http://osgnv.sourceforge.net/`

Name	Description	Website
osgOcean	Simulation toolkit for above and below water effects	`http://code.google.com/p/osgocean/`
osgPango	Improvements of the font rendering using the **Pango** library	`http://code.google.com/p/osgocean/`
osgQt	**Qt GUI** integration	In the core OSG source code
osgSWIG	Language bindings for Python and other languages	`http://code.google.com/p/osgswig/`
osgWidgets	3D widgets support	In the core OSG source code
osgVirtualPlanets	A framework of 3D GIS planets inside the **gvSIG**	`http://www.osor.eu/projects/osgvp/`
osgVisual	Scientific visualization and vehicle simulators	`http://www.osgvisual.org/projects/osgvisual/`
osgVolume	Volume rendering support	In the core OSG source code
osgXI	CgFx, 3D UI, and game developing components	`http://sourceforge.net/projects/osgxi/`
Maya2OSG	Maya's OSG scene importer/exporter	`http://maya2osg.sourceforge.net/`
VirtualPlanet Builder	Terrain database creation tool	`http://www.openscenegraph.org/projects/VirtualPlanetBuilder`

Summary

In this chapter, we discussed the most important visual components of a rendering API. These actually extend the core OSG elements by inheriting basic scene classes (for instance, `osg::Group`), re-implementing their functionalities, and adding derived objects to the **scene graph**. Because of the flexibility of **scene graph**, we can thus enjoy the new features of various customized **NodeKits** as soon as the simulation loop starts and traverses the scene nodes. It is never too difficult to design your own **NodeKits**, even if you don't have too much knowledge of all aspects of OSG.

In this chapter, we specifically covered:

◆ How to create special objects that face the viewer all of the time by using `osg::Billboard`

◆ How to create and set up texts with `osgText::Text` and `osgText::Text3D`, and how to specify a corresponding font with `osgText::Font` and `osgText::Font3D`

◆ The main components of a particle system, including the `osgParticle::Particle` and `osgParticle::ParticleSystem` classes, and the concepts of particle system updaters, emitters, programs, counters, shooters, placers, and operators

◆ The `osgShadow::ShadowScene` class and usable shadow techniques classes, and their utilizations in constructing a scene with shadows

◆ The implementation of special effects with the **osgFX** library

◆ More **NodeKits** in the current OSG distribution and third-party projects

12

Improving Rendering Efficiency

In this final chapter of this book, we are going to introduce the techniques necessary for building a fast, real-time rendering system that will help users to load, organize, and render massive datasets in an efficient manner. It is relatively easy to learn all the classes, methods, and global variables of a large set of API calls, but the way to put what has been learned into practical use, properly and efficiently, is another thing. The methods to improve rendering efficiency here may help to solve some engineering problems that we meet from time to time.

In this chapter, we will learn:

- ◆ The basic principles of implementing multithreaded operations and rendering in OSG
- ◆ The concept of scene culling and the occlusion culling technique
- ◆ Different ways to improve rendering performance, by modifying and sharing geometries and textures
- ◆ The dynamic paging mechanism and its utilization in handling huge datasets

OpenThreads basics

OpenThreads is a lightweight, cross-platform thread API for OSG classes and applications. It supports the fundamental elements required by a multithreaded program, that is, the thread object (`OpenThreads::Thread`), the mutex for locking data that may be shared by different threads (`OpenThreads::Mutex`), barrier (`OpenThreads::Barrier`), and condition (`OpenThreads::Condition`). The latter two are often used for thread synchronization.

To create a new thread for certain purposes, we have to derive the `OpenThreads::Thread` base class and re-implement some of its virtual methods. There are also some global functions for conveniently handling threads and thread attributes, for example:

- The `GetNumberOfProcessors()` function gets the number of processors available for use.
- The `SetProcessorAffinityOfCurrentThread()` function sets the processor affinity (that is, which processor is used to execute this thread) of the current thread. It should be called when the thread is currently running.
- The `CurrentThread()` static method of `OpenThreads::Thread` returns a pointer to the current running thread instance.
- The `YieldCurrentThread()` static method of `OpenThreads::Thread` yields the current thread and lets other threads take over the control of the processor.
- The `microSleep()` static method of `OpenThreads::Thread` makes the current thread sleep for a specified number of microseconds. It can be used in single-threaded applications, too.

Time for action – using a separate data receiver thread

In this example, we will design a new thread with the **OpenThreads** library and use it to read characters from the standard input. At the same time, the main process, that is, the OSG viewer and rendering backend will try retrieving the input characters and displaying them on the screen with the **osgText** library. The entire program can only quit normally when the data thread and main process are both completed.

1. Include the necessary headers:

```
#include <osg/Geode>
#include <osgDB/ReadFile>
#include <osgText/Text>
#include <osgViewer/Viewer>
#include <iostream>
```

2. Declare our new `DataReceiverThread` class as being derived from `OpenThreads::Thread`. Two virtual methods should be implemented to ensure that the thread can work properly: the `cancel()` method defines the cancelling process of the thread, and the `run()` method defines what action happens from the beginning to the end of the thread. We also define a **mutex** variable for inter-process synchronization, and make use of the singleton pattern for convenience:

```cpp
class DataReceiverThread : public OpenThreads::Thread
{
public:
    static DataReceiverThread* instance()
    {
        static DataReceiverThread s_thread;
        return &s_thread;
    }
    virtual int cancel();
    virtual void run();

    void addToContent( int ch );
    bool getContent( std::string& str );
protected:
    OpenThreads::Mutex _mutex;
    std::string _content;
    bool _done;
    bool _dirty;
};
```

3. The cancelling work is simple: set the variable _done (which is checked repeatedly during the `run()` implementation to `true`) and wait until the thread finishes:

```cpp
int DataReceiverThread::cancel()
{
    _done = true;
    while( isRunning() ) YieldCurrentThread();
    return 0;
}
```

4. The `run()` method is the core of a thread class. It usually includes a loop in which actual actions are executed all the time. In our data receiver thread, we use `std::cin.get()` to read characters from the keyboard input and decide if it can be added to the member string _content. When _done is set to `true`, the `run()` method will meet the end of its lifetime, and so does the whole thread:

```cpp
void DataReceiverThread::run()
{
```

```
        _done = false;
        _dirty = true;
        do
        {
            YieldCurrentThread();

            int ch = 0;
            std::cin.get(ch);
            switch (ch)
            {
            case 0: break;   // We don't want '\0' to be added
            case 9: _done = true; break;   // ASCII code of Tab = 9
            default: addToContent(ch); break;
            }
        } while( !_done );
    }
```

5. Be careful of the `std::cin.get()` function: it firstly reads one or more characters from the user input, until the *Enter* key is pressed and a `'\n'` is received. Then it picks characters one by one from the buffer, and continues to add them to the member string. When all characters in the buffer are traversed, it clears the buffer and waits for user input again.

6. The customized `addToContent()` method adds a new character to `_content`. This method is sure to be called in the data receiver thread, so we have to lock the mutex object while changing the `_content` variable, to prevent other threads and the main process from dirtying it:

```
void DataReceiverThread::addToContent( int ch )
{
    OpenThreads::ScopedLock<OpenThreads::Mutex> lock(_mutex);
    _content += ch;
    _dirty = true;
}
```

7. The customized `getContent()` method is used to obtain the `_content` variable and add it to the input string argument. This method, the opposite of the previous `addToContent()` method, must only be called by the following OSG callback implementation. The scoped locking operation of the mutex object will make the entire work thread-safe, as is done in `addToContent()`:

```
bool getContent( std::string& str )
{
    OpenThreads::ScopedLock<OpenThreads::Mutex> lock(_mutex);
    if ( _dirty )
    {
```

```
            str += _content;
            _dirty = false;
            return true;
        }
        return false;
    }
```

8. The thread implementation is finished. Now let's go back to rendering. What we want here is a text object that can dynamically change its content according to the string data received from the main process. An update callback of the text object is necessary to realize such functionality. In the virtual `update()` method of the customized update callback (it is for drawables, so `osg::NodeCallback` is not needed here), we simply retrieve the `osgText::Text` object and the receiver thread instance, and then reset the displayed texts:

```
class UpdateTextCallback : public osg::Drawable::UpdateCallback
{
public:
    virtual void update( osg::NodeVisitor* nv,
                         osg::Drawable* drawable )
    {
        osgText::Text* text =
            static_cast<osgText::Text*>(drawable);
        if ( text )
        {
            std::string str("# ");
            if ( DataReceiverThread::instance()->getContent(str) )
                text->setText( str );
        }
    }
};
```

9. In the main entry, we first create the `osgText::Text` drawable and apply a new instance of our text updating callback. The `setAxisAlignment()` here defines the text as a billboard in the scene, and `setDataVariance()` ensures that the text object is "dynamic" during updating and drawing. There is also a `setInitialBound()` method, which accepts an `osg::BoundingBox` variable as the argument. It forces the definition of the minimum bounding box of the drawable and computes the initial **view matrix** according to it:

```
osg::ref_ptr<osgText::Text> text = new osgText::Text;
text->setFont( "fonts/arial.ttf" );
text->setAxisAlignment( osgText::TextBase::SCREEN );
text->setDataVariance( osg::Object::DYNAMIC );
text->setInitialBound(
```

```
    osg::BoundingBox(osg::Vec3(), osg::Vec3(400.0f, 20.0f, 20.0f))
);
text->setUpdateCallback( new UpdateTextCallback );
```

10. Add the text object to an `osg::Geode` node and turn off lighting. Before starting the viewer, we also have to make sure that the scene is rendered in a fixed-size window. That's because we have to also use the console window for keyboard entry:

```
osg::ref_ptr<osg::Geode> geode = new osg::Geode;
geode->addDrawable( text.get() );
geode->getOrCreateStateSet()->setMode(
    GL_LIGHTING, osg::StateAttribute::OFF );

osgViewer::Viewer viewer;
viewer.setSceneData( geode.get() );
viewer.setUpViewInWindow( 50, 50, 640, 480 );
```

11. Start the data receiver thread before the viewer runs, and quit it after that:

```
DataReceiverThread::instance()->startThread();
viewer.run();
DataReceiverThread::instance()->cancel();
return 0;
```

12. Two windows will appear if you are compiling your project with your subsystem console. Set focus to the console window and type some characters. Press *Enter* when you are finished, and then press *Tab* followed by *Enter* in order to quit the receiver thread:

13. You will notice that the same characters come out in the OSG rendering window. This can be treated as a very basic text editor, with the text source in a separate receiver thread, and the drawing interface implemented in the OSG **scene graph**:

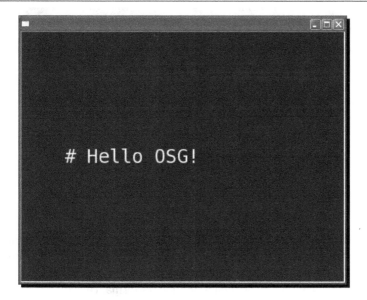

What just happened?

Introducing threads and multithreaded programming is beyond the scope of this book. However, it is already very common that applications use separate threads to load huge files from disk or from the Local Area Network (LAN). Other applications use threads to continuously receive data from the network service and client computers, or user-defined input devices including GPS and radar signals, which is of great speed and efficiency. Extra data handling threads can even specify an affinity processor to work on, and thus make use of today's dual-core and quad-core CPUs.

The **OpenThreads** library provides a minimal and complete object-oriented thread interface for OSG developers, and even general C++ threading programmers. It is used by the **osgViewer** library to implement multithreaded scene updating, culling, and drawing, which is the secret of highly efficient rendering in OSG. Note here, that **multithreaded rendering** doesn't simply mean executing OpenGL calls in different threads because the related rendering context (HGLRC under Win32) is thread-specific. One OpenGL context can only be current in one thread (using wglMakeCurrent() function). Thus, one OSG rendering window which wraps only one OpenGL context will never be activated and accept OpenGL calls synchronously in multiple threads. It requires an accurate control of the threading model to make everything work well.

There is a mutex object used both in the `addToContent()` and `getContent()` methods of the example `DataReceiverThread` class. It can prevent different threads from visiting the same data at the same time. Can you figure out what is the most likely time that the two methods may simultaneous operate on the conflicted `_content` variable? And what may happen if we don't use the mutex here?

Understanding multithreaded rendering

The traditional method of real-time rendering always involves three separate phases: user updating (UPDATE), scene culling (CULL), and executing OpenGL calls (DRAW).

User updating include all kinds of dynamic data modifications and operations, like changing the **scene graph** hierarchy, loading files, animating mesh vertices, and updating camera positions and attitudes. It then sends the scene graph to the culling phase, within which the scene is rebuilt, for the purpose of improving final rendering performance. Objects that are invisible in the viewing frustum or hidden for any reason will be removed, and the rest are sorted by rendering states and pushed into a drawing list. The list will be traversed in the final, drawing phase, and all OpenGL commands will be issued to the graphics pipeline for processing.

A single processor system would need to process all three phases serially, which may cause the one frame to be too long to fit user requirements.

In a system with multiple processors and multiple display devices, we can have more parallelizable CULL and DRAW tasks to speed up the frame rate. Especially when managing more than one rendering windows, it is necessary to have a new threading model with one CULL and one DRAW phase for each window, and execute them concurrently. This is, of course, more efficient than just using a single thread.

OSG provides a very convenient interface for choosing a threading model. Different threading models can be used in different circumstances, and have different efficiencies. In this example, we are going to show the difference between three common threading models when running a scene with a huge number of quad geometries, in three rendering windows of an `osgViewer::CompositeViewer`, synchronously.

1. Include the necessary headers:

    ```
    #include <osg/Group>
    #include <osgDB/ReadFile>
    #include <osgViewer/ViewerEventHandlers>
    #include <osgViewer/CompositeViewer>
    ```

2. The quads can be generated with the `osg::createTexturedQuadGeometry()` function. Their positions are decided simply by a random number generator. One such quad doesn't consume too much system resource. But a considerable number of these quads without using object sharing, will quickly waste system and video card memory (because of the construction of each geometry's display list), which is helpful for testing the system load capacity:

```
#define RAND(min, max) \
        ((min) + (float)rand()/(RAND_MAX+1) * ((max)-(min)))
osg::Geode* createMassiveQuads( unsigned int number )
{
    osg::ref_ptr<osg::Geode> geode = new osg::Geode;
    for ( unsigned int i=0; i<number; ++i )
    {
        osg::Vec3 randomCenter;
        randomCenter.x() = RAND(-100.0f, 100.0f);
        randomCenter.y() = RAND(1.0f, 100.0f);
        randomCenter.z() = RAND(-100.0f, 100.0f);

        osg::ref_ptr<osg::Drawable> quad =
            osg::createTexturedQuadGeometry(
                randomCenter,
                osg::Vec3(1.0f, 0.0f, 0.0f),
                osg::Vec3(0.0f, 0.0f, 1.0f)
            );
        geode->addDrawable( quad.get() );
    }
    return geode.release();
}
```

3. The composite viewer requires a separate `osgViewer::View` instance for the rendering windows. The window location and size are determined by the `setUpViewInWindow()` method:

```
osgViewer::View* createView( int x, int y, int w, int h,
                             osg::Node* scene )
{
    osg::ref_ptr<osgViewer::View> view = new osgViewer::View;
    view->setSceneData( scene );
    view->setUpViewInWindow( x, y, w, h );
    return view.release();
}
```

4. In the main entry, we first use an argument parser to select a threading model. By default, OSG will automatically choose the best threading strategy according to the number of processors and rendering windows of the application, that is, the `AutomaticSelection` case. But we can still specify a way to handle multithreaded rendering from inbuilt ones, including `SingleThreaded`, `ThreadPerContext`, and `ThreadPerCamera`:

```
osg::ArgumentParser arguments( &argc, argv );

osgViewer::ViewerBase::ThreadingModel th =
    osgViewer::ViewerBase::AutomaticSelection;
if ( arguments.read("--single") ) th =
    osgViewer::ViewerBase::SingleThreaded;
else if ( arguments.read("--useContext") ) th =
    osgViewer::ViewerBase::ThreadPerContext;
else if ( arguments.read("--useCamera") ) th =
    osgViewer::ViewerBase::ThreadPerCamera;
```

5. Create three rendering views and apply massive quad geometries to each of them. Totally, 20 thousand quads are allocated in this example for the purpose of illustrating different threading models:

```
osgViewer::View* view1 = createView( 50, 50, 640, 480,
    createMassiveQuads(10000) );
osgViewer::View* view2 = createView( 50, 550, 320, 240,
    createMassiveQuads(5000) );
osgViewer::View* view3 = createView( 370, 550, 320, 240,
    createMassiveQuads(5000) );
view1->addEventHandler( new osgViewer::StatsHandler );
```

6. Create a composite viewer and set the user-specified threading model. Note that the `setThreadingModel()` method here not only works for `osgViewer::CompositeViewer`, but is also available for more common `osgViewer::Viewer` instances:

```
osgViewer::CompositeViewer viewer;
viewer.setThreadingModel( th );

viewer.addView( view1 );
viewer.addView( view2 );
viewer.addView( view3 );
return viewer.run();
```

7. Compile the application (assuming that its name is `MyProject.exe`) and enter the following command in console mode:

```
# MyProject.exe --single
```

8. The result is shown in the following image. Notice that the frame rate is only 20 for the single threaded model, in which the update, cull, and draw phases are executed one by one in the same thread:

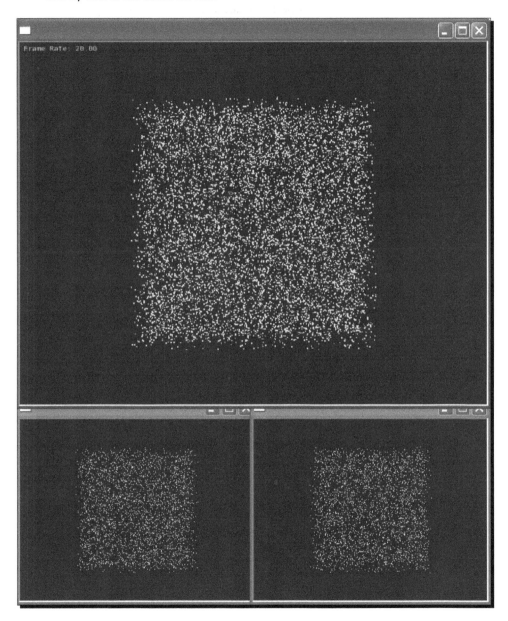

9. Change the argument `--single` to `--useContext` and start the test program again. This time you will find the frame rate has increased. This is because OSG uses separate threads for culling and drawing besides the user update phase, which improves the rendering performance a lot.

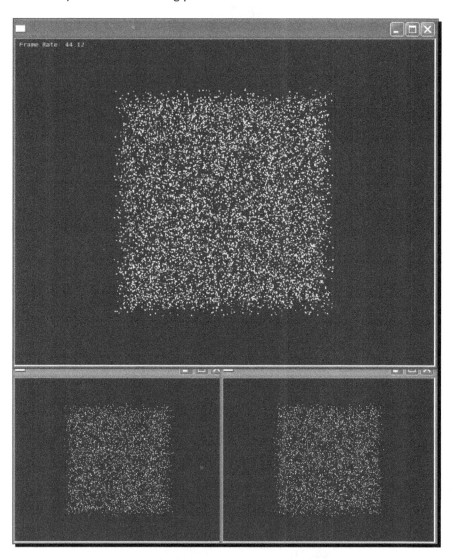

10. Change the command line to `--useCamera` and restart the program once more. This is actually the default strategy for most multi-processor computers these days. It should be even better than the second threading model, because it uses different threads for cameras and rendering windows, and runs threads on separate CPUs to obtain maximum efficiency:

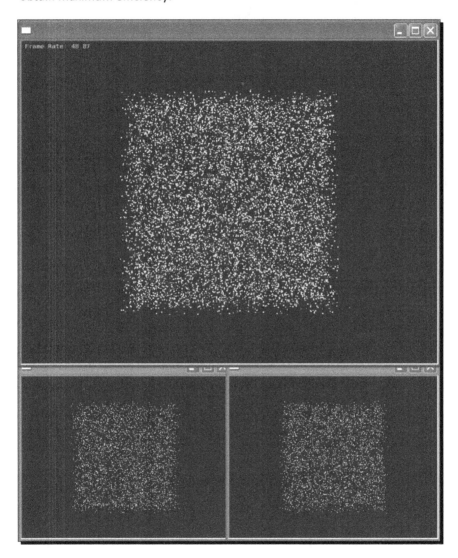

What just happened?

The SingleThreaded threading models can be demonstrated by the diagram below. The CULL and DRAW phases in each rendering window (view) may have different aggregated time, and one frame here is defined as the total time starting from the first view's CULL, and to the end of the last view's DRAW. User updating operations are ignored here because they always take the same aggregated time in all threading models:

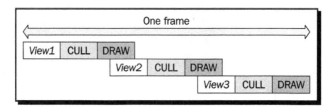

The updating, culling, and drawing operations are always executed in one thread. If there are multiple sub-views, that is, multiple culling and drawing tasks to finish, then they are going to be issued one by one. This is the most inefficient model of rendering the scene in OSG, but it is still useful for testing new functionalities. It also simplifies the integration with GUIs such as MFC and Qt. Because we do not care about thread conflicts, you may just put the run() method of osgViewer::Viewer or osgVIewer::CompositeViewer in a GUI timer event callback, instead of using an additional thread, as we have done in Chapter 9, *Interacting with Outside Elements*.

The ThreadPerContext model can be described by the following image:

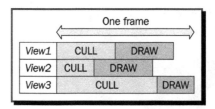

Every sub-view of the composite viewer will have its own thread in which to execute culling and drawing tasks. Because of the parallelization characteristic of threads, the execution time of a frame will be shorter than the total time of the longest CULL and DRAW pair. After all DRAW tasks are finished, the user update of the next frame will start immediately.

This is much better in rendering performance than the first single-threaded model. It can even make use of multiple processors because each thread can occupy an individual processor in order to maximize the use of hardware resources.

However, an even better solution is the `ThreadPerCamera` model. This separates the CULL phase of each view from the DRAW phase and implements them in threads, too. This means we can have at least one CULL thread and one DRAW thread for each rendering window and therefore can make full use of multi-processor systems. Because the culling operations must be related with an `osg::Camera` node (it manages view and projection matrices for **view-frustum culling**), we call this threading model a "thread per camera" model, as illustrated in the following image:

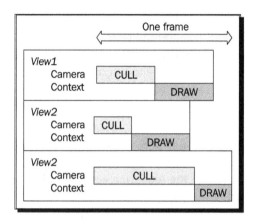

In this threading model, the DRAW phase is considered as two parallel processes, dispatching commands on the CPU side, and issuing a rendering buffer swap to execute them on the GPU side. The time-cost of swapping buffer operations can be unified and executed after all of the DRAW dispatching operations are done. But before that, this threading model starts the user UPDATE phase of the next frame in advance. This exciting work improves the rendering performance again, but may cause unexpected results if a user's updates change scene data that is being dispatched. That is why we are going to set a dynamic flag for scene objects that may be modified:

```
node->setDataVariance( osg::Object::DYNAMIC );
```

By default, OSG will suggest the `ThreadPerCamera` threading model, if a multi-processor system is detected.

Dynamic scene culling

The culling technique can be described easily: don't draw things you can't see. We can achieve this goal in two main ways: by reducing polygon faces that do not need to be detailed, and ignoring objects that are invisible in the current viewport.

The former is usually implemented by **level-of-detail (LOD)** algorithms, which in OSG is done by the `osg::LOD` class. The latter, which is actually the definition of scene culling, will aim to find objects in the **scene graph** that don't need to be rendered at all. There are several kinds of culling techniques assigned in OSG:

- **Back face culling**: This is implemented by the `osg::CullFace` class, which encapsulates OpenGL's `glCullFace()` function. It removes all polygons facing away from the camera from the rendering pipeline, thus reducing the memory traffic. This technique works well, especially for manifold watertight objects, but may be erroneous for transparent objects or objects with holes.

- **Small feature culling**: This technique enables the removal of objects that are too small to be seen, based on a visibility test, the outcome of which is the number of pixels that the object would affect if drawn. If that number is lower than the user-defined mini-pixel threshold, the object will be removed from the rendering list.

- **View-frustum culling**: The idea here is simply not to render what is outside of the viewing volume (often a truncated pyramid, that is, a frustum) defined by the view and projection matrices of the rendering window. This is one of the most efficient methods in modern rendering applications.

- **Occlusion culling**: This technique attempts to determine what objects are totally invisible because they are behind other objects. We will discuss this method soon, in the next section.

Note that the **small feature culling** method may cause actual geometry points to be not renderable. To disable this feature, we can make use of the `setCullingMode()` method of the camera node:

```
camera->setCullingMode(
    camera->getCullingMode() & ~osg::Camera::SMALL_FEATURE_CULLING );
```

Occluders and occludees

When rendering a complex scene, it is very common that two or more objects are overlapped, from the perspective of the viewer. This could lead to an overdraw, which means that pixels at the same location will be written to the **frame buffer** several times, while the final image only shows the last one. This causes efficiency losses because of multiple drawing that is not necessary (so called overdrawing).

The **Occlusion culling** technique simply increases the rendering performance by not rendering geometries hidden by other objects that are closer to the camera. The objects that cover other renderables are called occluders, and the rest of the **scene graph** can be treated as occludees (but it's not necessary to use such an unfamiliar word).

The general **occlusion culling** algorithm performs a visibility test on every object in the scene (of course, they should pass the **view-frustum culling** method first). The algorithm checks whether an object is occluded by an **occlusion representation**, which consists of some kind of occlusion information, for instance, polygonal clipping volumes, that can be used as occluders.

OSG provides the `osg::OccluderNode` class for implementing a basic occlude object. It is derived from `osg::Group`, and will check the relation between its **occlusion representation** and all scene nodes and objects except its children. This means that the `osg::OccluderNode`'s child nodes will never be occluded and can thus represent the geometry of the occluder.

Time for action – adding occluders to a complex scene

The scene which demonstrates how to use occlusion culling should have two parts: a huge number of geometries that must be culled sometime to improve the efficiency, and a few good enough `osg::OccluderNode` instances as occluders. Here we are going to create massive data once more, and create an occluder plane, which can speed up the rendering by removing quads that are behind it from the graphics pipeline.

1. Include the necessary headers:

    ```
    #include <osg/Geometry>
    #include <osg/Geode>
    #include <osgViewer/ViewerEventHandlers>
    #include <osgViewer/Viewer>
    ```

2. The massive quads creation function is listed here again. It is really helpful in this chapter's examples, but not good for practical use:

    ```
    #define RAND(min, max) \
            ((min) + (float)rand()/(RAND_MAX+1) * ((max)-(min)))
    osg::Geode* createMassiveQuads( unsigned int number )
    {
        osg::ref_ptr<osg::Geode> geode = new osg::Geode;
        for ( unsigned int i=0; i<number; ++i )
        {
            osg::Vec3 randomCenter;
            randomCenter.x() = RAND(-100.0f, 100.0f);
            randomCenter.y() = RAND(1.0f, 100.0f);
            randomCenter.z() = RAND(-100.0f, 100.0f);

            osg::ref_ptr<osg::Drawable> quad =
                osg::createTexturedQuadGeometry(
                    randomCenter,
                    osg::Vec3(1.0f, 0.0f, 0.0f),
    ```

```
                    osg::Vec3(0.0f, 0.0f, 1.0f)
            );
        geode->addDrawable( quad.get() );
    }
    return geode.release();
}
```

3. In the main entry, we first create the occluder node:

```
osg::ref_ptr<osg::OccluderNode> occluderNode = new
osg::OccluderNode;
```

4. The **occlusion representation** class is osg::ConvexPlanarOccluder, which is actually made up of a convex clipping polygon (defined by the getOccluder() method) with several holes (defined by the addHole() method). The polygon and hole vertices are added by the add() method of the osg::ConvexPlanarPolygon class. The **occlusion representation** must be set to the occluder node with the setOccluder() method:

```
osg::ref_ptr<osg::ConvexPlanarOccluder> cpo = new
    osg::ConvexPlanarOccluder;
cpo->getOccluder().add( osg::Vec3(-120.0f, 0.0f,-120.0f) );
cpo->getOccluder().add( osg::Vec3( 120.0f, 0.0f,-120.0f) );
cpo->getOccluder().add( osg::Vec3( 120.0f, 0.0f, 120.0f) );
cpo->getOccluder().add( osg::Vec3(-120.0f, 0.0f, 120.0f) );
occluderNode->setOccluder( cpo.get() );
```

5. We create a big geometry plane as the occlusion representation. To render its shape in the scene along with the massive occludees, we have to add the geometry that is created by osg::createTexturedQuadGeometry() as the occluder node's child:

```
osg::ref_ptr<osg::Geode> occluderGeode = new osg::Geode;
occluderGeode->addDrawable( osg::createTexturedQuadGeometry(
    osg::Vec3(-120.0f, 0.0f,-120.0f),
    osg::Vec3(240.0f, 0.0f, 0.0f),
    osg::Vec3(0.0f, 0.0f, 240.0f))
);
occluderNode->addChild( occluderGeode.get() );
```

6. When constructing the **scene graph**, the group node of the 100,000 objects and the occluder must be siblings under the same **root node**. We will also turn off lighting here in order to focus on observing if there are any efficiency improvements using occluders. After that, the `osgViewer::StatsHandler` is used to obtain scene statistics, and we can start the viewer:

```
osg::ref_ptr<osg::Group> root = new osg::Group;
root->addChild( createMassiveQuads(100000) );
root->addChild( occluderNode.get() );
root->getOrCreateStateSet()->setMode(
    GL_LIGHTING, osg::StateAttribute::OFF );

osgViewer::Viewer viewer;
viewer.addEventHandler( new osgViewer::StatsHandler );
viewer.setSceneData( root.get() );
return viewer.run();
```

7. Press the *S* key here to see the detailed frame rate. Drag the main camera with your left mouse button pressed to rotate the whole world in your eyes. The plane occluder can always cull away small quads that are totally hidden behind it, when looking from the current view point:

8. You may soon find that the maximum frame rate happens when the plane is completely in front of the eye point (as shown in the previous image), and the minimum one happens when the plane covers none of the massive number of quads (as shown in the following image):

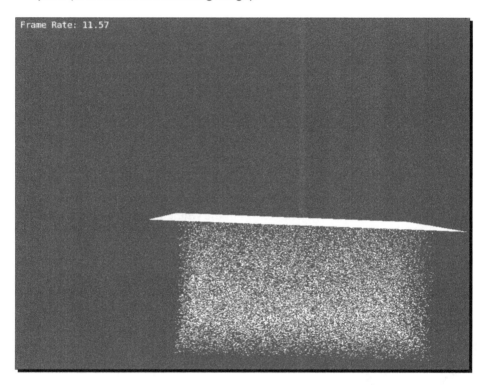

What just happened?

Somebody may think of implementing an algorithm that computes the occlusions between each of the two objects in the scene. Any object that may be hidden by one or more objects will thus be picked up and removed from the current drawing list. In this ideal situation, we don't need the concepts of occluders or occludes any more.

Unfortunately, this imagination is nearly impossible at present. An algorithmic approach to avoid inefficiency may cost too much in terms of speed. The previous example shows the time-cost of the culling work. The developer is working on a graphics system with the vertical synchronization (V-sync) at 60 Hz. The maximum frame rate should therefore be equal or less than 60 fps (frames per second). But here the maximum frame rate (when the occluder plane hides all other quads totally) is only about 40 fps, because of the dissipation of comparing the plane with 100,000 objects. Thus, an actual ideal efficient occlusion culling algorithm must perform simple enough tests, a limited number of times.

Have a go hero – adding holes to the occluder

The osg::ConvexPlanarOccluder class, which is the **occlusion representation** of osg::OccluderNode, accepts the osg::ConvexPlanarPolygon variable as the clipping component (via the setOccluder() method). Besides, it also accepts a number of holes to increase the complexity of the representation. Use the addHole() method with an osg::ConvexPlanarPolygon parameter to configure the osg::ConvexPlanarOccluder object, and don't forget to update the corresponding geometry representation, which is often placed as the child of the occlude node.

Improving your application

There are a lot of tricks to improve the rendering performance of applications with a large amount of data. But the essence of them is easy to understand: the smaller the number of resources (geometries, display lists, texture objects, and so on) allocated, the faster and smoother the user application is.

There are lots of ideas on how to find the bottleneck of an inefficient application. For example, you can replace certain objects by simple boxes, or replace textures in your application by 1x1 images to see if the performance can increase, thanks to the reduction of geometries and texture objects. The statistics class (osgViewer::StatsHandler, or press the *S* key in the osgviewer) can also provide helpful information.

To achieve a less-enough scene resource, we can refer to the following table and try to optimize our applications if they are not running in good shape:

Problem	Influence	Possible solution
Too many geometries	Low frame rate and huge resource cost	Use LOD and culling techniques to reduce the vertices of the drawables.
		Use primitive sets and the index mechanism rather than duplicate vertices.
		Merge geometries into one, if possible. This is because one geometry object allocates one display list, and too many display lists occupy too much of the video memory.
		Share geometries, vertices, and nodes as often as possible.

Problem	Influence	Possible solution
Too many dynamic objects (configured with the `setDataVariance()` method)	Low frame rate because the `DRAW` phase must wait until all dynamic objects finish updating	Don't use the `DYNAMIC` flag on nodes and drawables that do not need to be modified on the fly. Don't set the root node to be dynamic unless you are sure that you require this, because data variance can be inherited in the scene graph.
Too many texture objects	Low frame rate and huge resource cost	Share rendering states and textures as much as you can. Lower the resolution and compress them using the DXTC format if possible. Use `osg::TextureRectangle` to handle non-power-of-two sized textures, and `osg::Texture2D` for regular 2D textures. Use LOD to simplify and manage nodes with large-sized textures.
The scene graph structure is "loose", that is, nodes are not grouped together effectively.	Very high cull and draw time, and many redundant state changes	If there are too many parent nodes, each with only one child, which means the scene has as many group nodes as leaf nodes, and even as many drawables as leaf nodes, the performance will be totally ruined. You should rethink your scene graph and group nodes that have close features and behaviors more effectively.
Loading and unloading resources too frequently	Lower and lower running speed and wasteful memory fragmentation	Use the buffer pool to allocate and release resources. OSG has already done this to textures and buffer objects, by default.

An additional helper is the `osgUtil::Optimizer` class. This can traverse the **scene graph** before starting the simulation loop and do different kinds of optimizations in order to improve efficiency, including removing redundant nodes, sharing duplicated states, checking and merging geometries, optimizing texture settings, and so on. You may start the optimizing operation with the following code segment:

```
osgUtil::Optimizer optimizer;
optimizer.optimize( node );
```

 Some parts of the optimizer are optional. You can see the header file `include/osgUtil/Optimizer` for details.

Time for action – sharing textures with a customized callback

We would like to explain the importance of scene optimization by providing an extreme situation where massive textures are allocated without sharing the same ones. We have a basic solution to collect and reuse loaded images in a file reading callback, and then share all textures that use the same image object and have the same parameters. The idea of sharing textures can be used to construct massive scene graphs, such as digital cities; otherwise, the video card memory will soon be eaten up and thus cause the whole application to slow down and crash.

1. Include the necessary headers:

```
#include <osg/Texture2D>
#include <osg/Geometry>
#include <osg/Geode>
#include <osg/Group>
#include <osgDB/ReadFile>
#include <osgViewer/Viewer>
```

2. The function for quickly producing massive data can be used in this example, once more. This time we will apply a texture attribute to each quad. That means that we are going to have a huge number of geometries, and the same amount of texture objects, which will be a heavy burden for rendering the scene smoothly:

```
#define RAND(min, max) \
        ((min) + (float)rand()/(RAND_MAX+1) * ((max)-(min)))
osg::Geode* createMassiveQuads( unsigned int number,
                                const std::string& imageFile )
{
    osg::ref_ptr<osg::Geode> geode = new osg::Geode;
    for ( unsigned int i=0; i<number; ++i )
    {
        osg::Vec3 randomCenter;
        randomCenter.x() = RAND(-100.0f, 100.0f);
        randomCenter.y() = RAND(1.0f, 100.0f);
        randomCenter.z() = RAND(-100.0f, 100.0f);

        osg::ref_ptr<osg::Drawable> quad =
            osg::createTexturedQuadGeometry(
                randomCenter,
                osg::Vec3(1.0f, 0.0f, 0.0f),
                osg::Vec3(0.0f, 0.0f, 1.0f)
            );

        osg::ref_ptr<osg::Texture2D> texture = new osg::Texture2D;
        texture->setImage( osgDB::readImageFile(imageFile) );
        quad->getOrCreateStateSet()->setTextureAttributeAndModes(
            0, texture.get() );
```

```
                geode->addDrawable( quad.get() );
        }
        return geode.release();
}
```

3. The `createMassiveQuads()` function is, of course, awkward and ineffective here. However, it demonstrates a common situation: assuming that an application needs to often load image files and create texture objects on the fly, it is necessary to check if an image has been loaded already and then share the corresponding textures automatically. The memory occupancy will be obviously reduced if there are plenty of textures that are reusable. To achieve this, we should first record all loaded image filenames, and then create a map that saves the corresponding `osg::Image` objects.

4. Whenever a new `readImageFile()` request arrives, the `osgDB::Registry` instance will try using a preset `osgDB::ReadFileCallback` to perform the actual loading work. If the callback doesn't exist, it will call the `readImageImplementation()` to choose an appropriate plug-in that will load the image and return the resultant object. Therefore, we can take over the reading image process by inheriting the `osgDB::ReadFileCallback` class and implementing a new functionality that compares the filename and re-uses the existing image objects, with the customized `getImageByName()` function:

```
class ReadAndShareImageCallback : public osgDB::ReadFileCallback
{
public:
    virtual osgDB::ReaderWriter::ReadResult readImage(
        const std::string& filename, const osgDB::Options* options
);

protected:
    osg::Image* getImageByName( const std::string& filename )
    {
        ImageMap::iterator itr = _imageMap.find(filename);
        if ( itr!=_imageMap.end() ) return itr->second.get();
        return NULL;
    }

    typedef std::map<std::string, osg::ref_ptr<osg::Image> >
ImageMap;
    ImageMap _imageMap;
};
```

5. The `readImage()` method should be overridden to replace the current reading implementation. It will return the previously-imported instance if the filename matches an element in the `_imageMap`, and will add any newly-loaded image object and its name to `_imageMap`, in order to ensure that the same file won't be imported again:

```
osgDB::ReaderWriter::ReadResult ReadAndShareImageCallback::readIma
ge(
    const std::string& filename, const osgDB::Options* options )
{
    osg::Image* image = getImageByName( filename );
    if ( !image )
    {
        osgDB::ReaderWriter::ReadResult rr;
        rr = osgDB::Registry::instance()->readImageImplementation(
            filename, options);
        if ( rr.success() ) _imageMap[filename] = rr.getImage();
        return rr;
    }
    return image;
}
```

6. Now we get into the main entry. The file-reading callback is set by the `setReadFileCallback()` method of the `osgDB::Registry` class, which is designed as a singleton. Meanwhile, we have to enable another important run-time optimizer, named `osgDB::SharedStateManager`, that can be defined by `setSharedStateManager()` or `getOrCreateSharedStateManager()`. The latter will assign a default instance to the registry:

```
osgDB::Registry::instance()->setReadFileCallback(
    new ReadAndShareImageCallback );
osgDB::Registry::instance()->getOrCreateSharedStateManager();
```

7. Create the massive **scene graph**. It consists of two groups of quads, each of which uses a unified image file to decorate the quad geometry. In total, 1,000 quads will be created, along with 1,000 newly-allocated textures. Certainly, there are too many redundant texture objects (because they are generated from only two image files) in this case:

```
osg::ref_ptr<osg::Group> root = new osg::Group;
root->addChild( createMassiveQuads(500, "Images/lz.rgb") );
root->addChild( createMassiveQuads(500, "Images/osg64.png") );
```

8. The `osgDB::SharedStateManager` is used for maximizing the reuse of textures and state sets. It is actually a node visitor, traversing all child nodes' state sets and comparing them when the `share()` method is invoked. State sets and textures with the same attributes and data will be combined into one:

```
osgDB::SharedStateManager* ssm =
    osgDB::Registry::instance()->getSharedStateManager();
if ( ssm ) ssm->share( root.get() );
```

9. Finalize the viewer:

```
osgViewer::Viewer viewer;
viewer.setSceneData( root.get() );
return viewer.run();
```

10. Now the application starts with a large number of textured quads. With the `ReadAndShareImageCallback` sharing image objects, and the `osgDB::SharedStateManager` sharing textures, the rendering process can work without a hitch. Try commenting out the lines of `setReadFileCallback()` and `getOrCreateSharedStateManager()` and restart the application, and then see what has happened. The Windows Task Manager is helpful in displaying the amount of currently-used memory here:

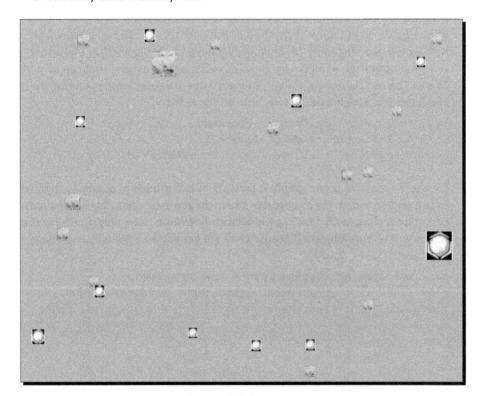

What just happened?

You may be curious about the implementation of osgDB::SharedStateManager. It collects rendering states and textures that firstly appear in the **scene graph**, and then replaces duplicated states of successive nodes with the recorded ones. It compares two states' member attributes in order to decide whether the new state should be recorded (because it's not the same as any of the recorded ones) or replaced (because it is a duplication of the previous one).

For texture objects, the osgDB::SharedStateManager will determine if they are exactly the same by checking the data() pointer of the osg::Image object, rather than by comparing every pixel of the image. Thus, the customized ReadAndShareImageCallback class is used here to share image objects with the same filename first, and the osgDB::SharedStateManager shares textures with the same image object and other attributes.

The osgDB::DatabasePager also makes use of osgDB::SharedStateManager to share states of external scene graphs when dynamically loading and unloading paged nodes. This is done automatically if getOrCreateSharedStateManager() is executed.

Have a go hero – sharing public models

Can we also share models with the same name in an application? The answer is absolutely yes. The osgDB::ReadFileCallback could be used again by overriding the virtual method readNode(). Other preparations include a member std::map for recording filename and node pointer pairs, and a user-defined getNodeByName() method as we have just done in the last example.

Paging huge scene data

Are you still struggling with the optimization of huge scene data? Don't always pay attention to the rendering API itself. There is no "super" rendering engine in the world that can work with unlimited datasets. Consider using the scene paging mechanism at this time, which can load and unload objects according to the current viewport and frustum. It is also important to design a better structure for indexing regions of spatial data, like **quad-tree**, **octree**, **R-tree**, and the **binary space partitioning** (BSP).

Making use of the quad-tree

A classic **quad-tree** structure decomposes the whole 2D region into four square children (we call them cells here), and recursively subdivides each cell into four regions, until a cell reaches its target capacity and stops splitting (a so-called leaf). Each cell in the tree either has exactly four children, or has no children. It is mostly useful for representing terrains or scenes on 2D planes.

The **quad-tree** structure is useful for **view-frustum culling** terrain data. Because the terrain is divided into small pieces that are a part of it, we can easily render pieces of small data in the frustum, and discard those that are invisible. This can effectively unload a large number of chunks of a terrain from memory at a time, and load them back when necessary—which is the basic principle of dynamic data paging. This process can be progressive: when the terrain model is far enough from the viewer, we may only handle its root and first levels. But as it is drawing near, we can traverse down to corresponding levels of the **quad-tree**, and cull and unload as many cells as possible, to keep the load balance of the scene.

Time for action – building a quad-tree for massive rendering

This is the last example in our OSG beginners' book, in which we would like to show how OSG handles massive data (often massive terrain data) with the **quad-tree** structure and paged nodes (osg::PagedLOD). We are going to construct a terrain model with fake elevation data, and use a recursion to build all child cells of a complete quad-tree. These cells are saved into separate files and managed by the osgDB::DatabasePager, which is introduced in brief in *Chapter 5, Managing Scene Graph*.

1. Include the necessary headers:

```
#include <osg/ShapeDrawable>
#include <osg/PagedLOD>
#include <osgDB/WriteFile>
#include <sstream>
```

2. Define some global variables. These will define the dimensions of a regularly-spaced grid of elevation points, including the data pointer (g_data), intervals of X and Y directions (g_dx and g_dy), rows and columns of the leaf cell in the quad-tree (g_minCols and g_minRows), and rows and columns of the entire dataset (g_numCols and g_numRows):

```
float* g_data = NULL;
float g_dx = 1.0f;
float g_dy = 1.0f;
unsigned int g_minCols = 64;
```

```
unsigned int g_minRows = 64;
unsigned int g_numCols = 1024;
unsigned int g_numRows = 1024;
```

3. The following figure shows how variables work here:

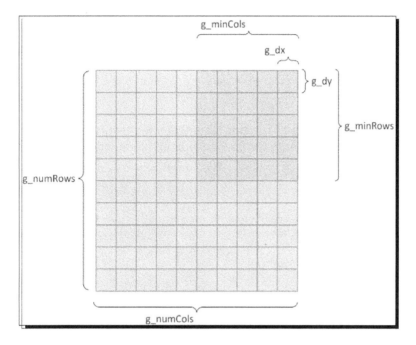

4. These preset global values indicate that we have a 1024x1024 area to be rendered, which contains over one million vertices. This already slows down the rendering of normal geometries, but it's far from enough for representing a digital terrain. Fortunately, we have the **quad-tree** and paging mechanism, which can solve the massive data problem in a nearly perfect way.

5. We will first fill the elevation grid (g_data) with random points. This is done via a simple `createMassiveData()` function. To retrieve an elevation at a certain column and row, we have to define an additional `getOneData()` function. This gets the minimum value between the input column/row number and the total value with the `osg::minimum()` function, and then finds the elevation data from the g_data pointer:

```
#define RAND(min, max) \
        ((min) + (float)rand()/(RAND_MAX+1) * ((max)-(min)))
void createMassiveData()
{
    g_data = new float[g_numCols * g_numRows];
```

```
        for ( unsigned int i=0; i<g_numRows; ++i )
        {
            for ( unsigned int j=0; j<g_numCols; ++j )
                g_data[i*g_numCols + j] = RAND(0.5f, 0.0f);
        }
    }
    float getOneData( unsigned int c, unsigned int r )
    {
        return g_data[osg::minimum(r, g_numRows-1) * g_numCols +
                      osg::minimum(c, g_numCols-1)];
    }
```

6. The `createFileName()` function is another important customized function for naming paged data files. It will be used later in this example:

```
std::string createFileName( unsigned int lv,
                            unsigned int x, unsigned int y )
{
    std::stringstream sstream;
    sstream << "quadtree_L" << lv << "_X" << x << "_Y" << y <<
".osg";
    return sstream.str();
}
```

7. The core of the **quad-tree** construction is the `outputSubScene()` function. This should be called recursively to build all child cells of a **quad-tree**, until an end condition is reached. The `lv`, `x`, and `y` parameters indicate the depth level of the **quad-tree** cell, as well as the X/Y indices in the current level. The `color` parameter is just used for distinguishing cells in a simple way:

```
osg::Node* outputSubScene( unsigned int lv,
                           unsigned int x, unsigned int y,
                           const osg::Vec4& color )
{
    ...
}
```

8. The indices of the cell don't equal the real position of the elevation value in the `g_data` pointer. Thus, we have to compute how many elevation points are contained in the current cell, along with the indices of the start/end column and row, and then save them for later use:

```
unsigned int numInUnitCol = g_numCols / (int)powf(2.0f,
    (float)lv);
unsigned int numInUnitRow = g_numRows / (int)powf(2.0f,
    (float)lv);
```

```
unsigned int xDataStart = x * numInUnitCol,
              xDataEnd = (x+1) * numInUnitCol;
unsigned int yDataStart = y * numInUnitRow,
              yDataEnd = (y+1) * numInUnitRow;
```

9. Assuming that the root level of a **quad-tree** is 0, we have a formula that explains the previous code segment: `(Points in a cell)` = `(Total points)` / `(level-th power of 2)`.

10. We can easily figure out that a level 1 cell contains a quarter of all points, and a level 2 cell contains one sixteenth of them. That means the rendering of four level 1 cells still requires all data to be drawn, if none of them are culled. So, is there a solution that can reduce the vertex number of these lower levels, that is, to downsample the height field in these cells? For example, each level 1 cell of a 1024x1024 dataset has 512x512 points. If these can be downsampled to 64x64, we will only have to render no more than 20,000 points at one time.

11. The answer is absolutely yes. As we have just discussed, the **quad-tree** can be progressively traversed as if it is a LOD (level-of-detail) based graph. Low levels work when the model is still far away and can't represent too many details, and leaf cells will come with uncompressed data only when the viewpoint is near enough.

12. We will create the downsampling height field for the current level using the `osg::HeightField` class, which is derived from `osg::Shape` and can be used by `osg::ShapeDrawable`. Its origin is defined as the bottom-left corner, and the skirt height can prevent gaps between two terrain cells:

```
bool stopAtLeafNode = false;
osg::ref_ptr<osg::HeightField> grid = new osg::HeightField;
grid->setSkirtHeight( 1.0f );
grid->setOrigin( osg::Vec3(g_dx*(float)xDataStart,
                           g_dy*(float)yDataStart, 0.0f) );
```

13. We will first check to see if the current cell reaches the last level, by comparing the start and end indices with the global `g_minCols` and `g_minRows`. If it does, we simply allocate the height field with the computed columns and rows and X/Y intervals, and read and set each point of the allocated elevation grid:

```
if ( xDataEnd-xDataStart<=g_minCols &&
     yDataEnd-yDataStart<=g_minRows )
{
    grid->allocate( xDataEnd-xDataStart+1, yDataEnd-yDataStart+1
);
    grid->setXInterval( g_dx );
    grid->setYInterval( g_dy );
    for ( unsigned int i=yDataStart; i<=yDataEnd; ++i )
```

```
    {
        for ( unsigned int j=xDataStart; j<=xDataEnd; ++j )
        {
            grid->setHeight( j-xDataStart, i-yDataStart,
                             getOneData(j, i) );
        }
    }
    stopAtLeafNode = true;
}
```

14. Otherwise, we should obtain downsampling data and keep the height field to a fixed, low resolution, using specific `g_minCols` and `g_minRows` variables. The simplest method here is to pick one point and add it to the `osg::HeightField` every few points. The X/Y intervals of the elevation grid should also be changed:

```
else
{
    unsigned int jStep = (unsigned int)ceilf(
        (float)(xDataEnd - xDataStart) / (float)g_minCols);
    unsigned int iStep = (unsigned int)ceilf(
        (float)(yDataEnd - yDataStart) / (float)g_minRows);
    grid->allocate( g_minCols+1, g_minRows+1 );
    grid->setXInterval( g_dx * jStep );
    grid->setYInterval( g_dy * iStep );
    for ( unsigned int i=yDataStart, ii=0; i<=yDataEnd;
          i+=iStep, ++ii )
    {
        for ( unsigned int j=xDataStart, jj=0; j<=xDataEnd;
              j+=jStep, ++jj )
        {
            grid->setHeight( jj, ii, getOneData(j, i) );
        }
    }
}
```

15. Set the height field to an `osg::ShapeDrawable` instance, and set the color. Add the shape to `osg::Geode`. If this is the leaf cell of the **quad-tree**, the recursion will end:

```
osg::ref_ptr<osg::ShapeDrawable> shape =
    new osg::ShapeDrawable( grid.get() );
shape->setColor( color );

osg::ref_ptr<osg::Geode> geode = new osg::Geode;
geode->addDrawable( shape.get() );
if ( stopAtLeafNode ) return geode.release();
```

16. Now we construct the paged nodes for the OSG scene. A **quad-tree** cell always has four children, except for leaf ones. Their levels and indices should be increased properly before starting the next level's recursion call. We also specify four different colors, red, green, blue and yellow, for rendering different child cells:

```
osg::ref_ptr<osg::Group> group = new osg::Group;
group->addChild(
    outputSubScene(lv+1, x*2, y*2, osg::Vec4(1.0f,0.0f,0.0f,1.0f))
);
group->addChild(
    outputSubScene(lv+1, x*2, y*2+1, osg::Vec4(0.0f,1.0f,0.0f,1.0f))
);
group->addChild(
    outputSubScene(lv+1, x*2+1,y*2+1,
osg::Vec4(0.0f,0.0f,1.0f,1.0f)) );
group->addChild(
    outputSubScene(lv+1, x*2+1, y*2, osg::Vec4(1.0f,1.0f,0.0f,1.0f))
);
```

17. The paged LOD node representing the current **quad-tree** level can be made up of two children: a rough model (the downsampled height field) that is cached for displaying at a far distance, and the fine "model" which actually consists of four cells describing the next level in the **quad-tree**. Because the next level can still be described as paged LOD nodes, we actually build a **quad-tree** style **scene graph** full of osg::PagedLOD nodes. The group node of next level cells can be saved into a separate file, with the filename being generated by createFileName():

```
osg::ref_ptr<osg::PagedLOD> plod = new osg::PagedLOD;

std::string filename = createFileName(lv, x, y);
plod->insertChild( 0, geode.get() );
plod->setFileName( 1, filename );

osgDB::writeNodeFile( *group, filename );
```

18. The paged LOD node must have a valid bounding sphere in order to make it correctly pass the **view-frustum culling**. Here, we have to successively set the center mode to user-defined, and define the center and radius of our customized bounding sphere. After that, we will set the visibility ranges of two child levels of the LOD node. The cutoff parameter is just an empirical value:

```
plod->setCenterMode( osg::PagedLOD::USER_DEFINED_CENTER );
plod->setCenter( geode->getBound().center() );
plod->setRadius( geode->getBound().radius() );
float cutoff = geode->getBound().radius() * 5.0f;
plod->setRange( 0, cutoff, FLT_MAX );
plod->setRange( 1, 0.0f, cutoff );
return plod.release();
```

19. In the main entry, the `createMassiveData()` function must be the first thing executed, in order to allocate the global terrain data. And we can add the root of the **quad-tree** to an `osg::Group` root node and save it into a file, too:

```
createMassiveData();

osg::ref_ptr<osg::Group> root = new osg::Group;
root->addChild(
    outputSubScene(0, 0, 0, osg::Vec4(1.0f, 1.0f, 1.0f, 1.0f)) );
osgDB::writeNodeFile( *root, "quadtree.osg" );

delete g_data;
return 0;
```

20. Assuming that the executable name is `MyProject.exe`. Now we can just enter the console mode and enter:

```
# MyProject.exe
# osgviewer quadtree.osg
```

21. The result is smooth and clear. We have just built a terrain model using customized elevation points. Looking from far away, it is obviously divided into four pieces, which is in fact the first four square cells of the **quad-tree**:

22. Move towards the terrain and you will see more detailed height fields within different cells of different levels:

23. The most detailed data will only be rendered when the viewer is very close to the ground. This is because the last four leaf cells of the **quad-tree** can only be loaded when the highest level of paged nodes is reached by the OSG backend:

What just happened?

In this last example of this book, we haven't provided anything new, but have only made use of the same, known node and drawable types (`osg::PagedLOD` and `osg::HeightField`) that we have already seen elsewhere in the book, as well as a world famous algorithm—**quad-tree**, to construct a complex scene graph that can perform dynamic scene paging, smoothly.

Obviously, there is a lot more work to do before we can put this small example into practical use. Terrain data with non-power-of-two row or column numbers may produce incorrect results at present. The concept of coordinate system datum (for instance, WGS84) is not included, so geometric earth models will not be creatable. The randomly-generated height data is also not ideal at all. Some `.geotiff` format imagery and elevation data may be good enough as a replacement, if you have an interest in extending the example in any way.

Pop quiz – number of created levels and files

The quad-tree creation example generates 86 files at one time in order to construct a complete quad-tree of four levels (L0-L3). Can you tell the reason why we have exactly four levels of terrain cells, and how each of the 86 files indicate their locations and indices within the tree hierarchy?

Have a go hero – testing a new terrain creation tool

Finally, we would like to introduce an independent terrain database creation tool named **VirtualPlanetBuilder** (or **VPB** for short), which reads a wide range of geospatial imagery and elevation data, and builds small pieces of terrain area with layers of paged LOD nodes. The previous example code actually comes from the theory of the **VPB** project.

VPB mainly depends on the OSG project and the third-party **GDAL** project. VPB is described and provided at: `http://www.openscenegraph.org/projects/VirtualPlanetBuilder`.

And **GDAL** can be found at:`http://www.gdal.org/`.

After downloading the source code, use CMake to build native solutions or makefiles, choose `ALL_BUILD` in your Visual Studio interface (or use `make install` in the UNIX shell), and obtain the **VPB** libraries and utilities. Use the `vpbmaster` executable to quickly build an OSG native format terrain from `.geotiff` files, such as:

```
# vpbmaster -d dem_file.tif -t dom_file.tif -o output.osgb
```

Because of the ability to handle a multi-terabyte database, create tiles across networks of computers, and read multi source imagery and DEM file formats, **VPB** can be used as a complete terrain-creation tool. You will always have the time to taste it and see if it can build the whole world for your applications. So good luck with it!

A demo database generated by **VPB** can be found on the web. You may use the `osgviewer` utility to view it, unless you don't have the `osgdb_curl` plug-in built (it requires the **libcurl** library):

```
# osgviewer http://www.openscenegraph.org/data/earth_bayarea/earth.ive
```

For more information about earth and terrain rendering, have a look at the **osgEarth** project (`http://osgearth.org/`). This does a similar job, by alternative creating terrain tiles offline or at run-time.

Summary

This beginners' book can only help you to develop a general ability to develop 3D applications with OSG, as well as looking for resources and implementations in the source code and community by themselves. But to master OSG's usage and construct your own projects with it, the only way to Rome will be to practice, practice, and practice. It is also a good practice to share your opinions, and contribute to the open source community all the time, because discussions and communications are always necessary processes to improve ourselves, too.

In this chapter, we specially covered:

◆ Making use of the **OpenThreads** library to develop multithreaded programs

◆ How to understand and choose different threading models in OSG, including the single-threaded, thread-per-graphics-context, and thread-per-camera models

◆ A basic occlusion culling implementation with the `osg::OccluderNode` class

◆ A basic texture sharing implementation for different external files using the `osgDB::ReadFileCallback` and `osgDB::SharedStateManager`

◆ The **quad-tree** structure and its initial implementation for building large terrain data in OSG, as well as a brief introduction of the professional creation tool **VPB**

Pop Quiz Answers

Chapter 2

Dependencies of osgviewer

It will certainly fail if you try to run the `osgviewer` executable and the model file on a clean system without necessary dependencies. You will at least need the `OpenThreads`, `osg`, `osgDB`, `osgUtil`, `osgGA`, `osgText`, and `osgViewer` libraries, as well as the `osgdb_osg` and `osgdb_deprecated_osg` plugins to make this simple scene work. The situation can be more complex if you are configuring a debug version of OSG (it may require additional C/C++ runtime libraries).

The difference between ALL_BUILD and 'build all'

The final outputs may be the same, but the process may not. The "batch building all" operation means you have to check and build every project in the solution, including `ALL_BUILD` and `INSTALL`. That will cause the projects handled by `ALL_BUILD` to be built twice! Although they won't be actually compiled again if already up-to-date, it is still a huge waste of time when compared with the standard steps.

Chapter 3

Configuring OSG path options yourselves

OSG_INCLUDE_DIR can be set to the include directory in the installation folder. OSG_LIBRARY must be set to the osg library (for example, osg.lib under Windows). Here, OSG_LIBRARY_DEBUG means the debug version (always with a postfix of "d", for example, osgd.lib). Others may be deduced by analogy.

Release a smart pointer

If the target object is not referenced by any other element before returning from the function, it will actually be deleted at the end of the function because the local osg::ref_ptr<> variable is out of scope. That makes the returned pointer invalid. The release() method solves the problem here. However, if you have some other element whose life is beyond the function referencing target before returning, try using target.get() instead, because the reference count should not be cleared this time.

Chapter 4

Results of different primitive types

The OpenGL documentation and some web tutorials can explain them clearly: http://www.opengl.org/sdk/docs/man/xhtml/glBegin.xml.

There is also an osggeometry example in the OSG source code, located at examples\osggeometry.

Optimizing indexed geometries

If you are drawing in GL_TRIANGLES mode without indexing, there will be up to 24 vertices allocated. GL_TRIANGLE_STRIPS works fine while triangles are connected in groups. For the case of representing an octahedron, we could use a triangle strip primitive set (2, 5, 3, 4, 1, 0, 2, 3, as shown in the figure in *the Drawing an octahedron* section) and two single triangles (4, 0, 3, and 5, 2, 1) to implement the same result.

Chapter 5

Fast dynamic casting

The `asGroup()` and `asGeode()` methods are virtual methods that could be re-implemented by subclasses such as `osg::Group` and `osg::Geode`. These methods actually don't do any runtime check and simply return `NULL` if not overridden, so they are always faster than `dynamic_cast<>`. The limitation here is that they only convert nodes into specify types, so if you are going to cast a certain node pointer to the `osg::LOD` type, use `dynamic_cast<>` instead:

```
osg::LOD* lod = dynamic_cast<osg::LOD*>(node);
```

Matrix multiplications

There is a website that excellently introduces the concepts here, as well as explains the reason why OSG does not use the **column major** and **prefix** notations that are introduced in OpenGL books: `http://www.openscenegraph.org/projects/osg/wiki/Support/Maths/MatrixTransformations`.

Chapter 6

Lights without sources

As lights are **positional states** in OpenGL, a light object attached to a node will always be affected by the node's local matrix. That is to say, the light will follow the node and work as a "headlight" of the moving vehicle. The `osg::LightSource` node can be used to fix the position of the light, with the `setReferenceFrame()` method. A fixed light can be treated as a "skylight" of the whole world.

Replacements of built-in uniforms

There are no standard ways to implement built-in uniforms. You could always use one or more of your own uniforms to emulate them, for example, use multiple vec4 variables (ambient, diffuse, specular, and so on) and float values (spot cut-off, attenuation) to deliver light parameters. The book *OpenGL Shading Language* written by Randi J. Rost should be good reading material for beginners.

Chapter 7

Changing model positions in the HUD camera

It will use the **projection matrix** of its parent camera (or main camera) when there is no preset one. A model filled the entire screen means that you can just wrap it up with a truncated pyramid (perspective) or cube (orthographic). An upside down effect can be implemented using:

```
setProjectionMatrixAsFrustum( left, right, top, bottom, near, far );
                    // Swapped top and bottom
```

To transform a specified part of 3D scenes into 2D images, you have to carefully set the view frustum. The following website may help in some ways: http://www.songho.ca/opengl/gl_projectionmatrix.html.

Another way to display the same scene in different views

The following example code segments will show the same scene in two cameras:

```
osg::ref_ptr<osg::Camera> camera1 = new osg::Camera;
camera1->setViewport( 0, 0, 400, 600 );
camera1->addChild( scene );
osg::ref_ptr<osg::Camera> camera2 = new osg::Camera;
camera2->setViewport( 400, 0, 400, 600 );
camera2->addChild( scene );
```

Consider setting a **view matrix** (using absolute or relative coordinates, as you wish) for each and then adding all sub-cameras to a **root node**.

Chapter 8

Adding or setting callbacks

Each nested callback is handled in the `traverse()` method of the last one, recursively. Reading the source code in `src/osg/NodeCallback.cpp` will also be helpful here. It is recommended to use `addUpdateCallback()` to add new callback objects in most situations because there may be other callbacks applied to the same node.

Choosing the alpha setter and the callback

Consider using RGBA textures with alpha values. Sometimes they are more preferred to be used to implement blending and transparent effects.

All kinds of update callbacks can be used to achieve fade-in and fade-out effects; just use a member variable in the callback class to record the material pointer.

As fade-in means to change the alpha value from 0 to 1, a fade-out effect should simply change it from 1 to 0. So the only line of code to change in the example is:

```
float alpha = 1.0f - _motion->getValue();
```

Chapter 9

Handling events within nodes

Node callbacks can directly perform node operations according to future user events, for example, moving the node when the user is pressing a key. Event handlers are more generic. They are useful in configuring global settings and handling events for all kinds of scene elements.

In this example, **event callback** is easier to implement than event handlers, but remember, too many callbacks may also cause performance problems.

Global and node-related events

Not at all. Timer and picking are all global behaviors that are not related to a certain node, so it is confusing if we implement them in a node callback without any more operations to the node itself.

Chapter 10

Getting rid of pseudo-loaders

OSG will look for plugins libraries according to the extension of the file. That said, the filename `movie.avi.ffmpeg` will be regarded as a `.ffmpeg` file and will be sent to the `osgdb_ffmpeg` plugins (with the same name), but never to the `osgdb_avi` plugins. So the fact is that we failed to find a suitable plugins to handle filenames, but not that the pseudo-loader lost its capability.

To make full use of your "own" osgdb_avi plugins (it can handle more than AVI files, in fact), you may read the *Handling the data stream* section in this chapter and try obtaining the osgDB::ReaderWriter pointer from the plugins for use.

Understanding the inheritance relations

The wrapper will still work, but properties such as node mask, state set, and applied callbacks will not be recorded again, because they are declared in the osg::Node class. Try using setNodeMask() to set a different mask to the ExampleNode instance and save it. See if there is any difference between using and not using osg::Node in the inheritance relations string of the wrapper.

Chapter 11

Text positions and the projection matrix

That is related to the view and projection matrix of the camera. As we could see in the example code, the HUD camera is using the absolute **reference frame** (not affected by parent ones) and the identity **view matrix** (the camera is facing towards the negative Z axis), which means that texts in the XOY plane can be fully displayed in the camera's view. While projected into a 2D orthographic camera, the text position should be set according to the clipping planes (0, 0) - (1024, 768). The bottom-right corner is near the coordinate (1024, 0) in this situation.

Chapter 12

Carefully blocking threads

The getContent() method is located in the text's **update callback**, so it will be called every frame while rendering. addContent() is always called when the thread is running and the user is providing input via the console. That means that the conflict of these two methods can occur all the time. Without a mutex or other protections, we can never determine what will happen (it may work for a while, receive unexpected characters sometime, or even crash).

Number of created levels and files

The total number of rows/columns is 1024, and the final number of each cell is 64. As every quad-tree cell can be replaced with 2x2 sub-cells while going nearer, we can easily deduce the size of cells in each level:

- Level 0 is 1024x1024 (1 cell)
- Level 1 is 512x512 (4 cells)
- Level 2 is 256x256 (16 cells)
- Level 3 is 128x128 (64 cells).

There is actually a level 4 (64x64), but it is not paged. So we finally have 85 paged files (1 + 4 + 16 + 64), and one root file for scheduling them.

Index

Symbols

2D textures
about 145
applying 143-145
loading 143-145
3DC Point cloud plug-in. *See* osgdb_3dc plug-in
3D texts
creating 300-303
.ini configuration file 20
<osgDB/ReadFile> header 47
.osg file format 264
<osgViewer/Viewer> header 47
--single argument 332
--useCamera command 333
--useContext argument 332

A

AC3D plug-in. *See* osgdb_ac plug-in
accept() method 110
acceptsExtension() method 276
Acrobat PDF plug-in. *See* osgdb_pdf plug-in
addChannel() method 220
addChild() method 94, 96, 101, 104
addDrawable() method 63, 292
addEventHandler() method 232
addFileExtensionAlias() method 265
addFileName() method 218
addImageFile() method 214
addImage() method 214
addParticleSystem() method 308
addPrimitiveSet() method 68, 71
addToContent() method 324
addUniform() method 154
addUpdateCallback() method 194

aircrafts
drawing, on loaded terrain 186-190
ALL_BUILD
and 'build all', differences 38
allocateImage() method 141
alpha attribute 251
anaglyph stereo scenes
rendering 183, 184
animation channels
managing 220-224
animation path
using 205-207
API documentation 24
Apple Quicktime plug-in. *See* osgdb_quicktime plug-in
applications
rendering performance, improving 341, 342
apply() method 82 117
array data
storing 66
AutoCAD 8
Autodesk 3DS plug-in. *See* osgdb_3ds plug-in
Autodesk DXF plug-in. *See* osgdb_dxf plug-in
Autodesk FBX plug-in. *See* osgdb_fbx plug-in
Autodesk FBX SDK
URL 267
AXIAL_ROT enumeration 292

B

back face culling 336
banners
creating 293-295
basic shapes
rendering 63
simple objects, creating 64

draw() method 86
DRAW phase 328, 334, 335
draw traversal 99
DriveManipulator 171
dynamic_cast<> operator 232
DYNAMIC object 199

E

ease motions
    about 204
    back function 204
    bounce effect function 204
    circle function 204
    cubic function (y = t3) 204
    elastic bounce function 204
    exponent function 204
    linear interpolation 204
    quad function (y = t2) 204
    quart function (y = t4) 204
    sine function 204
EmitVertex() function 159
enumerations
    AXIAL_ROT 292
    POINT_ROT_EYE 292
    POINT_ROT_WORLD 292
environment variables
    about 24, 25
    configuring 40
ESRI Shapefile plug-in. *See* osgdb_shp plug-in
event callback 194
event handlers 237
event traversal 98, 232, 237
event types, OSG
    about 233, 234
    DOUBLECLICK 233
    DRAG 233
    FRAME 233
    KEYDOWN 233
    KEYUP 233
    MOVE 233
    PUSH 233
    RELEASE 233
    SCROLL 233
    USER 234
extra plug-ins 24

F

FaceCollector structure 84
FFmpeg
    URL 267
FFmpeg library 270
FFmpeg plug-in. *See* osgdb_ffmpeg plug-in
fileExists() method 276
file I/O plug-ins, OSG 264
files
    reading, from internet 271, 272
find_package() macro 45, 88
first in first out (FIFO) list 239
fixed-function effects, OSG 131-133
fixed-function light sources, OSG 136
flashing spotlight
    rendering 215-218
Flight Gear
    URL 13
FlightManipulator 171
fog coordinate, vertex attribute 67
fog effect
    applying 134
fragment shaders 152, 155
frame buffer 61, 185
frame buffer object(FBO) 186
FRAME event 233 242
frame() method 172, 199, 254
FreeType
    about 276, 296
    URL 267
FreeType plug-in. *See* osgdb_freetype plug-in
FreeType support
    adding, for OSG 276
functor 81, 194

G

garbage collection
    need for 50
    working 50
GDAL
    about 356
    URL 267
GDAL plug-in. *See* osgdb_gdal
geode 62
Geode 62

H

handle() method 233
heads-up display camera. *See* **HUD camera**
height attribute 250
Hello World example
  improving 47
hierarchical graph 8
HUD camera
  about 168, 297
  creating 168, 169
  model positions, changing 170

I

ILM OpenEXR plug-in. *See* **osgdb_exr plug-in**
immediate mode 62
include subfolder 40
indexing primitives
  about 72
  indexed geometries, optimizing 76
in-graphics shaders
  animating 213
inheritedWindowData attribute 251
insertChild() method 94
insert() method 205
installation, OSG 21-23
instance() method 265
intersection strategy 243, 244
Inventor plug-in. *See* **osgdb_iv plug-in**
inverse() method 100
invert() method 100
I/O serialization 284
isPlaying() method 220
ITK
  URL 266

J

JasPer
  URL 267
JPEG 2000 plug-in. *See* **osgdb_jp2 plug-in**
JPEG plug-in. *See* **osgdb_jpeg plug-in**

K

keyboard events
  handling, with customized event handlers 233,
    234
KEYDOWN event 233
key-frame class
  DoubleKeyframe 219
  FloatKeyframe 219
  MatrixKeyframe 219
  QuatKeyframe 219
  Vec2Keyframe 219
  Vec3Keyframe 219
  Vec4Keyframe 219
KeySwitchMatrixManipulator 171
KEYUP event 233

L

leaf nodes 8, 78
level-of-detail technique. *See* **LOD**
libcurl
  about 266
  adding, to OSG 272-275
libraries, OpenSceneGraph (OSG)
  OpenThreads library 10
  osgDB library 10
  osg library 10
  osgUtil library 10
lib subfolder 40
light sources
  creating, in scene 137-140
Lightwave 3D Object plug-in. *See* **osgdb_lwo**
    plug-in
Lightwave 3D Scene plug-in. *See* **osgdb_lws**
    plug-in
linear interpolation 203
linear interpolation motion object
  creating 204
local coordinate system 164
LOD 107
LOD Cessna
  constructing 108, 109
log file
  saving 58, 59

osgParticle library 10
osgQt library 11
osgShadow library 11
osgSim library 11
osgTerrain library 11
osgText library 11
osgViewer library 11
osgVolume library 11
osgWidget library 11
nodes
  switching, in update traversal 195-197
NodeTrackerManipulator 171
non-full screen window
  viewing in 175
normalized device coordinate system 164
normal, vertex attribute 67
notifer
  redirecting 57
  tracing 57

O

occluders
  about 336
  adding, to complex scene 337-340
occlusion culling 336
occlusion culling algorithm 337
octahedron
  drawing 73-75
octree 347
OGR plug-in. *See* **osgdb_ogr plug-in**
on-demand rendering scheme 172
OpenFlight plug-in. *See* **osgdb_openflight**
      plug-in
OpenGL
  Bezier curve, generating 158-161
  objects, drawing 62
  state machine, encapsulating 124
  vertex attribute 67
OpenGL drawing calls
  creating 87-90
  using 87
OpenGL shading language. *See* **GLSL**
OpenGL teapot, creating
  OpenGL drawing calls, creating 87-90
Open Inventor 8

OpenInventor
  URL 267
OpenSceneGraph (OSG) architecture 12
OpenSceneGraph (OSG), benefits
  hardware portability 13
  high scalibility 12
  latest activity 13
  open source 13
  rigorous structure 12
  software portability 13
  superior performance 12
OpenThreads 322
OpenThreads::Barrier 322
OpenThreads::Condition 322
OpenThreads library 10
  about 327
  new thread, designing 322, 323
OpenThreads::Mutex 322
OpenThreads::Thread class
  about 322
  methods 322
OpenVRML
  URL 270
operator() method 194, 209
operator*() method 100
OSG
  3D texts, creating 300-303
  about 231
  architecture 12
  benefits 12
  billboards, creating in scene 292
  conflicted modifications, avoiding 198, 199
  culling techniques 335, 336
  customized events, adding 239
  development 9
  discussion groups 16
  environment variables, configuring 40
  event types 233, 234
  file I/O plug-ins 264
  fixed-function effects 131-133
  fixed-function light sources 136
  forum 16
  FreeType support, adding 276
  installer, URL 20
  installer, using 20
  installing 21-23

Y

Z

open source
community experience distilled

Blender 3D 2.49
Architecture, Buildings, and Scenery

Create photo-realistic 3D architectural visualizations of buildings,
interiors, and environmental scenery with Blender

Allan Brito   PACKT open source

Blender 3D 2.49 Architecture, Buildings, and Scenery

ISBN: 978-1-84951-048-6   Paperback: 376 pages

Create realistic models of building exteriors and
interiors, the surrounding environment, and scenery.

1. Study modeling, materials, textures, and light basics
   in Blender

2. Learn special tricks and techniques to create
   walls, floors, roofs, and other specific architectural
   elements

3. Create realistic virtual tours of buildings and scenes

Blender 3D 2.49
Incredible Machines

Modeling, rendering, and animating realistic machines with
Blender 3D

Allan Brito   PACKT

Blender 3D 2.49 Incredible Machines

ISBN: 978-1-847197-46-7   Paperback: 316 pages

Modeling, rendering, and animating realistic
machines with Blender 3D

1. Walk through the complete process of building
   amazing machines

2. Model and create mechanical models and vehicles
   with detailed designs

3. Add advanced global illumination options to the
   renders created in Blender 3D using YafaRay and
   LuxRender

Please check **www.PacktPub.com** for information on our titles

Away3D 3.6 Essentials

ISBN: 978-1-84951-206-0   Paperback: 416 pages

Take Flash to the next dimension by creating detailed, animated, and interactive 3D worlds with Away3D

1. Create stunning 3D environments with highly detailed textures

2. Animate and transform all types of 3D objects, including 3D Text

3. Eliminate the need for expensive hardware with proven Away3D optimization techniques, without compromising on visual appeal

OGRE 3D 1.7 Beginner's Guide

ISBN: 978-1-84951-248-0   Paperback: 300 pages

Create real time 3D applications using OGRE 3D from scratch

1. Motivate students from all backgrounds, generations, and learning styles

2. When and how to apply the different learning solutions with workarounds, providing alternative solutions

3. Easy-to-follow, step-by-step instructions with screenshots and examples for Moodle's powerful features

4. Especially suitable for university and professional teachers

Please check **www.PacktPub.com** for information on our titles